W9-ALZ-892

Spelling Workout

Phillip K. Trocki

Modern Curriculum Press
is an imprint of

Boston, Massachusetts

Chandler, Arizona

Glenview, Illinois

Upper Saddle River, New Jersey

COVER DESIGN: Pronk & Associates

ILLUSTRATIONS: Chris Knowles. 190: Jim Steck.

PHOTOGRAPHS: All photos © Pearson Learning unless otherwise noted.

Cover: Artbase Inc.
5: © Randy Harris/Fotolia.com. 8: Library of Congress. 9: © cyrano/Fotolia.com. 12: © Rudolf Tittelbach/Fotolia.com.
13: Library of Congress. 16: © Photos.com/Thinkstock. 17: © Photos.com/Thinkstock. 20: © SOMATUSCANI/Fotolia.com.
21: © Radu Razvan/Fotolia.com. 24: © Michael Matisse/PhotoDisc, Inc. 26: © Philipp Wininger/Fotolia.com. 29: © Brand X
Pictures/Thinkstock. 32: © Maximilian Effgen/Fotolia.com. 33: © Gina Smith/Fotolia.com. 36: © Jean-Marie MAILLET/Fotolia.
com. 37: © 2ndpic/Fotolia.com. 40: © godfer/Fotolia.com. 44: © Natalia Bratslavsky/Fotolia.com. 45: © chasingmoments/Fotolia.
com. 48: © Dima/Fotolia.com. 53: © Comstock. 56: © BlueOrange Studio/Fotolia.com. 57: © Keith Brofsky/PhotoDisc, Inc. 60:
© Piotr Marcinski/Fotolia.com. 61: NASA Jet Propulsion Laboratory Collection. 64: NASA Planetary Photo Journal Collection/
JPL. 65: Library of Congress. 69: © Steve Mason/PhotoDisc, Inc. 72: Library of Congress Digital. 77: © nsphotography/Fotolia.
com. 80: © oscar williams/Fotolia.com. 81: © Getty Images. 84: © Inna Sidorova/Fotolia.com. 85: © Medioimages/PhotoDisc/
Thinkstock. 88: Library of Congress. 89: © Gary/Fotolia.com. 92: © Goodshoot/Thinkstock. 93: © Jupiterimages/Thinkstock. 96:
© PhotoDisc, Inc. 99: © Jupiterimages/Thinkstock. 101: © Jupiterimages/Thinkstock. 104: © Michael Matisse/Thinkstock. 105:
© Jupiterimages/Thinkstock. 109: © Juraj/Fotolia.com. 110: *pos. 1:* © Keith Wheatley/Fotolia.com. *pos. 2:* © Paul837/Fotolia.com.
pos. 3: © Keith Wheatley/Fotolia.com. *pos. 4:* c/Fotolia.com. 112: © PaulPaladin/Fotolia.com. 113: © NickR/Fotolia.com. 116: ©
bat104/Fotolia.com. 117: © outdoorsman/Fotolia.com. 120: © grabj/Fotolia.com. 123: © Stephen Oliver/Dorling Kindersley. 125: ©
expsay/Fotolia.com. 128: © Artur Gabrysiak/Fotolia.com. 129: © Ryan McVay/Thinkstock. 132: © Comstock/Thinkstock. 133: © marc
hericher/Fotolia.com. 136: © Thinkstock. 137: © Jupiterimages/Thinkstock. 140: © PhotoDisc, Inc. 141: © Zoe/Fotolia.com. 144: ©
Photos.com/Thinkstock. 145: NASA/Spacesuit and Spacewalk History Image Gallery.

Acknowledgments
ZB font Method Copyright © 1996 Zaner-Bloser.

Some content in this product is based upon WEBSTER'S NEW WORLD DICTIONARY, 4/E. Copyright ©2013
by Houghton Mifflin Harcourt Publishing Company. Reprinted by permission of Houghton Mifflin Harcourt Publishing
Company. All rights reserved.

NOTE: Every effort has been made to locate the copyright owner of material reprinted in this book. Omissions
brought to our attention will be corrected in subsequent editions.

Copyright © 2002 Pearson Education, Inc., or its affiliates. All Rights Reserved. Printed in the United States of America. This publication is protected
by copyright, and permission should be obtained from the publisher prior to any prohibited reproduction, storage in a retrieval system, or transmission
in any form or by any means, electronic, mechanical, photocopying, recording, or likewise. For information regarding permissions, write to Pearson
Curriculum Group Rights & Permissions, One Lake Street, Upper Saddle River, New Jersey 07458.

Pearson, Prentice Hall, and Pearson Prentice Hall are trademarks, in the U.S. and/or other countries, of Pearson Education, Inc., or its affiliates.

Modern Curriculum Press
is an imprint of

ISBN–13: 978-0-7652-2487-3
ISBN–10:   0-7652-2487-9
26   18

Table of Contents

Learning to Spell a Word. 4

Keeping a Spelling Notebook 4

Lesson 1   Syllabication 5

Lesson 2   Words Ending with the Sound of əl 9

Lesson 3   Double Consonants 13

Lesson 4   Words with the Sound of ər 17

Lesson 5   Doubling Final Consonants 21

Lesson 6   Lessons 1–5 • Review. 25

Lesson 7   Prefixes for Numbers 29

Lesson 8   Prefixes **ante, epi, pre, pro**. 33

Lesson 9   Prefixes **ab, af, ag, an, anti** 37

Lesson 10   Prefixes **bene, beni, coll, com, contra, eu** 41

Lesson 11   Prefixes **mal, meta, de, dis**. 45

Lesson 12   Lessons 7–11 • Review. 49

Lesson 13   Latin Roots 53

Lesson 14   Latin Roots 57

Lesson 15   Latin Roots 61

Lesson 16   Latin Roots 65

Lesson 17   Challenging Words 69

Lesson 18   Lessons 13–17 • Review. 73

Lesson 19   Prefixes Meaning "Together" 77

Lesson 20   Prefixes Meaning "Not" 81

Lesson 21   Words of Latin Origin 85

Lesson 22   Words of Greek Origin. 89

Lesson 23   Words of Greek Origin. 93

Lesson 24   Lessons 19–23 • Review. 97

Lesson 25   Words Ending in **ize, ise, ent, ant**. 101

Lesson 26   Noun-Forming Suffix **ity** 105

Lesson 27   Words Ending in **ary, ory** 109

Lesson 28   Words of French Origin 113

Lesson 29   Challenging Words 117

Lesson 30   Lessons 25–29 • Review. 121

Lesson 31   Words from Science 125

Lesson 32   Words from Occupations. 129

Lesson 33   Words from Literature 133

Lesson 34   Words from Language Arts 137

Lesson 35   Challenging Words 141

Lesson 36   Lessons 31–35 • Review. 145

Writing and Proofreading Guide. 149

Using Your Dictionary 150

Spelling Workout Dictionary. 151

Spelling Notebook. 190

Learning to Spell a Word

1. Look at the word and say the letters.

2. Close your eyes and "picture" the word.

3. Spell the word silently.

4. Cover the word and write it on paper.

5. Check your spelling.

Keeping a Spelling Notebook

A spelling notebook will help you when you write.
Write the words you're having trouble with on a
separate sheet of paper or in the **Spelling Notebook**
at the back of the book.

Syllabication

Lesson 1

TIP

Study these rules of syllabication.

Divide words where natural breaks occur between prefixes, roots, and suffixes: un/doubt/ed/ly. When two consonants come between two vowels, divide between the consonants: com/mem/o/rate. When one consonant comes between two vowels, divide before the consonant if the first vowel is long: ex/po/sure. Divide after the consonant if the vowel is short: sat/u/rate. A vowel sounded alone can form a syllable: cur/i/os/i/ty.

Vocabulary Development

Write the **list word** that matches each definition.

1. celebrate something — commemorate
2. eagerness to know — curiosity
3. roast outdoors — barbeque
4. bring back to life — resurrect
5. leave behind — abandon
6. a trinket or decoration — ornament
7. necessary details — specifications
8. to determine — ascertain
9. soak — saturate
10. likely to act a certain way — tendency
11. thankfulness — gratitude
12. desire for food — appetite

LIST WORDS

1. abandon
2. commemorate
3. exposure
4. ornament
5. tendency
6. affidavit
7. consolidate
8. gratitude
9. resurrect
10. undoubtedly
11. appetite
12. curiosity
13. guardian
14. saturate
15. voluntary
16. barbecue
17. dominate
18. installation
19. specifications
20. ascertain

Dictionary Skills

Rewrite each of the following **list words** to show how they are divided into syllables.

1. gratitude — gra/ti/tude
2. voluntary — vo/lun/tary
3. guardian — guar/di/an
4. exposure — ex/po/sure
5. appetite — ap/pe/tite
6. affidavit — af/fi/dav/it
7. undoubtedly — un/doubt/ed/ly
8. consolidate — con/so/li/date
9. installation — in/stal/la/tion
10. dominate — do/mi/nate

5

Spelling Practice

DID YOU KNOW?

Dominate comes from the Latin word for "master," *dominus*, and so do the words *domineer* and *dominion*.

Word Analysis

Write the **list words** containing these double consonants:

1. rr   resurrect
2. ff   affidavite
3. pp   appetite
4. ll   installation
5. mm   commemorate

Write the **list words** containing these prefixes:

6. com   commemorate
7. con   consolidate
8. re   ressurect
9. ex   exposure
10. un   undoutedly

Write the **list words** containing five syllables.

11. Specifications   12. curiotity

Word Application

Replace the underlined word or words in each sentence with a **list word**. Write the **list word** on the line.

1. Rain fell so heavily that the water began to <u>soak</u> the dry earth.   saturate

2. We expressed our <u>thankfulness</u> by sending flowers.   gratitude

3. Please do not <u>leave</u> the grocery-store carts in the parking lot.   abandon

4. Tim will <u>head</u> the field of runners in the competition.   dominate

5. On July 4th, the United States will <u>celebrate</u> its birth.   consolidate

6. The committee will <u>place together</u> all of the smaller groups into one.   commemorate

7. Mr. Jackson has been selected as <u>overseer</u> of the club's investments.   guardian

8. You will find the <u>details</u> for building that boat in my book.   specifications

9. For dinner tonight, Dad and I will <u>roast</u> chicken on the grill.   barbeque

10. Too much <u>display</u> of skin to the sun can result in a sunburn.   exposure

11. The salesperson tried to <u>determine</u> what the customer wanted.   ascertain

12. Participation in the clothes drive is <u>your own choice</u>.   voluntary

13. The <u>likelihood</u> of the car to pull to the right on highways in annoying.   tendency

14. The vase of lilacs and tulips on that table is a lovely <u>decoration</u>.   ornament

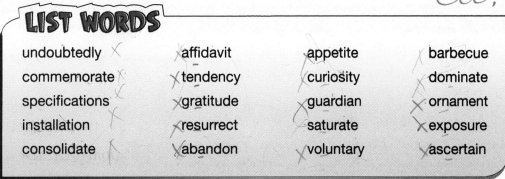

LIST WORDS

undoubtedly	affidavit	appetite	barbecue
commemorate	tendency	curiosity	dominate
specifications	gratitude	guardian	ornament
installation	resurrect	saturate	exposure
consolidate	abandon	voluntary	ascertain

Oct, 10, 2018

Puzzle

Use the **list words** to complete the crossword puzzle.

ACROSS

3. the act of letting something be seen
6. strong feelings of wanting to know or learn something
8. done of one's free will; by choice
9. placed in position
12. a person who guards or protects
15. the desire or wish for food
17. thankfulness
18. unite; merge; join together
19. likely to move or act in a certain way
20. a decoration

DOWN

1. to bring back to life
2. to soak through
4. without doubt; certainly
5. to honor or keep alive the memory of
7. a statement of all the necessary details, sizes, materials, etc.
10. to control or rule
11. to find out the facts
13. a statement written by one who swears it is the truth
14. meat roasted over an open fire
16. to give up completely; to leave

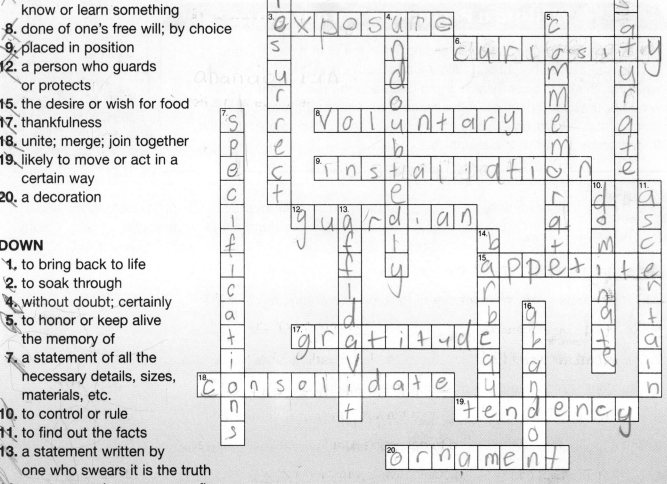

Proofreading

Use the proofreading marks to correct the mistakes in the biographical sketch. Then, write the misspelled **list words** correctly on the lines.

Robert Frost (1874–1963) is undoutedly oneof the greatest american poets of the twentieth century. Born in san Francisco, Frost moved with his family to New England after the death of his father in 1885. Frost's expozure tothe region's landscapes and speech mannerisms saterate many of his best poems. Yet scenic descriptions donot domminate all of frost's work The range of moods in his poetry is rich and varied, revealing a curoisity about human nature. Winner of the pulitzer Prize for poetry four times, there are now several books available that comemoarate Frost's work

Proofreading Marks

⬭ spelling mistake ⊙ add period
≡ capital letter # add space

1. dominate
2. commemorate
3. undoubted
4. exposure
5. saturate
6. curiosity

Writing a Persuasive Paragraph

In a Robert Frost poem called "Mending Wall" the poet writes, "Good fences make good neighbors." Write a persuasive paragraph to explain what you think the poet means. Try to persuade the reader that this is a wise—or unwise—statement. Give reasons for your opinion and use as many of the **list words** as you can. Proofread and revise your paragraph, then discuss it with your classmates.

BONUS WORDS

municipality	rural	commune	province	suburb
commonwealth	urban	residential	borough	colony

Write **bonus words** to answer the questions.

Which words describe the character or location of a community?

1. rural
2. urban
3. commune
4. residental

Which word names a territory distant from its parent country?

5. Colony

Which words name political communities that have governments of their own?

6. municipality
7. Commonwealth
8. Suburb
9. province
10. borough

100%

Words Ending with the Sound of əl

TIP

Many words end with the sound you hear at the end of <u>dismal</u>. This sound can be spelled in several different ways, as in <u>little</u>, <u>towel</u>, and <u>recital</u>. Remember that the words in this lesson all end with the same letters: **al**.

Vocabulary Development

Write the **list word** that matches each definition clue.

1. huge — colossal
2. reasonable — logical
3. forever — perpetual
4. not natural — artificial
5. dreary — dismal
6. by chance — accidental
7. additional — supplemental
8. lawless — criminal
9. mental — cerebral
10. financial — fiscal
11. hot and steamy — tropical
12. rebirth — revival

Dictionary Skills

Write the **list word** that matches each sound-spelling.

1. (up hē′v′l) — upheaval
2. (sen sā′shən ′l) — sensational
3. (his ter′i k′l) — histerical
4. (träp′i k′l) — tropical
5. (ik sper′ə men′t′l) — expeirimenta
6. (lit′ər əl) — literal
7. (sər vī′v′l) — servival
8. (ri sīt′′l) — recital
9. (ri vī′v′l) — revival
10. (in′tə grəl) — integral

LIST WORDS

1. accidental
2. dismal
3. integral
4. recital
5. survival
6. artificial
7. experimental
8. literal
9. revival
10. colossal
11. cerebral
12. fiscal
13. logical
14. sensational
15. tropical
16. criminal
17. hysterical
18. perpetual
19. supplemental
20. upheaval

9

Spelling Practice

DID YOU KNOW?

Dismal comes from a Middle English word which meant "unlucky days." Its Latin origins include *dis* or "day" and *mal* or "bad." Today, we use the word when we think something is gloomy, dreary, dreadful, hopeless, or depressing.

Word Analysis

Fill in the missing letters to form **list words**. Then, write the completed **list words** on the lines.

1. trop i c a l _____ tropical
2. fis c a l _____ fical
3. c ereb r a l _____ cerebral
4. art i fi c i a l _____ artificial
5. li b e r a l _____ literal
6. co l o s s a l _____ colossal
7. s u rviv a l _____ survival
8. in t e g r al _____ integral
9. a c cident a l _____ accidental
10. di s m a l _____ dismal

Word Application

Select a **list word** from the choices in parentheses to complete each sentence. Write the **list word** on the line.

1. That ___colossal___ stuffed animal is six-feet tall! (colossal, accidental)
2. ___Supplemental___ vitamins can't replace a meal. (Upheaval, Supplemental)
3. Falling off my bike was ___accidental___. (accidental, survival)
4. There is _____ activity even during sleep. (cerebral, tropical)
5. Human beings need food and water for their ___survival___. (survival, literal)
6. That ___dismal___ room is cold, damp, and gray. (accidental, dismal)
7. Take deep breaths to avoid becoming ___hysterical___. (perpetual, hysterical)
8. Natural light sources are better than ___artificial___ ones. (artificial, recital)
9. The ___perpetual___ noise kept her up all night. (perpetual, logical)
10. The earthquake caused a great ___upheaval___. (criminal, upheaval)
11. Stealing from banks is a ___criminal___ action. (revival, criminal)
12. "Using your head" can be ___literal___ if you hit the ball with your head while playing soccer. (recital, literal)
13. The quality of the ingredients is ___integral___ to the recipe. (integral, artificial)
14. Don't forget to memorize the music for your piano ___recital___. (experimental, recital)

LIST WORDS

fiscal	artificial	hysterical	criminal
dismal	logical	accidental	cerebral
revival	tropical	experimental	perpetual
recital	integral	sensational	upheaval
literal	survival	supplemental	colossal

11/13/18

Puzzle

This is a crossword puzzle without clues. Use the length and the spelling of each **list word** to complete the puzzle.

11/14.

Proofreading

Use the proofreading marks to correct the mistakes in the article below. Then, write the misspelled **list words** correctly on the lines.

Proofreading Marks

spelling mistake — delete word
? add question mark / small letter

The first (expiremental) Concord stagecoach was manufactured in 1827 by the Abbot-Downing Company. It created an (upheavel) in coach construction. The wheels were an an (intagral) part of the design. Made of oak, they were well-dried to withstand heat and cold, and would not shrink like other coach wheels. The body of the Coach was solid, resting on on thick leather braces. Even though the braces served to cushion and support the coach, do you think many Passengers enjoyed their ride Most described their travels as "dizmal" due to the (purpetual) motion of the coach.

1. Expeiremental
2. Integral
3. upheaval
4. dismal
5. perpetual

Writing a Description

In his book, *Roughing It*, Mark Twain described the Concord coach as "a cradle on wheels," and added, "It thrills me to think of the life and the wild sense of freedom on those fine overland mornings!" Write a description of what stagecoach travel might have been like, using as many of the **list words** as you can. Proofread and revise your description. Then, discuss your writing with your classmates.

 **BONUS WORDS**

11/14

automobile   hydroplane   ~~vessel~~   schooner   transcontinental
~~stagecoach~~   amphibious   ~~gasoline~~   tributary   propulsion

Write the **bonus word** that matches each clue.

1. driving force _____ gasoline
2. any boat or ship _____ vessel
3. horse-drawn carriage _____ stagecoach
4. from coast to coast _____
5. adapted for both land or water _____

6. river feeding another _____
7. one kind of fuel _____ gasoline
8. ship with two or more masts _____
9. this skims along the water's surface _____ hydroplane
10. four-wheeled motorized transportation _____ automobile

12

Go.

Double Consonants

Lesson 3

TIP

You may find it easier to spell a word that contains double consonants if you first divide the word into syllables. Pronounce each syllable of the following words, and listen for the sounds of the consonants.

ne/ces/si/ty   with/hold/ing

Vocabulary Development

Write the **list word** that matches each synonym.

1. restraining   _Suppress_
2. ruin   _Corrupt_
3. graciously   _cordially_
4. enormous   _immense_
5. need   _necessity_
6. sprinkle   _drizzle_
7. agreement   _acceptance_
8. juicy   _succulent_
9. squash   _oppress_
10. call   _summoned_
11. ownership   _possesion_
12. despair   _depression_

Dictionary Skills

Write the **list word** that comes between each pair of dictionary guide words.

1. succeed/succinct   _successive_
2. immerse/immortal   _immense_
3. denounce/drain   _drizzle_
4. access/assurance   _acceptance_
5. breeze/coral   _cancellation_
6. detour/drum   _depression_
7. polka/position   _pollen_
8. neck/policy   _oppress_
9. white/width   _withholding_
10. astute/canary   _boycott_
11. window/worry   _Wholly_
12. suppose/supreme   _Summon_

LIST WORDS

1. acceptance
2. corrupt
3. immigration
4. boycott
5. summon
6. assistance
7. depression
8. necessity
9. pollen
10. suppress
11. cancellation
12. drizzle
13. possession
14. succulent
15. wholly
16. cordially
17. immense
18. oppress
19. successive
20. withholding

SDP.

Spelling Practice

DID YOU KNOW ?

Around 1880, a man named Captain Charles Boycott acted as a rent collector for wealthy landowners in Ireland. Captain Boycott charged farmers extremely high rent for the land they worked. As a result, the farmers got together and refused to pay. Their tactics worked, and the rents were lowered. Soon, the term **boycott** became part of our language, meaning "a strike against unfair practices."

Word Analysis

Write **list words** to answer the following questions.

Which words contain the following suffixes?

ance	sion	ly
1. Acceptance	3. depression	5. wholly
2. assistance	4. posession	6. cordially

Which words contain the prefix **im**?

7. Immigration 8. immense

Analogies

Write a **list word** to complete each analogy.

1. Hurricane is to breeze as downpour is to _____.

2. Spending is to saving as giving is to _____.

3. Small is to tiny as large is to _____.

4. Resist is to resistance as assist is to _____.

5. Enemy is to cruelly as friend is to _____.

6. Something is to everything as partly is to _____.

7. Accept is to recruit as refuse is to _____.

8. Going out is to emigration as coming in is to _____.

9. Squirrel is to acorn as bee is to _____.

10. Show is to express as hide is to _____.

11. Accept is to renewal as reject is to _____.

12. Last is to previous as next is to _____.

13. Tasty is to savory as juicy is to _____.

14. Send away is to expel as call forth is to _____.

15. Clean is to pure as dirty is to _____.

16. Encourage is to uplift as burden is to _____.

17. Disapproval is to rejection as approval is to _____.

18. Happy is to elation as despondent is to _____.

19. Want is to desire as need is to _____.

LIST WORDS

acceptance	assistance	corrupt	cordially
cancellation	depression	drizzle	immense
immigration	necessity	boycott	oppress
possession	succulent	pollen	suppress
withholding	successive	wholly	summon

Puzzle

Use the **list words** to complete the crossword puzzle.

ACROSS

2. holding something by ownership
6. very large
8. the act of doing away with
9. deeply felt; sincere
10. the entire amount or degree
11. to refuse to buy, sell, or use
13. change from good to bad
14. yellow powder found on the stamen of flowers
15. coming in regular order without a break
16. help; aid
17. to put down by force; crush

DOWN

1. to rain lightly in fine drops
3. to call together
4. something necessary or needed
5. sadness; gloominess
6. the act of moving to a foreign country
7. taking willingly; responding in the affirmative
10. to keep from giving or granting
12. to burden; weigh down; worry
15. full of juice; juicy

Proofreading

Use the proofreading marks to correct the mistakes in the article below. Then, write the misspelled **list words** correctly on the lines.

Between 1881 and 1920, imigration to the United States skyrocketed. An imennse number of people—over 23 million—came to americas shores in succesive waves most of them from europe. They came for various reasons. Some wanted to escape from corupt political regimes, while others were fleeing economic depresion. All of them saw the United States as a land in which theyd be able to find new opportunities.

Proofreading Marks

◯ spelling mistake   ≡ capital letter

✓ add apostrophe   ⌃ add comma

1. _____

2. _____

3. _____

4. _____

5. _____

Writing Interview Questions

Imagine you are a reporter working for a big-city newspaper early in the twentieth century. What kind of questions would you want to ask a new immigrant to the United States? Write a list of interview questions, using as many **list words** as possible. Proofread and revise your questions, then use them to stage a question-and-answer session with another classmate.

BONUS WORDS

| commissioner | magistrate | coroner | attorney general | supervisor |
| superintendent | treasurer | secretary | vice-president | ambassador |

Write the **bonus word** that matches each clue.

1. title of some members of the president's cabinet _____

2. representative of one country to another country _____

3. minor official, such as a justice of the peace _____

4. country's top law official _____

5. official next in rank to a company's president _____

6. officer in charge of funds or finances _____

7. official who determines causes of death _____

8. official who heads a government department, such as fire or police _____

9. manager or director of a department or group _____

10. person in charge of a department or institution, such as a school _____

Words with the Sound of ər

 TIP

The **ər** sound that you hear at the end of <u>murmur</u>, <u>linear</u>, <u>alligator</u>, and <u>glacier</u> can be spelled many different ways. When you hear this sound in a word, pay close attention to how it is spelled. Remember, when the sound comes at the end of a word that names a person who does something, the sound is often spelled with **or**, as in <u>conqueror</u>.

Vocabulary Development

Write the **list word** that matches each synonym.

1. straight _____

2. crocodile _____

3. winner _____

4. faker _____

5. younger _____

6. whisper _____

7. forebears _____

8. warrior _____

9. pincers _____

10. teacher _____

11. vertical _____

12. specific _____

LIST WORDS

1. alligator
2. junior
3. incubator
4. murmur
5. reflector
6. ancestors
7. glacier
8. investor
9. particular
10. anchor
11. angular
12. gladiator
13. linear
14. perpendicular
15. tweezers
16. conqueror
17. impostor
18. moderator
19. professor
20. vinegar

Dictionary Skills

Write the **list word** that matches each sound-spelling.

1. (käŋ′kər ər) _____

2. (an′ses tərs) _____

3. (mäd′ə rāt′ər) _____

4. (iŋ′kyə bāt′ər) _____

5. (aŋ′gyə lər) _____

6. (im päs′tər) _____

7. (ri flek′tər) _____

8. (vin′i gər) _____

9. (in vest′ər) _____

10. (glā′shər) _____

11. (aŋ′kər) _____

12. (jōōn′yər) _____

Tweezers comes from an obsolete English word, *tweeses*, that meant "a case for small surgical instruments." That word came in turn from *etuis*, plural of a French word for a small case used to hold needles or other small implements.

Word Analysis

Write the **list words** in which the sound of /ər/ is spelled **ar**.

1. _____   4. _____

2. _____   5. _____

3. _____

Write the **list words** in which the sound of /ər/ is spelled **er**.

6. _____   8. _____

7. _____   9. _____

Write the **list word** in which the sound of /ər/ is spelled **ur**.

10. _____

Write the **list words** containing these double letters:

11. ee _____   13. ll _____

12. ss _____

Word Application

Replace the underlined word or words in each sentence with a **list word**. Write the **list word** on the line.

1. The two lines are <u>at right angles</u> to each other. _____

2. The recipe calls for just a dash of <u>a sour liquid</u>. _____

3. We are looking for a <u>specific</u> kind of mustard. _____

4. The trek will begin at the base of the <u>mountain of ice</u>. _____

5. Although the artist's drawings of people were rounded, the buildings had a <u>narrow, uniform</u> appearance. _____

6. Mrs. Greenbaum, a wealthy stockbroker, discussed the methods she used to become a successful <u>person who uses money or capital to gain a financial return</u>. _____

7. Mr. Olson moved the hen's eggs into the <u>place that is kept warm for hatching eggs</u>. _____

8. Captain Martinez ordered the sailors to drop the <u>heavy object that is put in water to keep a ship from drifting</u>. _____

LIST WORDS

linear	angular	professor	conqueror
junior	vinegar	gladiator	particular
glacier	investor	alligator	moderator
murmur	impostor	incubator	ancestors
anchor	reflector	tweezers	perpendicular

Puzzle

Use the **list words** to complete the crossword puzzle.

ACROSS

1. at right angles
6. a sour liquid
7. person in charge of conducting a debate
9. surface that reflects
11. large mass of snow and ice
12. in a line
14. small pincers for holding small items
16. having sharp corners
18. warm container for hatching eggs

DOWN

2. person who invests
3. distinct; not general
4. one who cheats or tricks people
5. one who overcomes another
8. teacher at college
10. people who come before others in a family line
11. ancient Roman fighter
13. large, lizard-like animal
15. low, steady sound
17. a younger person
19. heavy object that holds a boat in place

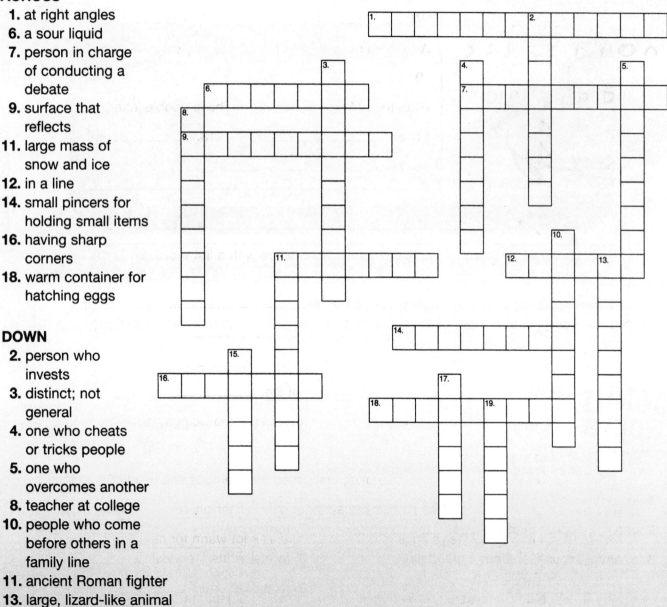

Proofreading

Use the proofreading marks to correct the mistakes in the article below. Then, write the misspelled **list words** correctly on the lines.

Proofreading Marks

↗ add comma   ⌒ℓ delete word

◯ spelling mistake

! add exclamation mark

Norway is known for its its scenery and a particuler glacior that is one of the largest in the world. A cruise along the Norwegian coast can be truly spectacular As your ship drops ancher perpindiculer to the steep mountain walls of a long narrrow bay known as a fjord listen for the murmer of a a distant waterfall. Many of these fjords have incredible vistas, with lush, green mountainsides that plunge straight into the water.

1. _____

2. _____

3. _____

4. _____

5. _____

Writing a Description

Write a description of what you might see from the deck of a ship that is traveling along the Norwegian coast. Use as many of the **list words** as you can. Proofread and revise your description, then read it aloud to your classmates.

BONUS WORDS

| petition | indictment | warrant | trespass | mandate |
| judicial | misdemeanor | property | subpoena | judgment |

Write the **bonus word** that matches each clue given.

1. legal decision _____

2. order to appear in court _____

3. a formal accusation from a grand jury

_____

4. written order to arrest _____

5. order from higher court _____

6. something that is owned _____

7. to enter illegally _____

8. formal written request _____

9. related to court _____

10. minor offense _____

Doubling Final Consonants

When a short-vowel word or syllable ends in a single consonant, usually double the final consonant before adding an ending or suffix that begins with a vowel.

> **unforget** + **able** = unforgettable
> overlap + **ing** = overlapping
> defer + **ed** = deferred
> propel + **er** = propeller

When adding **ly** to a word that ends in **l**, keep both **l**'s.

> usual + **ly** = usually

Vocabulary Development

Write the **list word** from column **B** that matches the clue in column **A**.

A		B
1. stopping	_____	permitted
2. came together	_____	omitted
3. memorable	_____	deferred
4. cast out	_____	deterring
5. cleared one's name	_____	conferred
6. chose a certain one	_____	unforgettable
7. postponed	_____	expelled
8. once in a while	_____	acquitted
9. allowed to act	_____	occasionally
10. left out	_____	preferred

Dictionary Skills

Rewrite the following **list words** to show how they are divided into syllables.

1. handicapped _____   **6.** controller _____

2. patrolled _____   **7.** occurring _____

3. forbidden _____   **8.** incurred _____

4. transmitting _____   **9.** propeller _____

5. overlapping _____   **10.** admitting _____

LIST WORDS

1. controller
2. patrolled
3. forbidden
4. conferred
5. preferred
6. unforgettable
7. deferred
8. expelled
9. transmitting
10. deterring
11. occasionally
12. occurring
13. incurred
14. propeller
15. admitting
16. omitted
17. permitted
18. acquitted
19. overlapping
20. handicapped

Spelling Practice

DID YOU KNOW ?

There was a form of bartering in the 1660s in which two people wishing to exchange items would get together with an umpire. All three parties would put a small amount of money into a hat. Eventually, the owners would insert a hand into the hat, or *hand in cap*. Depending on whether the owners withdrew their hands with money determined the outcome of the deal. The term *handicap* was used in rules for horse racing in the late 1600s. Today, it applies to a disadvantage in a sporting event, like golf, or it describes something that holds a person back or that makes things harder for him or her.

Word Analysis

Write the **list word** formed by adding one of the following endings or suffixes to each of the words given: **er, ed, en, ing, ly**.

1. admit _____
2. confer _____
3. omit _____
4. forbid _____
5. permit _____
6. defer _____
7. patrol _____
8. control _____
9. occur _____
10. occasional _____
11. propel _____
12. handicap _____
13. incur _____
14. overlap _____
15. prefer _____
16. acquit _____
17. expel _____
18. deter _____

Word Application

Write a **list word** to complete each sentence.

1. The directors of the manufacturing firm _____ about how to increase production.

2. Unfortunately, Ian _____ his name from his project.

3. Lisa was _____ from the program because she broke the rules.

4. The breathtaking view from the top of Mt. Washington was _____.

5. A new local television station will begin _____ programs next week.

6. Mrs. Chase is the air-traffic _____ who will be guiding the disabled jet through the landing.

7. The guard dogs are doing a fine job of _____ trespassers.

8. After weeks of testimony, the jury _____ the defendant.

9. A solar eclipse will be _____ at the beginning of next month.

10. Any bills that have been _____ during your stay will be paid by the company.

11. Although Jon enjoyed snowboarding, he really _____ summer sports.

12. Since their vacations are _____, they plan to spend some time together at the beach.

13. State troopers _____ the highway in unmarked cars.

LIST WORDS

controller	permitted	omitted	occasionally
patrolled	admitting	expelled	unforgettable
forbidden	occurring	incurred	transmitting
conferred	acquitted	propeller	overlapping
preferred	deterring	deferred	handicapped

Puzzle

Write the **list word** that is a synonym for each word given to complete the crossword puzzle.

ACROSS

1. disabled
5. happening
6. director
8. policed
9. ejected
11. postponed
15. sending
18. confessing
19. allowed
20. preventing

DOWN

2. cleared
3. outlawed
4. rotor blades
7. sometimes
10. favored
12. eliminated
13. memorable
14. consulted
16. overlaid
17. acquired

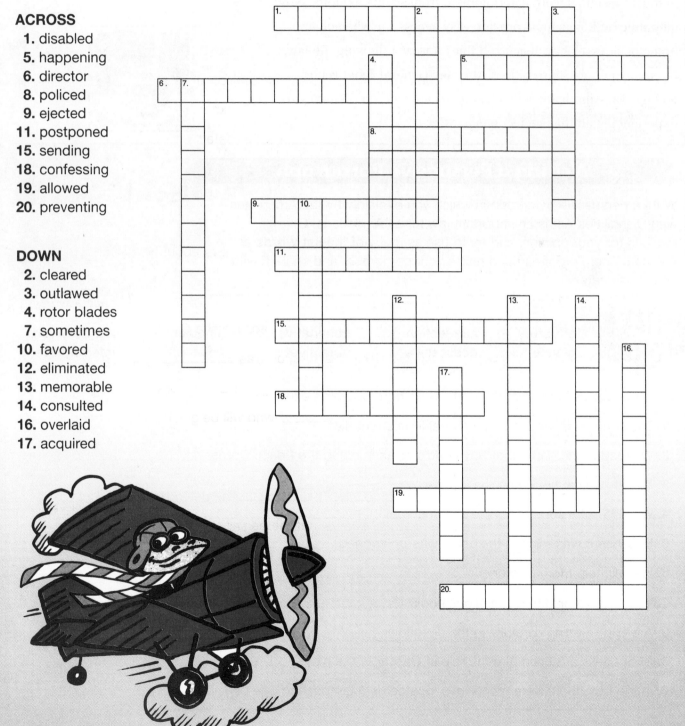

Proofreading

Use the proofreading marks to correct the mistakes in the article below. Then, write the misspelled **list words** correctly on the lines.

Proofreading Marks

⬯ spelling mistake   ⊙ add period
≡ capital letter   ⌃ add comma

On July 26 2000 the americans with Disabilities Act celebrated its tenth anniversary This historic law confered on handicaped people throughout america the right to greater access, admiting them to buildings nationwide. Before 1990, for example, many people in wheelchairs found that the stairs in most museums were detering them from seeing exhibits. Now, all public buildings must provide easy access for wheelchairs. Some businesses have encurred fines for not following the law, but many people share retired Attorney General Janet reno's feeling that Americans with disabilities are well on their way to experiencing all that society has to offer.

1. _____

2. _____

3. _____

4. _____

5. _____

Writing a Persuasive Paragraph

Write a persuasive paragraph in which you explain why the Americans with Disabilities Act is an important law for all Americans. Give reasons for your opinion, and try to use as many of the **list words** as you can. Then, proofread and revise your paragraph, and share it with your classmates.

BONUS WORDS

adverb	interjection	nominative	singular	auxiliary verb
clause	possessive	objective	adjective	interrogative

Write the **bonus word** that the underlined word or words exemplify.

1. <u>They</u> arrived in time to see the opening ceremonies. _____

2. We read in the paper that <u>Raymond's</u> brother joined the Peace Corps. _____

3. Tina drove <u>cautiously</u> on the icy road. _____

4. <u>Wow!</u> What a surprise it is to see you again! _____

5. <u>Because it was raining,</u> the game was postponed. _____

6. We <u>will</u> help Mom fix dinner. _____

7. You have to read this <u>marvelous</u> book. _____

8. <u>Are you</u> listening carefully to the directions? _____

9. Miss Lewis assigned <u>him</u> the role of Caesar in the play. _____

10. In the box, there were magazines, postcards, stamps, and one <u>pencil</u>. _____

- Dividing words into syllables can help you spell them. Usually, you can divide between a root or base word and a prefix or suffix, as in re/act. You can divide between two consonants that come between two vowels, as in col/lect. When only one consonant comes between two vowels, divide after the first vowel if it is long, as in pro/tect, and after the consonant if the vowel is short, as in sat/is/fy. A vowel can also form its own syllable, as in vi/o/lent.

- Pay particular attention to the spelling of word endings. Words ending with **al**, such as fiscal, may sound as if they end with **le** or **el**. The /ər/ sound you hear at the end of junior can be spelled many ways, as in murmur, grammar, humor, and super.

- Pay attention to words that have endings beginning with vowels. These may have had their final consonants doubled if the vowel before the consonant is short, as in trotting and permitted.

Lesson 1

List Words

affidavit

appetite

commemorate

tendency

voluntary

resurrect

dominate

guardian

saturate

installation

_____

_____

Write a **list word** to complete each sentence.

1. Tomatoes have a _____ to grow best during hot, sunny weather.

2. The _____ the witness signed was given to the judge.

3. Your idea didn't work last year, but let's _____ it and see if we have better luck this year.

4. A sprinkler is the easiest way to _____ a lawn with an inch of water.

5. A child's _____ is an adult who is authorized to make decisions for the child.

6. A contribution of $10.00 is _____, not required.

7. The _____ of an antenna can improve TV reception.

8. A water tower that is as large as a skyscraper will _____ the landscape.

9. My parents will plant a cherry tree to _____ my sister's birth.

10. After a workout, it takes a lot more than one sandwich to satisfy my _____.

List Words

artificial
criminal
experimental
hysterical
revival
tropical
logical
perpetual
colossal
accidental

_____
_____

Write a **list word** to complete each analogy.

1. Huge is to small as _____ is to tiny.

2. Cold is to hot as arctic is to _____.

3. Careful is to thoughtless as _____ is to irrational.

4. Death is to burial as rebirth is to _____.

5. Serenity is to disorganization as tranquil is to _____.

6. Genuine is to authentic as _____ is to unnatural.

7. Eternity is to momentary as _____ is to temporary.

8. Honorable is to dishonorable as legal is to _____.

9. Purposeful is to scheduled as _____ is to unscheduled.

10. Photography is to artistic as chemistry is to _____.

List Words

possession
summon
cancellation
successive
acceptance
assistance
depression
immense
necessity
immigration

_____
_____

Write **list words** to answer the questions. Some words are used more than once.

Which words contain double **m**?

1. _____

2. _____

3. _____

Which words contain double **s**?

4. _____

5. _____

6. _____

7. _____

8. _____

Which words end in **ance**?

9. _____

10. _____

Which words end in **ation**?

11. _____

12. _____

Which words end in **sion**?

13. _____

14. _____

Lesson 4

List Words

ancestors
investor
particular
perpendicular
reflector
murmur
vinegar
glacier
conqueror
angular

_____
_____

Write the **list word** that matches each clue.

1. found in a cold place _____
2. a gentle sound _____
3. shines light back at you _____
4. someone with money to loan _____
5. not rounded _____
6. not slanted _____
7. ingredient in salad dressing _____
8. great-grandparents, for instance _____
9. a winner _____
10. separate or special _____

Lesson 5

List Words

admitting
deferred
incurred
omitted
preferred
conferred
handicapped
occurring
occasionally
unforgettable

_____
_____

Unscramble the **list words** to complete the crossword puzzle.

ACROSS
2. INROCRUCG
4. LYANSOACLOCI
7. REPFREDER
8. UCRINDRE
9. FRONDRECE

DOWN
1. LABEFUNGETORT
2. TOMIDET
3. REFEDDER
5. ENPAIDDPACH
6. INTAMGTID

Show What You Know

One word is misspelled in each set of **list words**. Fill in the circle next to the **list word** that is spelled incorrectly.

1. ○ artificial   ○ abandon   ○ conqueror   ○ cancelation
2. ○ drizle   ○ impostor   ○ wholly   ○ experimental
3. ○ exposure   ○ possession   ○ literal   ○ moderater
4. ○ succulant   ○ revival   ○ professor   ○ ornament
5. ○ vinegar   ○ tendency   ○ colossal   ○ comemorate
6. ○ affidavet   ○ cordially   ○ cerebral   ○ controller
7. ○ patrolled   ○ fiscall   ○ consolidate   ○ immense
8. ○ graditude   ○ oppress   ○ logical   ○ forbidden
9. ○ resurrect   ○ sensational   ○ conferred   ○ succesive
10. ○ tropical   ○ undoubtedly   ○ prefered   ○ withholding
11. ○ criminal   ○ appetite   ○ alligater   ○ unforgettable
12. ○ hystericle   ○ junior   ○ curiosity   ○ deferred
13. ○ incubator   ○ perpetuel   ○ expelled   ○ guardian
14. ○ murmer   ○ saturate   ○ transmitting   ○ supplemental
15. ○ voluntary   ○ reflector   ○ upheeval   ○ occasionally
16. ○ deterring   ○ ancestors   ○ barbaque   ○ acceptance
17. ○ dominate   ○ corrupt   ○ glacier   ○ occuring
18. ○ investor   ○ imigration   ○ incurred   ○ installation
19. ○ boycott   ○ propellor   ○ particular   ○ specifications
20. ○ anchor   ○ ascertain   ○ admiting   ○ summon
21. ○ accidental   ○ anguler   ○ assistance   ○ omitted
22. ○ gladiator   ○ permitted   ○ dizmal   ○ depression
23. ○ nescessity   ○ integral   ○ linear   ○ acquitted
24. ○ recital   ○ overlapping   ○ pollen   ○ perpendiculer
25. ○ survival   ○ supress   ○ tweezers   ○ handicapped

Prefixes for Numbers

 TIP

Prefixes with Greek or Latin roots can indicate "how much." Here are some examples.

Prefix	Origin	Meaning	Prefix	Origin	Meaning
milli	Latin	"one-thousandth"	**duo**	Latin	"two"
centi	Latin	"one-hundredth"	**deca**	Greek	"ten"
deci	Latin	"one-tenth"	**kilo**	Greek	"one thousand"
semi	Latin	"half"	**myria**	Greek	"countless"
mono	Greek	"one"			

Vocabulary Development

Write the **list word** that matches each clue.

1. music for two people _____

2. speech by one person _____

3. on one tone _____

4. 1,000 watts _____

5. not of high value _____

6. total control _____

7. 0.1 liter _____

8. 0.01 meter _____

9. 0.001 liter _____

10. large stone block _____

11. ten years _____

12. king or queen _____

Dictionary Skills

Write the **list word** that matches each sound-spelling.

1. (sem′i an′yoo wəl) _____

2. (des′ə mēt′ər) _____

3. (sen′tə grād) _____

4. (män′ə lôg) _____

5. (mil′ə gram) _____

6. (kil′ə lēt′ər) _____

7. (des′ə m′l) _____

8. (mir′ē əd) _____

9. (doo′pleks) _____

10. (män′ərk) _____

LIST WORDS

1. centigrade
2. decimal
3. kiloliter
4. monolith
5. monarch
6. centimeter
7. deciliter
8. kilowatt
9. monopoly
10. myriad
11. decade
12. duet
13. milligram
14. monotone
15. semiannual
16. decimeter
17. duplex
18. milliliter
19. monologue
20. semiprecious

29

DID YOU KNOW ?

Kilowatt means "1,000 watts." A watt is a unit of electric power that was named for Scottish inventor James Watt, best known for his contributions to the development of the steam engine in the late 1700s.

Word Analysis

Write the **list word** derived from the Greek or Latin root given.

1. Greek **polein** ("to sell") _____

2. Greek **plax** ("surface") _____

3. Greek **lithos** ("stone") _____

4. Latin **annus** ("year") _____

5. Greek **tonos** ("tone") _____

6. Greek **archein** ("to rule") _____

7. Latin **gradus** ("degree") _____

8. Greek **legein** ("to speak") _____

9. Latin **gramma** ("small weight") _____

10. Latin **pretium** ("price") _____

Syllabication

Write each **list word** under the correct heading.

Words with Two Syllables

1. _____

2. _____

3. _____

4. _____

Words with Five Syllables

5. _____

Words with Three Syllables

6. _____

7. _____

8. _____

9. _____

10. _____

11. _____

12. _____

13. _____

Words with Four Syllables

14. _____

15. _____

16. _____

17. _____

18. _____

19. _____

20. _____

Word Application

Underline the **list word** that is used incorrectly in each sentence. Write the correct **list word** on the line.

1. The library has a monopoly of books to choose from. _____

2. That person speaks in an uninteresting myriad. _____

3. Does the company have a monotone on cable-TV service? _____

LIST WORDS

centigrade	decimal	decade	decimeter
monotone	deciliter	duet	semiannual
kiloliter	kilowatt	myriad	centimeter
monolith	monopoly	milliliter	monologue
monarch	milligram	duplex	semiprecious

Classification

Write a **list word** to complete each series.

1. Fahrenheit, Celsius, _____

2. weekly, monthly, _____

3. solo, _____, trio

4. home, _____, apartment

5. year, _____, century

6. _____, gram, kilogram

Puzzle

Use **list words** to complete the crossword puzzle.

ACROSS

1. period of ten years
3. large block of stone
7. owned or controlled by one person or group
8. maintaining the same tone or pitch
9. one-thousandth of a gram
10. having two units or parts
14. thermometer based on 0° as the freezing point of water
16. one-tenth of a meter
17. large, indefinite number or variety
18. 1,000 liters
19. one-thousandth of a liter

DOWN

1. counted by tens
2. long speech by one person
4. king, queen, or emperor
5. happening twice a year
6. not highly valuable
11. one-tenth of a liter
12. one-hundredth of a meter
13. 1,000 watts
15. music for two voices

Proofreading

Use the proofreading marks to correct the mistakes in the article below. Then, write the misspelled **list words** correctly on the lines.

Proofreading Marks

⬭ spelling mistake   ⊙ add period

? add question mark   ⌃ add comma

Have you ever seen a picture of Stonehenge. A miriyad of giant stones form this ruin in southern England. It is not a single edifice, but a circular stone structure that was built beginning around 3,100 B.C. Each monnolith that makes up Stonehenge weighs several tons. Over a dekade ago, scientists proposed the theory that the structure was an early observatory. In England, some people believe that Queen Boudicca a monarck of the Celtic people built Stonehenge as her monument Today many people come on a semianual basis to celebrate the summer and winter solstices at Stonehenge.

1. _____

2. _____

3. _____

4. _____

5. _____

Writing Interview Questions

What kind of questions would you like to ask scientists about their work at Stonehenge? Write a set of interview questions, using as many **list words** as possible. Proofread and revise your questions. Then, use your questions to stage a question-and-answer session with another classmate.

BONUS WORDS

genetics	reproduction	pregnancy	fetus	identical
heredity	umbilical cord	fertilization	embryo	fraternal

Write the **bonus word** to complete each sentence.

1. Twins from the same egg are _____.

2. _____ twins come from two different eggs and do not look identical.

3. The branch of biology that deals with heredity and variation in living things is _____.

4. The _____ is the source of nourishment for a fetal mammal.

5. The transmission of traits from parent to offspring is called _____.

6. Animals create new members of the species through the process of _____.

7. _____ is the state of a female animal as she carries her unborn child.

8. Through _____, the female's egg begins to develop into offspring.

9. An _____ is an animal's fertilized egg in the earliest stage of development.

10. In its later stages of development, the unborn offspring is called the _____.

Prefixes ante, epi, pre, pro

 TIP

Some prefixes give "when" or "where" clues. The prefixes **ante**, **epi**, **pre**, and **pro** can refer to time or place. An understanding of these prefixes can help you spell many words. Look at the chart below.

Prefix	Meaning	Example	Meaning
ante	"before," "in front of"	anteroom	"entrance room"
epi	"on the outside," "over"	epidermis	"outer skin layer"
pre	"in front," "earlier"	premature	"happening early"
pro	"forward," "ahead"	protrude	"to stick out"

Vocabulary Development

Write the **list word** that matches each synonym.

1. event _____
2. first _____
3. letter _____
4. assume _____
5. early _____
6. overhang _____
7. foreseer _____
8. parade _____
9. skin _____
10. forerunner _____
11. forward _____
12. forewarning _____

Dictionary Skills

Rewrite each of the following **list words** to show how they are divided into syllables.

1. protocol _____
2. presuppose _____
3. prelude _____
4. epitaph _____
5. anteroom _____
6. proposal _____
7. premonition _____
8. epilogue _____
9. anterior _____
10. prejudice _____

LIST WORDS

1. antecedent
2. epilogue
3. episode
4. premier
5. protrude
6. anterior
7. premonition
8. preamble
9. prejudice
10. procession
11. epitaph
12. anteroom
13. presuppose
14. premature
15. prophet
16. epistle
17. epidermis
18. prelude
19. proposal
20. protocol

Spelling Practice

DID YOU KNOW ?

Premonition comes from the Latin word *monere*, meaning "to warn." This word is, in turn, related to the Latin word *memini*, meaning "I remember." Thus, a premonition could be considered a reminder that occurs beforehand, or a forewarning.

Word Analysis

Write the missing prefixes to form **list words** that complete the definitions.

1. _____ **dermis**, the outer layer of skin

2. _____ **monition**, a preconceived notion

3. _____ **trude**, to stick out

4. _____ **suppose**, to suppose beforehand

5. _____ **tocol**, a code of proper behavior

6. _____ **room**, an outside chamber

7. _____ **posal**, a suggestion

8. _____ **judice**, judging beforehand

9. _____ **logue**, a speech at the end of a play

10. _____ **taph**, words engraved on a tombstone

11. _____ **mature**, before the proper or usual time

12. _____ **lude**, a preliminary part

Word Application

Replace the underlined words in each sentence with **list words**. Write the **list words** on the lines.

1. As we entered the <u>front part</u> of the park, we saw a long <u>parade</u> of musicians marching in

   formation. _____ _____

2. During his life, he was considered a great <u>seer</u>, which is why the <u>inscription on his gravestone</u>

   refers to him as a man of wisdom and faith. _____ _____

3. If it weren't for the unpleasant <u>event</u> with the doorman, no one would have known that our

   arrival was <u>too early</u>. _____ _____

4. <u>Correct behavior</u> dictates that we must wait in the <u>front room</u> before all the elders have taken

   their seats. _____ _____

5. The <u>beginning</u>, or opening paragraph, of the Constitution is a kind of <u>introduction</u> for the

   rest of the document. _____ _____

6. It is of <u>the first</u> importance that this <u>letter</u> be sent immediately!

   _____ _____

LIST WORDS

anterior	antecedent	epidermis	epistle
epilogue	premonition	anteroom	epitaph
episode	presuppose	preamble	prelude
proposal	premature	prejudice	premier
protrude	procession	prophet	protocol

Puzzle

This is a crossword puzzle without clues. Use the length and the spelling of each **list word** to complete the puzzle.

Proofreading

Use the proofreading marks to correct the mistakes in the article below. Then, write the misspelled **list words** correctly on the lines.

Proofreading Marks

⬭ spelling mistake ⌗ add space
⌢ delete word / small letter

The Great Circus Parade was first presented in Milwaukee, Wisconsin, in 1963, but ithas its anticedent in the circus parades of Europe. In fact, the circus as an American Amusement Institution was born in 1793 when John Ricketts, who had worked in a circus in London, England, presented a performance in Philadelphia, Pennsylvania. It was a a preloode to the big-top shows people enjoy today. The proposel for the Great Circus Parade came from the director of a circus museum, and the procesion now includes 60 historic circus wagons from around the world. Each year, the Parade is is the most exciting epesode ofa week-long festival of circus activities in Milwaukee.

1. _____

2. _____

3. _____

4. _____

5. _____

Writing a Description

Think of an interesting job in a circus, such as an animal trainer or keeper, a high-wire performer, or a clown. Write a brief description of the job, including what you might like about it, and what might be unpleasant or dangerous. Use some **list words** in your description. Proofread and revise your writing, then share it with classmates. Discuss which jobs seem the most interesting.

BONUS WORDS

| musician | horticulturist | psychiatrist | meteorologist | dental hygienist |
| dietitian | chiropractor | metallurgist | mathematician | physical therapist |

Write the **bonus word** to complete each series.

1. ores, smelting, mines, _____

2. weather, clouds, winds, _____

3. nerves, spinal column, joints, _____

4. songs, performances, instruments, _____

5. trees, shrubs, gardens, _____

6. food, nutrition, vitamins, _____

7. teeth, dentist, X-rays, _____

8. numbers, formulas, equations, _____

9. psychoses, neuroses, depression, _____

10. hydrotherapy, exercises, massage, _____

Prefixes ab, af, ag, an, anti

When added to base words or roots derived from Latin roots, the prefix **ab** usually means "away," "from," or "down." The prefixes **af**, **ag**, and **an** usually mean "to," "at," or "toward." The prefix **anti** means "against."

Latin Root	Meaning	Example	Meaning
horrere	"to shudder"	abhor (verb)	"to dislike intently"
filius	"son"	affiliate (verb)	"to connect with"
gravis	"heavy"	aggravate (verb)	"to make something worse"
nihil	"nothing"	annihilate (verb)	"to destroy completely"
socius	"companion"	antisocial (adj.)	"unfriendly"

Vocabulary Development

Write the **list word** that matches each synonym or definition.

1. friendly _____

2. positive _____

3. to refrain willingly _____

4. to free from guilt _____

5. pushy; assertive _____

Dictionary Skills

Write the **list words** beginning with **ab** in alphabetical order.

1. _____ 4. _____

2. _____ 5. _____

3. _____ 6. _____

Write the **list words** beginning with **af** and **ag** in alphabetical order.

7. _____ 10. _____

8. _____ 11. _____

9. _____ 12. _____

Write the **list words** beginning with **an** in alphabetical order.

13. _____ 17. _____

14. _____ 18. _____

15. _____ 19. _____

16. _____ 20. _____

LIST WORDS

1. abhor
2. abstain
3. affirmative
4. announcement
5. annul
6. abolish
7. absolve
8. affiliate
9. annotate
10. antibiotic
11. absurd
12. affable
13. aggravate
14. annihilate
15. antihistamine
16. abstract
17. affluent
18. aggressive
19. annex
20. antisocial

Spelling Practice

DID YOU KNOW ?

Aggravate comes from a Latin word which means "to make heavier" and is related to the word *gravity*. When a problem is aggravated, it is made heavier or greater than it was.

Word Analysis

Write the **list word** derived from the Latin root given.

1. **notare** ("to mark") _____

2. **fluere** ("to flow") _____

3. **nectere** ("to bind") _____

4. **nullum** ("nothing") _____

5. **biosis** ("life") _____

6. **solvere** ("to release") _____

7. **firmare** ("to make firm") _____

8. **abolere** ("to destroy") _____

9. **nuntiare** ("to report") _____

10. **surdus** ("dull; insensible") _____

Analogies

Write a **list word** to complete each analogy.

1. Dessert is to meal as _____ is to building.

2. Artistic is to painter as _____ is to companion.

3. Feed is to hunger as _____ is to guilt.

4. Fast is to slow as specific is to _____.

5. "Yes, please" is to accept as "No, thank you" is to _____.

Word Application

Select a **list word** from the choices in parentheses to complete each sentence. Write the **list word** on the line.

1. Many nations _____ with the United Nations. (affiliate, annul, aggravate)

2. People on low-fat diets _____ from rich foods. (absolve, abstain, aggravate)

3. This storm will _____ the river's flooding. (abhor, aggravate, annul)

4. I don't mean to be _____, but I'd like to be alone. (affluent, affable, antisocial)

5. We _____ termites before they ruin a house! (absolve, annihilate, annex)

6. Both parties voted to _____ the bad agreement. (annul, absolve, abstract)

7. An _____ family donated funds for the hospital wing. (antibiotic, affluent)

LIST WORDS

aggressive	aggravate	absurd	annul
antisocial	absolve	affluent	affable
affirmative	annihilate	abolish	abhor
announcement	annotate	affiliate	annex
antihistamine	antibiotic	abstract	abstain

Puzzle

Use the **list words** to complete the crossword puzzle.

ACROSS

1. to put in notes
5. something that is announced
6. to put an end to or cancel
8. friendly or easy to talk to
11. medicine used to fight hay fever or colds
12. saying "yes"
14. to make worse
15. disliking company
16. ridiculous
17. to free of guilt
18. to get rid of

DOWN

2. wealthy or rich
3. to destroy completely
4. addition to a building
7. eager to fight
8. unlike real things
9. to become associated with
10. detest or hate
11. to hold oneself back
13. something used to kill germs

Proofreading

Use the proofreading marks to correct the mistakes in the article. Write the misspelled **list words** correctly on the lines.

Proofreading Marks

⬭ spelling mistake ⊙ add period

ⱱ add apostrophe ¶ new paragraph

The aptly named common cold is the most frequent infection in the United States, and one that most people abhore. Its hard to remain afable when you dont feel well Cold symptoms begin when an aggresive virus attaches itself to the lining of your nasal passages or throat. Your immune system then attacks the germs with white blood cells, which is what causes the symptoms of a cold.

Millions eagerly await the anouncement of a cure. In the meantime, an antihistamene may temporarily relieve symptoms, but an antebiotic will have no effect on a cold, since it doesnt kill viruses.

1. _____

2. _____

3. _____

4. _____

5. _____

6. _____

Writing a List

Write a list of steps people can take to both prevent catching a cold, and to feel better if they do catch one. Use as many **list words** as you can. When finished, proofread and revise your list, then share it with others. Use the lists to create a group poster entitled "The Common Cold—Prevention and Cures."

BONUS WORDS

cliché	obsolete	slang	superfluous	verbose
jargon	colloquial	trite	redundant	vernacular

Write a **bonus word** to match each etymology.

1. Greek **tryein** ("to wear away") _____

2. Latin **ob** ("toward") + **exolescere** ("out of use") _____

3. Latin **super** ("above") + **fluctus** ("wave") _____

4. Latin **verna** ("native population") _____

5. German **klitsch** ("clump of clay") _____

6. Latin **com** ("together") + **loqui** ("to speak") _____

7. Latin **verbum** ("word") _____

8. Latin **re** ("again") + **undare** ("to swell") _____

Write a **bonus word** to define each example.

9. Path noise disrupted the radio transmission. _____

10. Those wheels will run you about ten grand. _____

Prefixes bene, beni, coll, com, contra, eu

TIP

The prefixes **bene**, **beni**, **coll**, **com**, **contra**, and **eu** refer to place or value. Knowing and recognizing these prefixes can help you spell many words.

Prefix	Meaning	Example	Meaning
bene or **beni**	"good"	benign	"not harmful"
coll	"with; together"	collect	"to gather"
com	"with; together"	commerce	"buying and selling"
contra	"against," "opposite"	contradict	"to express opposition"
eu	"good"	eulogy	"public praise after a person's death"

Vocabulary Development

Write the **list word** that matches each definition clue.

1. something sold _____
2. public or shared _____
3. beginning _____
4. happiness; giddiness _____
5. to compare _____
6. different; opposed _____
7. smuggled goods _____
8. a crash _____
9. remark _____
10. a promise or pledge _____
11. not harmful _____
12. fellow worker _____

Dictionary Skills

Write the **list word** that matches each sound-spelling.

1. (kə lab′ə rāt) _____
2. (käm′ərs) _____
3. (ben′ə fak′tər) _____
4. (kə lek′shən) _____
5. (yo͞o lə jē) _____
6. (ben′ə fit) _____
7. (kän trə dikt′) _____
8. (bi nīn′) _____
9. (käl′ēg) _____
10. (kə myo͞ot′) _____

LIST WORDS

1. benefactor
2. colleague
3. commute
4. communal
5. contradict
6. benign
7. collection
8. comment
9. commencement
10. contrast
11. benefit
12. collaborate
13. commitment
14. contraband
15. eulogy
16. collision
17. commodity
18. commerce
19. contrary
20. euphoria

Spelling Practice

DID YOU KNOW ?

Euphoria once meant "relief that comes from a medical procedure." This meaning, in turn, came from a Greek word meaning "power of bearing children easily." Today, euphoria no longer refers to medical procedures, but is used to describe an extreme feeling of well-being.

Word Analysis

Write each **list word** under its prefix.

bene, beni

1. _____   3. _____

2. _____

coll

4. _____   6. _____

5. _____   7. _____

eu

8. _____   9. _____

contra

10. _____   12. _____

11. _____   13. _____

com

14. _____   18. _____

15. _____   19. _____

16. _____   20. _____

17. _____

Classification

Write a **list word** to complete each series.

1. accident, crash, _____   **2.** harmless, favorable, _____

Word Application

Write a **list word** to complete each sentence.

1. This new gymnasium will _____ everyone in the entire city!

2. Professor Katz and Dr. Sanchez will _____ on a new book.

3. At the funeral, the minister gave a beautiful _____.

4. If we receive funds, we will make a _____ to this new project.

5. All the animals, both horses and cattle, drank from one _____ trough.

LIST WORDS

benefactor	benign	commencement	comment
colleague	contrary	collaborate	collision
commute	eulogy	commitment	commerce
communal	contrast	contraband	collection
contradict	benefit	commodity	euphoria

Puzzle

Use the **list words** to complete the crossword puzzle.

ACROSS

2. a crash or clash

5. a person who works in the same office or field as another

6. anything that is bought or sold

7. a person who helps those in need

10. to travel to a particular place on a regular basis

11. kindly, good-natured

13. smuggled goods

15. a feeling of high spirits

16. a remark expressing an opinion

17. in opposition

18. something gathered

DOWN

1. to work together in preparing something

2. a promise; a pledge

3. anything that helps

4. buying or selling; trade

8. belonging to the community; public

9. to say the opposite of

10. a beginning or a start; a graduation ceremony

12. to compare in a way that shows differences

14. a speech or writing praising a person who has died

Proofreading

Use the proofreading marks to correct the mistakes in the following article. Then, write the misspelled **list words** correctly on the lines.

Proofreading Marks

⬭ spelling mistake ＝ capital letter

🖑🖑 add quotation marks

! add exclamation mark

The College of philadelphia was one of the first American colleges to grant degrees. The school held its first comencement in 1757. In comtrast with other schools, the program was conducted with prayers and sermons. In 1783, an early benefacter of the school, george washington, received an honorary degree. Imagine the students' excitement In 1823, the ceremony was moved to Masonic Hall, which was the work of architect William Strickland. Architectural historians have made the commint that the Hall is "one of the earliest important American buildings in the Gothic style. Now known as the university of pennsylvania, the college offers degrees in everything from comerce to art history.

1. _____

2. _____

3. _____

4. _____

5. _____

Writing a Graduation Speech

Imagine that you have been chosen to speak at your school's graduation ceremony. Write a short speech that tells your hopes for the future and your feelings about your school. Include as many **list words** as you can. Then, proofread and revise your speech, and read it aloud to your classmates.

BONUS WORDS

philharmonic	classical	virtuoso	a cappella	crescendo
conservatory	soloist	vibrato	cadence	decrescendo

Write the **bonus word** that matches each definition clue.

1. highly skilled performer _____

2. one who performs alone _____

3. society of music lovers

_____

4. music in the European tradition

_____

5. voices without instrumental accompaniment

_____

6. pulsating musical effect _____

7. beat or rhythm _____

8. getting louder and louder

_____

9. getting less and less loud

_____

10. place where musicians study and learn

_____

Prefixes <u>mal</u>, <u>meta</u>, <u>de</u>, <u>dis</u>

The prefixes **mal, de**, and **dis** have Latin roots. The prefix **mal** usually means "bad." The prefix **de** often means "away from" or "undo." The prefix **dis** often means "not" or "apart." The prefix **meta** has Greek roots. It can mean "with, after, behind, beyond, among, about."

Root	Meaning	English Word	Meaning
functio	"to perform"	malfunction	"to function incorrectly"
morphe	"form; shape"	metamorphosis	"a change in form"
cedere	"to go forward"	deceased	"dead"
solvere	"to free"	dissolve	"to break apart in liquid"

Vocabulary Development

Write the **list word** that matches each definition clue.

1. argument _____

2. twist; deform _____

3. displeasure _____

4. drawback; minus _____

5. ill will _____

6. complete change _____

7. break apart in liquid _____

Dictionary Skills

Under each heading, write the **list words** in alphabetical order.

Words with Prefix **de**

1. _____

2. _____

3. _____

4. _____

5. _____

6. _____

7. _____

8. _____

Words with Prefix **mal**

9. _____

10. _____

11. _____

12. _____

Words with Prefix **meta**

13. _____

14. _____

15. _____

LIST WORDS

1. malfunction
2. detour
3. metaphor
4. disadvantage
5. decompose
6. malevolent
7. dissatisfaction
8. metamorphosis
9. distort
10. decanter
11. metabolism
12. dissolve
13. decline
14. maladjusted
15. dispute
16. descendant
17. malice
18. deception
19. deplete
20. deceased

Spelling Practice

Word Analysis

Write the **list word** derived from the Latin root given.

1. **clinare** ("to bend") _____

2. **deplere** ("to empty") _____

3. **satis** ("enough") _____

4. **torquere** ("to twist") _____

5. **volens** ("to wish") _____

6. **functio** ("to perform") _____

7. **componer** ("to put together") _____

8. **scandere** ("to climb") _____

9. **cedere** ("to go forward") _____

10. **justus** ("just") _____

Antonyms

Write the **list word** that matches each antonym.

1. satisfaction _____

2. truth _____

3. accept _____

4. agreement _____

5. ancestor _____

6. kind _____

7. goodwill _____

8. alive _____

9. permanent form _____

10. benefit _____

Word Application

Select a **list word** from the choices in parentheses to complete each sentence. Write the **list word** on the line.

1. Through _____, the body regulates its flow of energy. (metaphor, metabolism, malice)

2. The crystal _____ was filled with cold water. (decanter, deplete, maladjusted)

3. Fallen trees will eventually _____ and enrich the forest soil. (dispute, decompose, distort)

4. The _____ around the construction is clearly marked. (dispute, deplete, detour)

5. "Life is just a bowl of cherries" is a _____. (decanter, metaphor, malice)

LIST WORDS

malice	malevolent	deplete	descendant
detour	dissatisfaction	metaphor	malfunction
dispute	metamorphosis	deception	decompose
distort	disadvantage	decanter	metabolism
decline	maladjusted	dissolve	deceased

Puzzle

Each of the following clues is an example, or illustration, of a **list word**. Write the associated **list words** in the answer spaces. Then, transfer the numbered letters to the spaces below to answer the riddle.

1. "No, thank you." — — — — — —
                        7   23

2. Traffic is diverted. — — — — — —
                          14   5

3. grandchild — — — — — — — — — —
                    24   2

4. "Truth is beauty." — — — — — — — —
                         1   20

5. Flowers wither. — — — — — — — —
                         12 19

6. "I'm not pleased." — — — — — — — — — — — — — —
                              8   4

7. false advertising claims — — — — — — — — — —
                                      17 6

8. Stir sugar in water. — — — — — — —
                             22 3

9. revenge — — — — — —
                16   9

10. Exaggerate the facts. — — — — — —
                              10 18

11. cemetery occupants — — — — — —
                           13   15

12. fairy-tale dragon — — — — — — — — —
                               21   11

RIDDLE: How did the caterpillar turn into an elephant?

ANSWER: through a 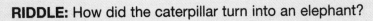 — — — — — — — — — — — of
                     1 2 3 4 5 6 7 8 9 10 11

— — — — — — — — — — — — —
12 13 14 15 16 17 18 19 20 21 22 23 24

Proofreading

Use the proofreading marks to correct the mistakes in the following paragraphs. Then, write the misspelled **list words** correctly on the lines.

Proofreading Marks

⬭ spelling mistake   ⌃ add comma

/ small letter

? add question mark

Monarch butterflies go through many stages in their metamorphisis from egg to adult. First, the female lays her eggs on a Milkweed plant. When the caterpillar has grown, it forms a cocoon called a chrysalis. The Monarch has a fast metabolizm and can sometimes change into a butterfly in about a week. Even so, due to habitat loss, their numbers are in dicline around the world.

Did you know that birds avoid Monarchs When monarchs feed on milkweed, they collect a poison that makes them distasteful to birds, putting other insects at a disatvantage. Birds learn to spot the monarch's pattern and avoid it. Viceroy butterflies share similar markings, a deseption that keeps birds from eating them too.

1. _____

2. _____

3. _____

4. _____

5. _____

Writing a Descriptive Paragraph

Migratory groups of monarch butterflies gather each winter at places in California and central Mexico. Write a description of what it might be like to stumble upon one of these gatherings. Use as many **list words** as you can. Proofread and revise your description, then read it aloud to your classmates.

BONUS WORDS

arcade	façade	geodesic	Doric	colonnade
buttress	frieze	Corinthian	Ionic	gargoyle

Write the **bonus word** that matches each definition clue.

1. ornamental "creature" _____

2. with a gridlike frame _____

3. projecting support structure _____

4. row of columns _____

5. band of sculpture _____

6. front of building _____

7. arched, covered passageway _____

Write the **bonus words** that name types of columns.

8. _____   9. _____   10. _____

- Some Greek and Latin prefixes can be added to roots and base words to indicate time, place, direction, or value. Here are some examples.

Prefix	Meaning	English Word	Meaning
ab	"away; from; down"	abhor	"to dislike intensely"
af, ag, an	"to; at; toward"	affiliate	"to join with"
ante	"before; in front"	anterior	"toward the front"
anti	"against"	antisocial	"unfriendly"
bene, beni	"good"	benefit	"advantage"
coll, com	"with; together"	commerce	"business; trade"
contra	"against"	contradict	"disagree; dispute"
de	"apart; undo"	detour	"alternative route"
dis	"apart; not"	dissatisfied	"not satisfied"
epi	"outside; over"	epidermis	"outside skin layer"
eu	"good"	eulogy	"funeral tribute"
mal	"bad"	malevolent	"evil"
meta	"with; beyond"	metaphor	"exaggerated comparison"
pre	"infront; earlier"	preview	"glimpse of future event"
pro	"forward; ahead"	protrude	"stick out in front"

- Other Greek and Latin prefixes, such as **duo** and **deca**, indicate number. A <u>duet</u> is music for two voices. A <u>decade</u> is ten years.

Lesson 7

Write prefixes and **list words** to complete this chart.

List Words

centimeter

monologue

semiprecious

decade

myriad

kilowatt

semiannual

deciliter

milligram

duplex

_____

_____

	Prefix	English Word	Meaning
1.	_____	_____	ten years
2.	_____	_____	one-tenth of a liter
3.	_____	_____	an extreme amount
4.	_____	_____	one-thousandth of a gram
5.	_____	_____	1,000 watts
6.	_____	_____	occurring twice a year
7.	_____	_____	one-hundredth of a meter
8.	_____	_____	having two units
9.	_____	_____	speech by one person
10.	_____	_____	not of the highest value

List Words

- antecedent
- epilogue
- epidermis
- prejudice
- procession
- preamble
- premier
- epistle
- anterior
- epitaph
- _____
- _____

Write a **list word** to complete each sentence.

1. In the _____, the author explained what happened to the explorers following their discovery.

2. The humorous poet Dorothy Parker once suggested this _____ for her own tombstone: "Excuse My Dust."

3. As the maid of honor, I was next to last in the bridal _____.

4. The _____ of the U.S. Constitution begins, "We the People of the United States. . . ."

5. In an _____ to his editor, the author F. Scott Fitzgerald introduced a writer named Ernest Hemingway.

6. A pronoun must agree in number with its _____.

7. The _____ lobe is in the front part of the brain.

8. _____ can cause people to dislike strangers.

9. Sunburn is an inflammation of the _____.

10. Wheat and corn are two of the _____ agricultural products of America's midwestern states.

List Words

- abhor
- affiliate
- absurd
- antisocial
- annihilate
- antihistamine
- affirmative
- aggressive
- announcement
- aggravate
- _____
- _____

Write a **list word** to answer each definition clue.

1. medicine to relieve allergy symptoms _____
2. silly or foolish _____
3. unfriendly _____
4. ready to argue or fight _____
5. to become a member _____
6. to destroy completely _____
7. a public message _____
8. positive or bold _____
9. dislike intently _____
10. to make worse or to annoy _____

List Words

contrast

collision

eulogy

contrary

benign

contradict

benefactor

commencement

collaborate

colleague

_____

_____

Each of these sentences contains the wrong **list word**. Cross out the word, and write the correct **list word** on the line.

1. A kind eulogy donated funds. _____

2. The contrary damaged my car. _____

3. The two writers agreed to contradict on a book. _____

4. Doctors must be both intelligent scientists and contrast listeners.

   _____

5. At the memorial, an eloquent commencement was delivered. _____

6. Compare and collaborate the music of Mozart and Bach. _____

7. After the benefactor ceremony, the graduates shook hands.

   _____

8. Your collision, or associate, left this message for you. _____

9. In the debate, Frank used established facts to colleague the position

   of his opponent. _____

10. Although we're friends, Jim and I have benign ideas on many

    subjects. _____

List Words

deception

deplete

dissolve

malice

distort

descendant

metamorphosis

decompose

malevolent

metaphor

_____

_____

Use the **list words** to complete the crossword puzzle.

ACROSS
1. to rot or erode
4. to twist or bend
5. active ill will; spite
7. to use up a supply
8. evil or mean

DOWN
1. child of future generation
2. dramatic change in form
3. fraud or falsehood
4. to break apart in liquid
6. figurative comparison

Show What You Know

One word is misspelled in each set of **list words**. Fill in the circle next to the **list word** that is spelled incorrectly.

1. ○ centigrade   ○ colision   ○ absurd   ○ anterior
2. ○ agravate   ○ premonition   ○ decimal   ○ commodity
3. ○ preamble   ○ commerce   ○ affable   ○ kilolitre
4. ○ contrary   ○ monolithe   ○ prejudice   ○ annihilate
5. ○ monarch   ○ procession   ○ euphoria   ○ antihystamine
6. ○ centimeter   ○ epitaphe   ○ abstract   ○ malfunction
7. ○ antiroom   ○ metaphor   ○ affluent   ○ deciliter
8. ○ aggressive   ○ killowatt   ○ detour   ○ presuppose
9. ○ monopoly   ○ premature   ○ annex   ○ disadvantige
10. ○ myried   ○ decompose   ○ prophet   ○ antisocial
11. ○ milligram   ○ benefacter   ○ decade   ○ malevolent
12. ○ colleague   ○ epidirmis   ○ epistle   ○ dissatisfaction
13. ○ prelude   ○ commute   ○ duet   ○ metamorfosis
14. ○ communal   ○ monotone   ○ distort   ○ proposel
15. ○ decanter   ○ semiannual   ○ protocal   ○ contradict
16. ○ decimeter   ○ maladjusted   ○ benign   ○ metabolizm
17. ○ dessolve   ○ collection   ○ duplex   ○ abstain
18. ○ comment   ○ affirmative   ○ decline   ○ mililiter
19. ○ monologe   ○ semiprecious   ○ abhor   ○ commencement
20. ○ contrast   ○ anouncement   ○ annul   ○ dispute
21. ○ anticedent   ○ descendant   ○ benefit   ○ abolish
22. ○ malise   ○ collaborate   ○ absolve   ○ epilogue
23. ○ episode   ○ commitment   ○ afiliate   ○ deception
24. ○ premier   ○ contraband   ○ deplete   ○ anotate
25. ○ antibiotic   ○ deceased   ○ protrude   ○ uelogy

Latin Roots

TIP

A root is a word part that gives the word its basic meaning. Here are some English words that are based on Latin roots.

Latin Roots	Meaning	English Word	Meaning
aqua	"water"	aquatic	"growing or living in water"
hosp, host	"guest; visitor"	hostel	"inn; inexpensive lodging"
hostis	"stranger; enemy"	hostile	"warlike; unfriendly"
later	"side"	lateral	"toward the side"
mort	"death"	mortal	"that which will die"
sim	"like; same"	simultaneous	"occurring at once"
liber	"free"	liberate	"to set free"

Vocabulary Development

Write **list words** with the same Latin root as the word given.

latitude   1. _____   3. _____

         2. _____

mortality 4. _____   6. _____

         5. _____   7. _____

simile   8. _____   10. _____

         9. _____

liberty   11. _____   12. _____

hospital   13. _____   14. _____

hostess   15. _____   16. _____

Dictionary Skills

Write the **list words** that come between each pair of dictionary guide words. Write the words in alphabetical order.

apt/arid   **hose/hot**

1. _____   4. _____

2. _____   5. _____

3. _____   6. _____

                             7. _____

                             8. _____

LIST WORDS

1. aquarium
2. hostel
3. lateral
4. mortuary
5. simultaneous
6. dissimilar
7. hostage
8. aquatic
9. mortgage
10. simulate
11. hospitalize
12. hostile
13. liberal
14. mortician
15. unilateral
16. hospice
17. mortal
18. aquamarine
19. quadrilateral
20. liberate

DID YOU KNOW?

Mortgage comes from two words in Old French, *mort* and *gage*, that meant "dead" and "pledge." The pledge would be "dead" to the lender if the borrower paid the debt and kept the property that had been pledged. The pledge would also be "dead" to the borrower if he or she failed to pay the debt and lost the property.

Spelling Practice

Word Analysis

Write **list words** to answer the following questions.

Which words contain the Latin root that means "free"?

1. _____ 2. _____

Which words contain the Latin root that means "death"?

3. _____ 5. _____

4. _____ 6. _____

Which words contain the Latin root that means "like" or "same"?

10. _____ 12. _____

11. _____

Which word contains the Latin root that means "stranger"?

13. _____

Which words have the Latin root **hosp** that means "guest"?

14. _____ 15. _____

Which words contain the Latin root that means "water"?

16. _____ 18. _____

17. _____

Word Application

Write a **list word** to complete each sentence.

1. Have you seen every fish in the _____?

2. An ordinary sheet of paper has a _____ shape.

3. It will take 20 more years to pay the _____ on the house.

4. We should _____ all the enslaved people in the world.

5. The _____ will help us take care of the funeral proceedings.

6. I am afraid of my neighbor's _____ dogs, so I try to avoid passing his house.

7. Amanda turned on a fan indoors to _____ the wind for her science project.

8. He and his sister are very _____; they enjoy none of the same things!

9. In skiing, _____ movement helps to avoid going forward too fast.

10. He can afford _____ contributions to charity because he is very wealthy.

LIST WORDS

aquarium	hospice	hostel	mortgage
hospitalize	hostage	hostile	unilateral
aquamarine	aquatic	liberal	mortician
quadrilateral	liberate	lateral	mortuary
simultaneous	simulate	mortal	dissimilar

Puzzle

Use the **list words** to complete the crossword puzzle.

ACROSS

1. growing or living in water
6. happening at the same time
9. to admit to a medical care facility
10. bluish-green color
12. a prisoner taken by an enemy
13. in a sideward direction
14. a health-care facility with a home-like feeling
15. free-thinking; generous
18. an overnight shelter used by hikers and other travelers
19. place where corpses are kept before funeral

DOWN

2. a figure with four sides and four angles
3. to pretend; to act like
4. a person who prepares bodies for burial
5. a long-term loan on a piece of property
7. to set free
8. not alike; different
11. one-sided
12. warlike; unfriendly
16. a place where fish are exhibited
17. that which will die

Proofreading

Use the proofreading marks to correct the mistakes in the article below. Then, write the misspelled **list words** correctly on the lines.

The newly remodeled akuarium recently hired an agency to handle their advertisingcampaign. The campaign was designed to release simultainious printand media ads.

The newspaper and magazine ads were not dissimmilar—both featured full-color photos of the diverse acquatic life that can be seen in the many tanks on display. The television ad was able to simmulate an underwater dive where viewers were treated to the beauty of a coral reef. The advertising agencys production department outdid itself and created a great campaign, which generated increased ticket sales in a matter of weeks.

Proofreading Marks

⬭ spelling mistake   ⌗ add space
˅ add apostrophe   ¶ new paragraph

1. _____
2. _____
3. _____
4. _____
5. _____

Writing a Commercial

Write a script for a radio commercial advertising a new aquarium. You may wish to write a dialogue between two people who visited the aquarium and who were very impressed with what they saw. Include dialogue for an announcer and use as many **list words** in your ad as you can. After proofreading and revising your script, work with a small group to present your ad to the class. Later, discuss what made each ad effective.

BONUS WORDS

telecast	ad-libbed	production	technological	frequencies
audition	videotape	amplifier	closed circuit	broadcasting

Write the **bonus word** that matches each clue given.

1. cable-TV program _____
2. TV transmission _____
3. technical progress _____
4. transmitted TV signals _____
5. a TV presentation _____

6. spoken without preparation _____
7. to broadcast by TV _____
8. device to increase sound _____
9. a prerecorded TV program _____
10. to try out for a TV show _____

Latin Roots

TIP

Recognizing Latin roots in words can help you determine the meanings of unfamiliar words. Here are some examples.

Latin Roots	Meaning	English Word	Meaning
plic, plex	"fold"	complication	"something that confuses"
rupt	"break"	interrupt	"break in on"
pend	"hang"	suspended	"hanging down"
struct	"build"	structural	"suitable for building"

Look for the Latin roots in the **list words**.

Vocabulary Development

Write the **list word** from column **B** that matches the synonym in column **A**.

A		**B**
1. puzzling	_____	implicate
2. disturb	_____	bankrupt
3. individually	_____	impending
4. involve	_____	duplicate
5. unexplainable	_____	destruction
6. sudden	_____	perplexing
7. impoverished	_____	independently
8. threatening	_____	inexplicable
9. copy	_____	disrupt
10. wreckage	_____	abrupt

Dictionary Skills

Write the **list word** that matches each sound-spelling.

1. (pen′joo ləm) _____

2. (sə spend′ed) _____

3. (in struk′shən) _____

4. (ap′li kə b'l) _____

5. (käm′plə kā′shən) _____

6. (struk′chər əl) _____

7. (sə spens′) _____

8. (pen′dənt) _____

9. (kəm pleks′) _____

10. (in tə rupt′) _____

LIST WORDS

1. abrupt
2. complex
3. implicate
4. inexplicable
5. structural
6. applicable
7. disrupt
8. independently
9. pendulum
10. suspended
11. bankrupt
12. duplicate
13. instruction
14. pendant
15. suspense
16. complication
17. impending
18. interrupt
19. destruction
20. perplexing

Spelling Practice

DID YOU KNOW?

Bankrupt comes from two Italian words meaning "broken bench." Moneylenders used to carry on their business at a bench or table. They would be put out of business if the bench were broken, just as nowadays people are put out of business if they cannot pay their debts.

Word Analysis

Write **list words** to answer the following questions.

Which words contain the Latin root that means "hang"?

1. _____   4. _____

2. _____   5. _____

3. _____   6. _____

Which words contain the Latin root that means "build"?

7. _____   9. _____

8. _____

Which words contain the Latin root that means "break"?

10. _____   12. _____

11. _____   13. _____

Which words contain the Latin root that means "fold"?

14. _____   18. _____

15. _____   19. _____

16. _____   20. _____

17. _____

Word Application

Replace each underlined word or words in the sentences with a **list word**. Write the **list word** on the line.

1. The <u>confusing</u> page design suffers from unnecessary <u>intricacy</u>.

   _____   _____

2. He said he saw a UFO <u>hanging</u> in midair, but when asked how it could be flying, he said that it was <u>unexplainable</u>. _____   _____

3. When we tried to <u>repeat</u> the experiment, the weather was no longer <u>suitable</u>.

   _____   _____

4. They didn't want their phones to <u>cause a break in</u> the experiment, so they turned them off. _____

5. Since the president didn't want the weather to <u>disturb</u> the meeting, she called it off until the <u>threatening</u> storm passed by. _____   _____

LIST WORDS

abrupt	inexplicable	bankrupt	pendulum
complex	destruction	duplicate	impending
pendant	independently	instruction	structural
disrupt	complication	implicate	applicable
interrupt	suspended	suspense	perplexing

Puzzle

Use the **list words** to complete the crossword puzzle.

ACROSS

3. something that is taught

7. an object hung from a fixed point so as to swing freely

9. uncertain; doubtful; confusing

13. an exact copy or reproduction

16. the act or process of being destroyed

17. relevant; appropriate

18. to break in on a discussion

19. hanging from a support

DOWN

1. to disturb the orderly course of a meeting or other social affair

2. financially broke

4. not simple; complicated

5. used in or suitable for building

6. state of anxious uncertainty

8. involve in a crime

10. freely; without influence or assistance

11. about to happen

12. not able to be explained or understood

14. a hanging ornamental object

15. something that is hard to solve or untangle

17. sudden

Proofreading

Use the proofreading marks to correct the mistakes in the article below. Then, write the misspelled **list words** correctly on the lines.

If someone becomes bankrupped, it often means that he or she has no income and is unable to pay bills or it may result because a person cannot control his or her spending.

People can have their credit cards suspendid because they owe too much money Although filing for bankruptcy can be purplexing, a bank official can offer instruktion on how to proceed. still, many recommend it only as a last resort. having a bankruptcy show up on your credit report can disruppt your life and make buying a car or house, renting an apartment, or obtaining a credit card very difficult.

1. _____

2. _____

3. _____

4. _____

5. _____

Writing a Persuasive Paragraph

Imagine that you are a bank official. Write a persuasive paragraph explaining why bankruptcy should be avoided if at all possible. Give convincing reasons for your opinion, and try to use as many **list words** in your writing as you can. Proofread and revise your paragraph, then share it with your classmates.

 **BONUS WORDS**

| chandelier | pedestal | parquet | mahogany | canopy |
| draperies | ottoman | upholstery | veneer | davenport |

Write the **bonus word** that matches each definition clue.

1. thin surface layer of fine wood _____

2. large couch or sofa _____

3. curtains of heavy material _____

4. a lighting fixture hanging from a ceiling _____

5. a roof-like covering over a bed _____

6. a column-like stand for displaying art _____

7. dark, reddish-brown wood _____

8. inlaid wood flooring _____

9. materials used to cover furniture _____

10. low cushioned seat without back or arms _____

Latin Roots

Here are some common Latin roots and their meanings.

Latin Roots	Meaning	English Word	Meaning
voc, vok	"voice"	vocalize	"speak or sing"
var	"different"	variety	"number of different things"
vag	"wander"	vagabond	"wanderer"
centr	"center"	centralize	"to bring to the center"
term	"end; limit"	terminal	"at the end"
terr	"land"	territory	"large tract of land"

Vocabulary Development

Write the **list word** from column **B** that matches the definition or synonym in column **A**.

A

1. unclear _____
2. assortment _____
3. annoy _____
4. tramp _____
5. destroy _____
6. odd _____
7. land _____
8. patio _____
9. sing _____
10. conclude _____

B

vagabond

eccentric

terrace

terrain

provoke

exterminate

determine

vocalize

variety

vague

Dictionary Skills

Write the **list word** that matches each sound-spelling.

1. (ver′ē ā′shən) _____
2. (ver′ē əs) _____
3. (kən sen′trik) _____
4. (ri vōk′) _____
5. (sen′trə līz) _____
6. (prə vōk′) _____
7. (vā′grənt) _____
8. (ad′və kāt) _____
9. (ter′ə tôr′ē) _____
10. (tʉr′mə n′l) _____

LIST WORDS

1. advocate
2. centralize
3. terrain
4. vagabond
5. variety
6. concentric
7. exterminate
8. terrace
9. vague
10. various
11. determine
12. provoke
13. territory
14. vagrant
15. vocation
16. eccentric
17. revoke
18. terminal
19. variation
20. vocalize

DID YOU KNOW ?

Determine literally means "to mark off the end." It was used to refer to verdicts reached in courts of law. That is exactly what is done when we determine something—we reach an end or conclusion.

Word Analysis

Write **list words** to answer the following questions.

Which words contain the Latin root that means "wander"?

1. _____ 2. _____ 3. _____

Which words contain the Latin root that means "voice"?

4. _____ 6. _____ 8. _____

5. _____ 7. _____

Which words contain the Latin root that means "center"?

9. _____ 10. _____ 11. _____

Which words contain the Latin root that means "different"?

12. _____ 13. _____ 14. _____

Which words contain the Latin root that means "end" or "limit"?

15. _____ 16. _____ 17. _____

Which words contain the Latin root that means "land"?

18. _____ 19. _____ 20. _____

Word Application

Replace the underlined word or words in each sentence with a **list word**. Write the **list word** on the line.

1. Do you think Uncle Harold is an <u>odd or unusual</u> person? _____

2. The supermarket has a <u>generous selection</u> of fruits and vegetables. _____

3. Priests, ministers, and rabbis have a religious <u>profession</u>. _____

4. What is the northwest <u>border country</u>? _____

5. The new house is being built on hilly <u>ground</u>. _____

6. The design in the painting was made with <u>the same center</u> circles. _____

7. His music included a <u>change</u> of a familiar theme. _____

8. A consumer <u>rights speaker</u> met with a group of concerned citizens. _____

9. If you drink and drive, the police may <u>take back</u> your driver's license. _____

10. Go left at the next block to get to the bus <u>station</u>. _____

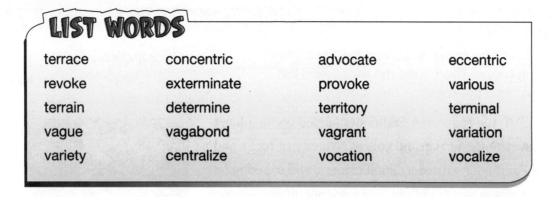

LIST WORDS

terrace	concentric	advocate	eccentric
revoke	exterminate	provoke	various
terrain	determine	territory	terminal
vague	vagabond	vagrant	variation
variety	centralize	vocation	vocalize

Puzzle

Use the **list words** to complete the crossword puzzle.

ACROSS

2. the main station of a railroad
5. person with no obvious means of support
6. to anger or irritate
7. a paved area near a house
8. ground or area of land
12. not definite or distinct
13. several or many
14. to speak or sing
17. person who wanders from place to place
18. to find out exactly
19. one's profession or occupation
20. the land ruled by a nation or state

DOWN

1. to gather together
3. to kill or destroy
4. sharing the same center
9. to speak or write in support of something
10. change in form or appearance
11. to take back or put an end to
15. not usual or normal
16. number of different things

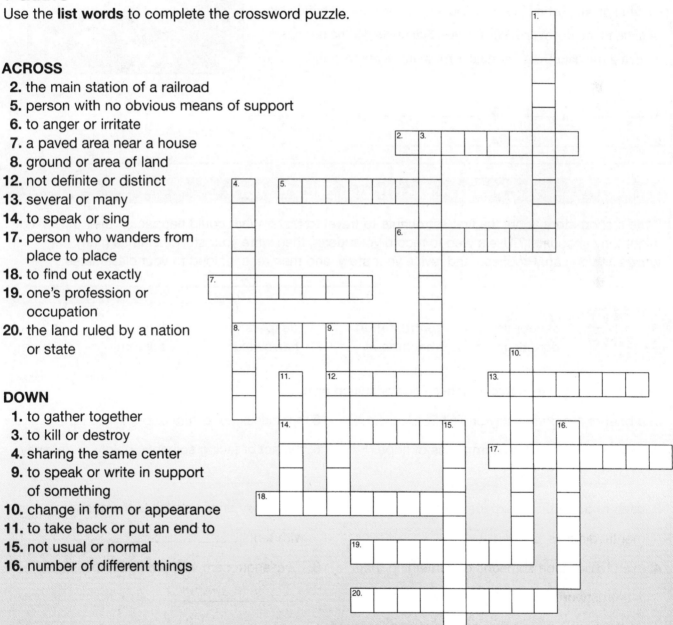

Proofreading

Use the proofreading marks to correct the mistakes in the paragraph below. Then, write the misspelled **list words** correctly on the lines.

Proofreading Marks

⬭ spelling mistake   ℓ delete word
⊙ add period   ⌃ add comma

On July 4 1997, the spacecraft Pathfinder landed on the planet Mars to investegate the terrian and collect a vareity of rocks and soil samples Pathfinder carried a digital camera, and a a complete meteorology package that could measure vareation in temperature, pressure, and wind at at different heights above the surface. This would help scientists on Earth ditermine whether Mars might be capable of supporting life. Pathfinder sent back over 2 billion bits of data, including over 16000 images. Scientists will be be studying the data from Pathfinder for many years to come.

1. _____ 3. _____ 5. _____

2. _____ 4. _____

Writing a Short Story

Write a short story about the first astronauts to travel to Mars. What could happen on their trip? What might they encounter? Use a web to record your ideas, then write your story, using as many **list words** as you can. Proofread and revise your story, and then read it aloud to your classmates.

BONUS WORDS

| escapade | confrontation | desperation | bivouac | intrepid |
| dauntless | treacherous | harrowing | sojourn | courier |

Write the **bonus word** that matches each definition clue.

1. a brief or temporary stay or visit _____

2. recklessness resulting from a loss of hope

_____

3. used to describe an experience that causes

mental distress _____

4. used to describe someone or something that

is untrustworthy _____

5. a reckless adventure or prank _____

6. the act of facing someone boldly or defiantly

_____

7. temporary encampment in the open

with tents _____

8. messenger sent with an urgent message

_____

Write the **bonus words** that are synonyms for <u>fearless</u>.

9. _____ **10.** _____

Latin Roots

 TIP

These common Latin roots can help you determine the meanings of many English words.

Latin Roots	Meaning	English Word	Meaning
spec	"see; look at"	perspective	"a particular view"
spir	"breathe"	expire	"to come to an end"
clu, clud	"shut"	exclude	"keep out"
mater, matri	"mother"	maternal	"motherly"

Study the Latin roots to determine the meanings of the **list words**.

Vocabulary Development

Write the **list word** that matches each definition clue.

1. to make impossible _____

2. a grand event _____

3. privacy; isolation _____

4. critical examination _____

5. a stimulation to do something creative _____

6. an unlawful plot _____

7. of the soul rather than the body _____

8. to think about _____

9. happened _____

10. making a part of a whole _____

LIST WORDS

1. conspiracy
2. expire
3. inspiration
4. matrimony
5. spectacle
6. disrespect
7. expectation
8. maternity
9. perspective
10. speculate
11. exclusive
12. including
13. matron
14. preclude
15. spiritual
16. exclude
17. inspection
18. maternal
19. seclusion
20. transpired

Dictionary Skills

Identify the **list words** that come between each pair of dictionary guide words. Write the words in alphabetical order.

conspire/external   **mate/precious**

1. _____   6. _____

2. _____   7. _____

3. _____   8. _____

4. _____   9. _____

5. _____   10. _____

Spelling Practice

DID YOU KNOW ?

Spectacle, **spectacular**, **spectator**, **spectroscope**, and **spectrum** all come from the Latin word *spectare*, meaning "to behold" or "to watch." All of these words have to do with someone seeing or with something seen or used in seeing.

Word Analysis

Write **list words** to answer the following questions.

Which words contain the Latin root that means "breathe"?

1. _____   3. _____   5. _____

2. _____   4. _____

Which words contain the Latin root that means "see"?

6. _____   8. _____   10. _____

7. _____   9. _____   11. _____

Which words contain the Latin root that means "shut"?

12. _____   14. _____   16. _____

13. _____   15. _____

Which words contain the Latin root that means "mother"?

17. _____   19. _____   20. _____

18. _____

Analogies

Write a **list word** to complete each analogy.

1. Fatherhood is to paternity as motherhood is to _____.

2. Guess is to predict as think is to _____.

3. Allow is to forbid as permit is to _____.

4. Body is to soul as physical is to _____.

5. Ordinary is to common as unique is to _____.

Word Application

Replace each underlined word or words in the sentences with **list words**. Write the **list words** on the lines.

1. The privacy of the hillside cabin allowed Martin to change his view on life.

   _____   _____

2. He found that the solitude of the mountains gave him the uplifting experience he needed

   to reaffirm his religious beliefs. _____   _____

3. A dramatic change had occurred within him. _____

LIST WORDS

conspiracy	disrespect	exclusive	exclude
expectation	inspection	including	matron
inspiration	maternity	seclusion	expire
matrimony	spectacle	preclude	maternal
perspective	speculate	transpired	spiritual

Puzzle

Unscramble the **list words** to complete the crossword puzzle.

ACROSS

1. NPRTADEISR
6. CSUVIEELX
8. PCUSALETE
9. OYISCPNARC
12. REUEPCLD
15. LANEMTRA
16. ESLSUNCIO
17. NIEPSNCITO
18. IEDTRSEPSC
19. NLIDCGUIN

DOWN

2. UPIIRLSTA
3. RXIEPE
4. ECPTSLEAC
5. RPPVEECSETI
6. EEUXLCD
7. TNRPNISIAIO
10. YENAMTRIT
11. PECXTENTAIO
13. RNAMTO
14. ROYTAIMMN

Proofreading

Use the proofreading marks to correct the mistakes in the article below. Then, write the misspelled **list words** correctly on the lines.

Proofreading Marks

⬭ spelling mistake   ? add question mark

ˇ add apostrophe   / small letter

Matrimmony during the Middle Ages was considered a family affair, and weddings themselves were not often lavish. From our purspective, they offered little in the way of spectakle for members of the community. In Italy, for example, a couple exchanged gifts, such as a piece of fruit, in the seklusion of the Brides house. The "vows" could be as simple as "Will you marry me" "I will." The presence of a state or religious official, includeing a priest or rabbi, was not even necessary. The role of a religious leader at a medieval Wedding was simply to bless the couple after the ceremony.

1. _____   4. _____

2. _____   5. _____

3. _____

Writing a Friendly Letter

Imagine that you have a relative in medieval Italy who is going to be married. Write a letter to a friend in which you describe the preparations for the ceremony. Use as many of the **list words** as you can. Include all the parts of a friendly letter, such as the date, greeting, and closing. When finished, proofread and revise your letter, then read it to your classmates.

BONUS WORDS

Sierra Leone	Chile	Yugoslavia	Pakistan	Zimbabwe
El Salvador	Portugal	Guatemala	Morocco	Indonesia

Write the **bonus words** that match each geographical location given.

Africa   1. _____   2. _____   3. _____

Asia   4. _____   5. _____

Europe   6. _____   7. _____

Central America 8. _____   9. _____

South America   10. _____

Challenging Words

 TIP

Some words are especially difficult to spell because they contain sounds that can be spelled by different letters. For example, the soft **c** sound in <u>fallacy</u> sounds very similar to the **s** sound in <u>defenseless</u>. In other challenging words, letters may stand for unusual sounds. For example, in <u>especially</u> the **c** stands for the sound of **sh**. Memorize the spellings of the **list words** so that you aren't fooled by their subtle "tricks."

Vocabulary Development

Write the **list word** that matches each synonym or definition.

1. costs _____
2. totally _____
3. client _____
4. traditional _____
5. lessen _____

6. unmerciful _____
7. polite behavior _____
8. easily provoked _____
9. worry or fear _____
10. particularly _____

Dictionary Skills

Write the **list word** that comes between each pair of dictionary guide words.

1. **entrance/equation** _____
2. **sorrow/south** _____
3. **deal/defeat** _____
4. **common/count** _____
5. **ember/empty** _____
6. **sole/soup** _____
7. **examine/exchange** _____
8. **decoy/dill** _____
9. **either/emigrate** _____
10. **fabulous/fame** _____
11. **anvil/anything** _____
12. **couple/cover** _____

LIST WORDS

1. anxiety
2. customer
3. diminish
4. entirely
5. expenses
6. controversial
7. customary
8. eloquent
9. equally
10. fallacy
11. courtesy
12. decision
13. eminent
14. excitable
15. source
16. cruel
17. defenseless
18. sophomore
19. excess
20. especially

Spelling Practice

DID YOU KNOW ?

The study of knowledge and ideas is called *sophiology*. **Sophomore** comes from the Greek word *sophos*, for "wise," and *mros*, meaning "dull." Together, they mean "a wise fool." We use *sophomore* as a name for a person who is in the second year of high school or college. It is believed that the name came from the notion that sophomores are usually wiser than freshmen, but foolish enough to think that they "know it all."

Word Analysis

Write **list words** to answer the following questions. Some words will be used more than once.

Which words contain the double consonant **ll**?

1. _____ 2. _____ 3. _____

Which words contain the letter **x**?

4. _____ 6. _____ 7. _____

5. _____

Which words contain the letter **q**?

8. _____ 9. _____

Which words contain no more than two syllables?

10. _____ 11. _____ 12. _____

Analogies

Write a **list word** to complete each analogy.

1. Fat is to thin as increase is to _____.

2. Kind is to happiness as _____ is to sorrow.

3. Calm is to still as _____ is to active.

4. Two is to three as _____ is to junior.

5. Disagree is to _____ as agree is to acceptable.

6. Profits are to in as _____ are to out.

7. Contentment is to happy as _____ is to worried.

Word Application

Complete each of the following phrases by writing a **list word** to replace the word or words in parentheses.

1. the (famous) author _____

2. (origin) of the problem _____

3. common (polite behavior) _____

4. (too much) baggage _____

5. (completely) correct _____

6. a complete (falsehood) _____

7. a (helpless) animal _____

8. the (expressive) poet _____

9. travel (costs) _____

10. a difficult (choice) _____

11. (student class) dance _____

12. his (usual) route _____

LIST WORDS

anxiety	controversial	courtesy	equally
customer	customary	decision	fallacy
diminish	especially	eminent	source
entirely	defenseless	excitable	excess
expenses	sophomore	eloquent	cruel

Puzzle

Use the **list words** to complete the crossword puzzle.

ACROSS

2. easily provoked or excited
4. polite behavior
5. second year of high school or college
7. to lessen
9. helpless; unable to stand up for oneself
10. starting point; origin
12. totally
14. false or mistaken idea
15. mean; unmerciful
17. client or purchaser of goods or services
18. extreme concern, worry, or fear

DOWN

1. settlement, conclusion, or choice
2. costs; money spent
3. debatable; subject to divided opinions
6. distinguished; famous; above others in rank
8. following tradition, custom, or usual routine
11. in identical portions, sizes, or values
12. particularly
13. well-spoken; expressive; poetic
16. too much; more than enough

Proofreading

Use the proofreading marks to correct the mistakes in the article below. Then, write the misspelled **list words** correctly on the lines.

Proofreading Marks

⬭ spelling mistake   # add space

≡ capital letter   ⊙ add period

In America, the first newspaper appeared in boston in 1690. As it was published without British authority, itwas considered controvershul, and its emenint publisher was arrested The first successful newspaper was *The Boston News-Letter*, begun by postmaster john campbell in 1704. Expensis were high, however, and finding a custumer willing to pay the costly price ofa subscription was difficult. By the eve of the Revolutionary War, though, some two dozen papers were issued in all the colonies. Eluquent articles in these papers were amajor force that influenced public opinion in America over the fight for independence.

1. _____

2. _____

3. _____

4. _____

5. _____

Writing a News Story

Write a news story about a recent event that took place in your school. Start with a lead paragraph and answer the questions *who? what? where? when?* and *why?* in the body of the story. Use **list words** if possible. When finished, proofread and revise your story. Put it together with other stories to create a class or school newspaper.

Bonus Words

editorial	journalism	lithography	libelous	investigative
obituary	distribution	censorship	muckrake	commentaries

Write a **bonus word** to complete each sentence.

1. _____ of the press could harm a newspaper's ability to publish important facts.

2. Study _____ in school if you want to become a newspaper reporter.

3. Several columnists write _____ to air their views on newsworthy issues.

4. On the _____ page, the newspaper presents its opinions on current issues.

5. Some newspapers published in the United States have worldwide _____.

6. Many newspapers are printed by using a process called _____.

7. Following a person's death, the _____ summarizes the events of his or her life.

8. _____ reporters aim to find the facts behind a mystery or unsolved crime.

9. A story may be judged _____ if it unfairly injures or ridicules an individual.

10. To _____ is to write a news story to expose corruption in business or politics.

- Latin roots can help you determine the meanings of unfamiliar words. Knowing how a Latin root is spelled can help you figure out how to spell a difficult word. Here are some examples:

Latin Root (Meaning)	English Word	Latin Root (Meaning)	English Word
aqua ("water")	aquatic	**voc/vok** ("voice")	vocalize
later ("side")	unilateral	**var** ("different")	variety
sim ("like")	simulate	**vag** ("wander")	vagrant
liber ("free")	liberal	**centr** ("center")	centralize
host/hosp ("guest")	hostel	**term** ("end")	terminal
hostis ("warlike")	hostile	**terr** ("land")	terrace
mort ("death")	mortal	**spec** ("see")	inspection
plic/plex ("fold")	complex	**spir** ("breathe")	spiritual
rupt ("break")	abrupt	**clu/clud** ("shut")	preclude
pend ("hang")	pendant	**mater** ("mother")	maternity
struct ("build")	construct		

- Words that do not follow ordinary spelling rules present a challenge. Memorize and practice spelling tricky words such as these: <u>customer</u>, <u>eloquent</u>, and <u>eminent</u>.

Lesson 13

List Words

aquarium

lateral

hospice

dissimilar

hostage

mortgage

hospitalize

simultaneous

quadrilateral

liberate

_____

_____

Write **list words** to answer the questions.

Which **list words** have the Latin root **host** or **hosp** that means "guest"?

1. _____   3. _____

2. _____

Which **list word** contains the Latin root **aqua** that means "water"?

4. _____

Which **list word** contains the Latin root **mort** that means "death"?

5. _____

Which **list words** contain the Latin root **sim** that means "like"?

6. _____   7. _____

Which **list words** contain the Latin root **later** that means "side"?

8. _____   9. _____

Which **list word** contains the Latin root **liber** that means "free"?

10. _____

Write a **list word** to complete each sentence.

List Words

inexplicable

instruction

destruction

independently

suspended

duplicate

structural

suspense

interrupt

applicable

_____

_____

1. If you do a project without a partner, you work

   _____.

2. If you see something you can't explain, it is _____.

3. If you read mystery stories, you enjoy _____.

4. If a tornado whips through town, it causes _____.

5. If a remark is off the subject, it is not _____.

6. When you _____ something, you make an identical copy of it.

7. If a building collapses, it probably has _____ deficiencies.

8. A balloon flying high is _____ in the air.

9. If you break into a conversation,

   you _____.

10. To learn how to play the violin,

    you look for _____.

Write a **list word** to match each clue.

List Words

advocate

terrain

concentric

exterminate

vague

various

determine

eccentric

territory

variation

_____

_____

1. circles   _____

2. a change   _____

3. destroy   _____

4. unclear   _____

5. different   _____

6. a region   _____

7. odd   _____

8. supporter   _____

9. land   _____

10. figure out   _____

Fill in the puzzle by writing a **list word** to match each synonym.

List Words

- conspiracy
- inspiration
- matrimony
- spectacle
- disrespect
- maternal
- perspective
- speculate
- exclude
- seclusion

_____

_____

ACROSS
2. keep out
7. privacy
8. view
9. display
10. marriage

DOWN
1. conjecture
3. plot
4. rudeness
5. encouragement
6. motherly

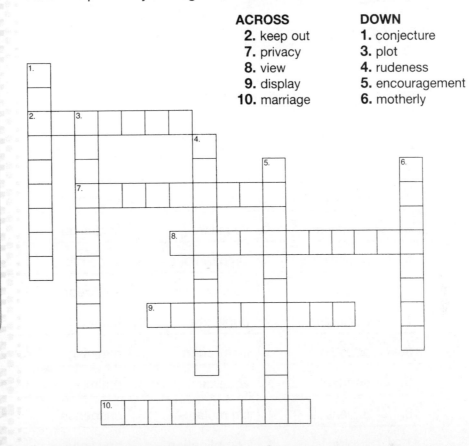

Write the **list words** that come between each pair of dictionary guide words. Write the words in alphabetical order.

List Words

- anxiety
- cruel
- customary
- fallacy
- courtesy
- decision
- excitable
- controversial
- defenseless
- especially

_____

_____

answer/deal

1. _____
2. _____
3. _____
4. _____
5. _____

debt/fawn

6. _____
7. _____
8. _____
9. _____
10. _____

Show What You Know

One word is misspelled in each set of **list words**. Fill in the circle next to the **list word** that is spelled incorrectly.

1. ○ exclude ○ acquarium ○ provoke ○ applicable
2. ○ disrupt ○ territory ○ hostal ○ inspection
3. ○ maternel ○ lateral ○ vagrant ○ independently
4. ○ pendalum ○ vocation ○ seclusion ○ mortuary
5. ○ transpired ○ simultanious ○ eccentric ○ suspended
6. ○ revoke ○ controversial ○ bankrupt ○ disimilar
7. ○ customer ○ duplicate ○ hostege ○ terminal
8. ○ aquadic ○ instruction ○ diminish ○ variation
9. ○ pendant ○ vocalize ○ entirely ○ mortgadge
10. ○ expenses ○ simmulate ○ suspense ○ conspiracy
11. ○ expire ○ complication ○ angziety ○ hospitalize
12. ○ hostile ○ customery ○ interrupt ○ impending
13. ○ elloquent ○ destruction ○ liberal ○ inspiration
14. ○ matrimoney ○ mortician ○ equally ○ perplexing
15. ○ spectacle ○ advocate ○ falacy ○ unilateral
16. ○ courtesy ○ hospice ○ disrespect ○ centralise
17. ○ mortal ○ expectasion ○ terrain ○ decision
18. ○ vagabond ○ aquamarine ○ eminnent ○ maternity
19. ○ excitable ○ purspective ○ variety ○ quadrilateral
20. ○ source ○ concentric ○ liberate ○ speckulate
21. ○ exclusive ○ defensless ○ abrupt ○ exterminate
22. ○ complex ○ including ○ terrace ○ sophemore
23. ○ vage ○ implicate ○ cruel ○ matron
24. ○ preclude ○ various ○ especialy ○ inexplicable
25. ○ excess ○ determine ○ structural ○ spirtual

Prefixes Meaning "Together"

The prefixes **co** and **syn** mean "together." However, the prefix **syn** changes the spelling to **syl** when it is used before words beginning with **l**; it changes to **sym** when it is used before words beginning with **b**, **m**, or **p**. Notice the spelling of these example words.

coauthor	syntheses	syllable
symbolize	symmetry	symptom

Vocabulary Development

Write the **list word** that matches each synonym or definition.

1. balance _____

2. sentence structure _____

3. a temple _____

4. to be identical or in accord _____

5. live together _____

6. understandable _____

7. musical _____

8. a medical indicator _____

9. an outline of a course of study _____

10. bring together _____

11. word part _____

12. guaranteed by property _____

Dictionary Skills

Write the **list word** that matches each sound-spelling.

1. (kō′pī lət) _____

2. (sim′b'l īz) _____

3. (kō′in sīd′) _____

4. (simp′təm) _____

5. (kō ô′thər) _____

6. (sin′taks) _____

7. (sim pō′zē əm) _____

8. (sin′thə sis) _____

9. (siŋ′krə nīz) _____

10. (siŋ′kə pāt) _____

11. (kō äp′ər ə tiv) _____

12. (kō hir′ənt) _____

LIST WORDS

1. coauthor
2. collateral
3. copilot
4. symptom
5. synagogue
6. coexist
7. coordinate
8. syllable
9. symmetry
10. synchronize
11. coherent
12. cooperative
13. symphonic
14. synthesis
15. syncopate
16. coincide
17. symbolize
18. symposium
19. syntax
20. syllabus

DID YOU KNOW?

A **syncope** is a word that is made shorter by cutting out sounds in the middle. For example, writing *ne'er* in place of *never* would be a syncope. In music, to syncopate means "to make a rhythm feel shorter by cutting out beats in the middle."

Word Analysis

Write the **list word** that has the same root or base word as the word given.

1. syncopation _____
2. synthetic _____
3. authorize _____
4. autopilot _____
5. cooperation _____
6. coincidence _____
7. synchronicity _____
8. symphony _____
9. coexistence _____
10. symmetrical _____
11. coordination _____
12. symbolic _____
13. symptomatic _____
14. coherence _____

Write the **list words** that contain double letters.

15. _____
16. _____
17. _____
18. _____
19. _____
20. _____

Word Application

Select a **list word** from the choices in parentheses to complete each sentence. Write the **list word** on the line.

1. A symposium on _____ music will be held tomorrow night. (syntax, symphonic)

2. A _____ assists a pilot in flying a plane. (collateral, copilot)

3. The contestants had to _____ their watches before the race. (synchronize, symbolize)

4. "What do the stripes on our flag _____?" asked a student. (coincide, symbolize)

5. We heard a _____ speech on the importance of computers. (syllable, coherent)

6. What beautiful symmetry of design on that _____! (synagogue, syntax)

7. Tomatoes and carrots are companion plants that _____ well in the garden. (coauthor, coexist)

8. Mr. Warren said, "Learn to spell each _____ in this word." (syllabus, syllable)

9. David and his coauthor attended the _____ introducing new science-fiction writers and the techniques that they use. (symposium, synthesis)

10. The sentence _____ can give you clues to a word's meaning. (syllable, syntax)

11. Sometimes _____ is needed in order to purchase expensive items. (coordinate, collateral)

LIST WORDS

coauthor	coexist	synchronize	coherent
collateral	syntax	cooperative	symbolize
symmetry	syllable	symphonic	synthesis
symptom	coincide	symposium	coordinate
syllabus	copilot	synagogue	syncopate

Puzzle

Use the **list words** to complete the crossword puzzle.

ACROSS

1. having to do with the sounds a symphony makes

5. a writer who works with another writer

6. a meeting to discuss some particular subject

8. the assistant pilot of an airplane

9. a word or part of a word

12. the putting together of parts or elements to make a whole

16. speaking or thinking in a way that makes sense

17. the way words are put together in sentences; sentence structure

18. to be the symbol of something; represent

DOWN

2. to bring together in a proper relation

3. a sign that something else exists, especially in sickness

4. helpful; willing to cooperate

5. to happen at the same time

7. an outline or summary

9. a temple where Jewish people gather for worship

10. property given as a pledge to repay a loan

11. to make agree in time or rate of speed

13. to shift the musical accent of a beat

14. balance or harmony

15. living together in peace

Proofreading

Use the proofreading marks to correct the mistakes in the article below. Then, write the misspelled **list words** correctly on the lines.

Through a coperative effort with the Chicagoschool system, The Youth Education programs of the Chicago Symphony Orchestra providein-depth classical music experiences to more than 100,000 area children each year. The school system works with the symphony to coordenate the program so that it will coinside with the school yearcalendar. Activities include an extensive series of Symphomic Concerts for schools, a sympozium for teachers, and opportunities for talented young musicians. "Our Concert was the best we have ever attended, wrote one teacher after this year's first show.

Proofreading Marks

⬭ spelling mistake   ⌗ add space

╱ small letter

❦❦ add quotation marks

1. _____

2. _____

3. _____

4. _____

5. _____

Writing a Review

Write a review of a book you have read, a musical performance you have heard or a movie, TV show, or play you have seen recently. Give your opinion and explain why you liked or disliked it. Use as many **list words** as you can, then proofread and revise your review. Compile your work with that of other classmates in a book. Add new reviews to the book periodically.

BONUS WORDS

| amphitheater | coliseum | prologue | pageant | critique |
| melodrama | soliloquy | vaudeville | scenario | cinema |

Write **bonus words** to answer the questions.

Which word relates to film or movies?

1. _____

Which word might discuss a play or film in a critical way?

2. _____

Which words name buildings or structures?

3. _____ 4. _____

Which words describe or name kinds of performances?

5. _____ 6. _____ 7. _____

Which words name particular parts of plays?

8. _____ 9. _____ 10. _____

Prefixes Meaning "Not"

TIP

Many different prefixes mean "not." Some of these prefixes change their spellings before certain letters. The prefix **a**, for example, becomes **an** before a vowel. The prefix **in** becomes **im** before **m**, **b**, and **p**. Look at how these words are spelled:

anarchy   incognito   immobilize   impromptu

Other prefixes meaning "not" include **non** and **neg**, as in nonexistent and negative.

Vocabulary Development

Write the **list word** that matches each definition or synonym.

1. unfavorable _____

2. idle _____

3. in disguise _____

4. without advance planning _____

5. unnamed _____

6. null and void _____

7. cool and composed _____

8. prevent movement _____

9. clean _____

10. mimic or copy _____

11. incorrect _____

12. hesitant _____

LIST WORDS

1. anarchy
2. imprudent
3. impersonate
4. incognito
5. negligent
6. anesthesia
7. immobilize
8. impatiently
9. indecisive
10. negative
11. anemia
12. immaculate
13. inaccurate
14. invalid
15. nonchalant
16. anonymous
17. impromptu
18. inactive
19. neglect
20. nonexistent

Dictionary Skills

Rewrite each of the following **list words** to show how they are divided into syllables.

1. neglect _____
2. anemia _____
3. anarchy _____
4. invalid _____
5. negligent _____

6. impatiently _____
7. anesthesia _____
8. immobilize _____
9. nonexistent _____
10. imprudent _____

Spelling Practice

DID YOU KNOW ?

Nonchalant is a word borrowed from the French language and comes from two Latin words meaning "to be not warm." A person who is nonchalant does not get warm or passionate about things, but seems always to be cool or lukewarm.

Word Analysis

Write the **list word** formed by adding a prefix that means "not" to each base word given.

1. valid _____

2. decisive _____

3. mobilize _____

4. accurate _____

5. prudent _____

6. active _____

7. patiently _____

8. existent _____

Word Application

Replace the underlined word or words in each sentence with a **list word**. Write the **list word** on the line.

1. Make sure you do not <u>abandon</u> your duty. _____

2. These troops are <u>not on active duty</u>. _____

3. Ellen is so <u>composed</u>, and I am so nervous. _____

4. First, the doctor will have to <u>prevent motion of</u> that broken leg. _____

5. We could not identify the voice of the <u>nameless</u> caller. _____

6. The party was not planned; it was <u>spur-of-the-moment</u>. _____

7. To avoid photographers, the celebrity traveled <u>in disguise</u>. _____

8. This surgery will require only local <u>painkiller</u>. _____

9. Make sure you do not make <u>wrong</u> claims about your product. _____

10. The Washington family keeps their home <u>very clean</u>. _____

11. The nurse will test you for <u>a blood disorder</u>. _____

12. In the fog, my ocean view was <u>not there</u>. _____

13. People often try to <u>pretend they are</u> famous people. _____

14. Spending all your money would be <u>unwise</u>. _____

15. A leader is not allowed to be <u>wavering</u>. _____

16. After the revolution, <u>an absence of government</u> ruled. _____

17. The driver was <u>careless</u> in maintaining his car's brakes. _____

18. The critic gave the movie a <u>bad</u> review. _____

19. My sister waited <u>with annoyance</u> for me to finish brushing my teeth. _____

LIST WORDS

anarchy	negligent	impatiently	anonymous
invalid	immobilize	immaculate	impromptu
neglect	incognito	inaccurate	anesthesia
anemia	indecisive	imprudent	impersonate
inactive	negative	nonchalant	nonexistent

Puzzle

This is a crossword puzzle without clues. Use the length and the spelling of each **list word** to complete the puzzle.

Proofreading

Use the proofreading marks to correct the mistakes in the paragraphs below. Then, write the misspelled **list words** correctly on the lines.

The comic character Superman was created in the 1930s by Jerry Siegel and Joe Shuster Superman was first conceived as a negetive character, a villain with superior strength, but Siegel became indicisive as the character developed. The idea to to make him a hero from another planet who fights against annarchy and and who can immobolise a villain with one blow, came to Jerry in the middle of the night. The next day, the first Superman story was written

In 1938, Superman's alter ego, reporter Clark Kent, began working inkognito at *The Daily Star*, which later became *The Daily Planet*. He has worked there now for for over 60 years!

Proofreading Marks

⬭ spelling mistake

! add exclamation mark

⊙ add period ↶ delete word

1. _____

2. _____

3. _____

4. _____

5. _____

Writing a Comic Strip

Create a superhero comic strip about a character whose incredible powers save an entire city from destruction. Write an introductory paragraph that tells the character's name and describes her or his super-human traits. Use as many **list words** as you can. After proofreading and revising your paragraph, illustrate and write the dialogue for the comic strip. Publish your comic strip in a class or school newspaper or newsletter.

BONUS WORDS

| altruistic | articulate | arduous | unscathed | boisterous |
| laudable | winsome | staunch | vindictive | dynamic |

Write the **bonus word** that matches each synonym.

1. vengeful _____

2. difficult _____

3. intelligible _____

4. energetic _____

5. cute _____

6. loud _____

7. loyal _____

8. charitable _____

9. uninjured _____

10. praiseworthy _____

Words of Latin Origin

You have already studied several words and prefixes that have Latin roots. Knowing the meanings of Latin roots that appear frequently in English words will help you to analyze unfamiliar words for correct meaning and spelling.

Latin Root	Meaning	English Words	Meaning
documentum	"lesson; example"	document documentary	"paper relied on for proof" "film that teaches"
optio	"wish; desire"	option optional	"the power to choose" "not mandatory; elective"
opticus	"eye"	optician	"one who makes eyeglasses"

Vocabulary Development

Write the **list word** that matches each definition clue.

1. law _____

2. excessive _____

3. young _____

4. choice _____

5. wealthy _____

6. bug poison _____

7. promotion _____

8. political party _____

9. eye specialist _____

10. nonfiction film _____

Dictionary Skills

Write the **list word** that matches each etymology.

1. Latin **sub** ("under; near") + **urbs** ("town") _____

2. Latin **vermis** ("worm") _____

3. Latin **vere** ("truly") + **dictum** ("said") _____

4. Latin **dominus** ("master") _____

5. Latin **regere** ("to rule") _____

6. Latin **ex** ("intensive") + **hilaris** ("glad") _____

7. Italian **quaranta** ("forty") from Latin **quattuor** ("four") _____

8. Latin **audire** ("to hear") _____

9. Latin **maximus** ("greatest") _____

10. Latin **moles** ("mass") _____

LIST WORDS

1. auditor
2. exorbitant
3. molecular
4. ordinance
5. Republican
6. documentary
7. insecticide
8. optician
9. publicity
10. suburban
11. dominion
12. juvenile
13. option
14. quarantine
15. vermin
16. exhilarated
17. maximum
18. opulent
19. regime
20. verdict

Spelling Practice

Word Analysis

Write the **list word** with the same Latin root as the word given.

1. order _____
2. maxim _____
3. dominate _____
4. quarter _____
5. orbit _____
6. urban _____
7. adopt _____
8. audition _____

Analogies

Write a **list word** to complete each analogy.

1. Cell is to cellular as molecule is to _____.
2. Communist is to Socialist as Democrat is to _____.
3. Question is to answer as evidence is to _____.
4. Adult is to mature as adolescent is to _____.
5. Rat is to _____ as lion is to predators.
6. Tooth is to dentist as eye is to _____.
7. Real is to _____ as make-believe is to fiction.
8. Bed is to sleep as hospital is to _____.
9. Least is to minimum as greatest is to _____.

Word Application

Select a **list word** from the choices in parentheses to complete each sentence. Write the **list word** on the line.

1. Ralph used _____ to rid his garden of aphids and beetles. (vermin, publicity, insecticide)

2. I was shaken but _____ by the roller coaster ride. (exhilarated, exorbitant, opulent)

3. Your posters provided great _____ for my campaign. (publicity, dominion, documentary)

4. The movie was set in the _____ palace of Catherine the Great. (maximum, opulent, exhilarated)

5. The _____ of Queen Victoria lasted from 1837 to 1901. (opulent, regime, verdict)

maximum	documentary	dominion	option
exorbitant	insecticide	juvenile	auditor
molecular	exhilarated	optician	vermin
ordinance	Republican	publicity	regime
suburban	quarantine	opulent	verdict

Puzzle

Use the **list words** to complete the crossword puzzle.

ACROSS

4. related to the particles in an element or compound

5. related to young people

7. a law, especially one made by a city government

11. excessive in number or size

13. rule or power to rule

15. period of time in which a certain person is in power

16. person who makes eye-care products

17. nonfiction film

18. insects or small animals, such as termites and rats

19. material geared to announce events or provide information to the public

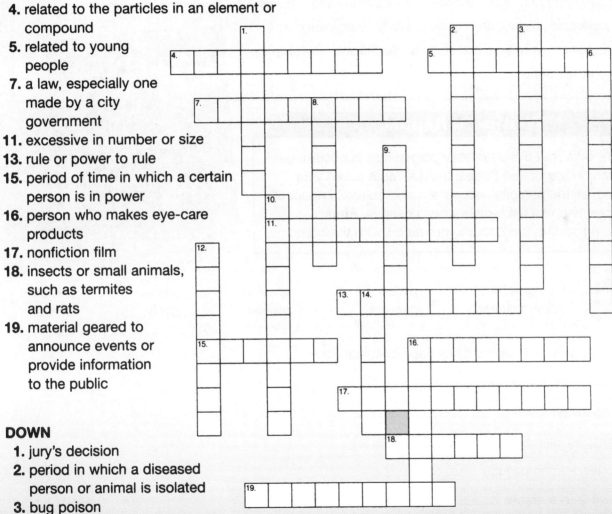

DOWN

1. jury's decision

2. period in which a diseased person or animal is isolated

3. bug poison

6. feeling cheerful and lively

8. person who checks financial accounts and records

9. the greatest possible amount

10. a political party in the United States

12. related to areas situated near a city

14. power to choose; one particular choice

16. rich or luxurious

Proofreading

Use the proofreading marks to correct the mistakes in the article. Write the misspelled **list words** correctly on the lines.

The plague known as the Black Death erupted in the gobi Desert in mongolia in the late 1320s. No one knows why. Whatever the reason, Scientists know that the outbreak began there and spread outward, taking an exorbitent toll on the Earths population. The bacteria that causes the Plague is carried by fleas that travel on virmin. In the middle ages, however, no one knew what caused the disease, and the only opshun people had when it appeared was to try and leave their town or city. Some city officials tried to qwarentine plague sufferers, and in Italy an ordnance was issued forbidding anyone who had come in contact with the plague to leave his or her home.

Proofreading Marks

⬭ spelling mistake	⌄ add apostrophe
☰ capital letter	/ small letter

1. _____

2. _____

3. _____

4. _____

5. _____

Writing a Report

Write a report about a modern-day plague that is occurring or could occur in the United States. Include facts about your topic, such as the personal, economic, and cultural impact of the disease, and use **list words** when possible. After proofreading and revising, share your report with the class.

BONUS WORDS

topography	avalanche	erosion	mesa	crevasse
sedimentary	igneous	geyser	atoll	alluvial

Write the **bonus word** that matches each definition clue.

1. deep crack in land or ice _____

2. wearing away of soil _____

3. ring-shaped island _____

4. high, steep-sided plateau _____

5. study of land surfaces _____

6. boiling spring _____

7. containing matter deposited by water or wind, as sand or soil _____

8. made up of sand or clay washed down by flowing water _____

9. matter produced by the action of volcanoes or other intense heat _____

10. sudden, swift slide of a mass of loosened snow, earth, or rocks _____

Words of Greek Origin

Many English words have Greek origins. Knowing the meanings of Greek roots and prefixes will help you spell and define unfamiliar words.

Prefix + Root	Meaning	English Word	Meaning
meter + polis	"mother" + "city"	metropolis	"major city"
theos + logos	"god" + "word"	theology	"religious studies"
archi + tekton	"chief" + "builder"	architect	"building designer"

Vocabulary Development

Write the **list word** that matches each synonym or definition clue.

1. school _____
2. ancient _____
3. rubbery _____
4. urgent _____
5. find fault _____
6. universe _____
7. government rules _____
8. document library _____
9. careful study _____
10. word puzzle _____
11. worldwide _____
12. attractive _____

Dictionary Skills

Write a **list word** to match each Greek etymology.

1. **aēr** ("air") + **naus** ("ship") _____
2. **theo** ("god") + **logos** ("word") _____
3. **dēmos** ("the people") + **kratos** ("strength") _____
4. **Magnētis** ("stone from Magnesia") _____
5. **politikos** ("of a citizen") _____
6. **elatos** ("to beat out") _____
7. **Akadēmos** ("figure in Greek myths") _____
8. **ana** ("back") + **gamma** ("letter") _____
9. **oikos** ("house") + **nomos** ("one who manages") _____
10. **archi** ("chief") + **tekton** ("builder") _____
11. **ana** ("up") + **lysis** ("loosening") _____
12. **ek** ("out") + **leipein** ("to leave") _____

LIST WORDS

1. academy
2. archive
3. cosmopolitan
4. economical
5. metropolis
6. aeronautics
7. archaic
8. criticize
9. elastic
10. democracy
11. analysis
12. architect
13. crisis
14. cosmos
15. politics
16. anagram
17. bureaucracy
18. eclipse
19. magnetic
20. theology

Spelling Practice

DID YOU KNOW ?

Academy comes from the Greek word for "a grove of trees near Athens." Plato, an ancient Greek philosopher and teacher, taught his students in that grove. The Greeks thought that it had once belonged to a hero in a Greek legend named Akadēmos.

Word Analysis

Write the **list word** that has the same root as the word given.

1. polite _____
2. magnesium _____
3. economy _____
4. Minneapolis _____
5. analyze _____
6. airplane _____
7. academic _____
8. telegram _____

Analogies

Write a **list word** to complete each analogy.

1. Difficult is to easy as _____ is to modern.
2. Communism is to Cuba as _____ is to the United States.
3. Portrait is to artist as building is to _____.
4. Brittle is to break as _____ is to stretch.
5. Archaeology is to early civilizations as _____ is to religious doctrines.
6. Applaud is to "yes" as _____ is to "no."
7. Library is to book as _____ is to document.
8. Island is to ocean as galaxy is to _____.

Word Application

Select a **list word** from the choices in parentheses to complete each sentence. Write the **list word** on the line.

1. Red tape is a slang term for the complexities of _____. (aeronautics, bureaucracy, crisis)

2. A _____ person travels all over the world with ease. (politics, cosmopolitan, democracy)

3. Scientists who design rockets are experts in _____. (aeronautics, metropolis, crisis)

4. The moon may totally cover the sun in a solar _____. (bureaucracy, cosmos, eclipse)

5. The tornado created a _____ in the city. (metropolis, crisis, cosmos)

6. His lawyer's _____ of the problem was helpful. (anagram, criticize, analysis)

LIST WORDS

crisis	aeronautics	analysis	anagram
archive	bureaucracy	architect	academy
criticize	cosmopolitan	archaic	metropolis
elastic	economical	cosmos	magnetic
eclipse	democracy	politics	theology

Puzzle

Use the **list words** to complete the crossword puzzle.

ACROSS

1. universe
2. the science of aircraft
5. study of religion
9. able to fit into any culture
10. government by the people
11. hiding of the sun or moon
14. the most important city
15. person who designs buildings
16. rubbery
17. outdated or seldom used
18. to be critical of

DOWN

1. great danger
2. word made by changing the order of letters in another word
3. place of study
4. examination
6. where records are stored
7. saving money
8. attracting others
12. the science of government
13. government by officials who always obey all rules

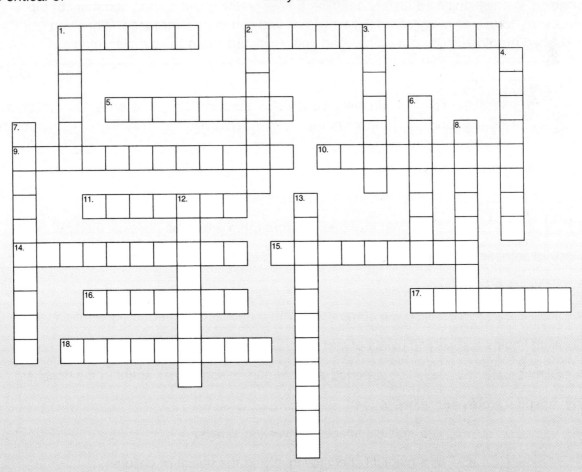

Proofreading

Use the proofreading marks to correct the mistakes in the article below. Then, write the misspelled **list words** correctly on the lines.

Did you know that cities exist for many reasons. In ancient times, cities could provide protection in times of crysis. During attacks, the population could flee behind the city walls Today, with libraries and museums, many cities are an arkive for information, as well as centers for manufacturing. They also serve as hubs for state and federal burocracy. Washington, D.C, for example, displays the monumental buildings and large public spaces typical of a capital metropoliss.

In ancient times and today, however, cities have always provided fertile ground for the development of human culture, with their cozmopolitan mixture of different people and ideas.

Proofreading Marks

◯ spelling mistake   ? add question mark

¶ new paragraph   ⊙ add period

1. _____

2. _____

3. _____

4. _____

5. _____

Writing a Postcard

What cities have you visited? What cities around the world would you like to visit? Write a travel postcard in which you provide a friend with some details about your trip to the city of your choice. A travel postcard usually contains a brief greeting and a short summary of trip highlights. Try to use as many of the **list words** as you can in your message. When you have finished proofreading and revising, read your postcard aloud to your classmates.

BONUS WORDS

therapeutic	convalescent	surgery	gurney	dispensary
rehabilitate	intravenous	pediatrics	syringe	radiology

Write a **bonus word** to complete each sentence.

1. A _____ is a stretcher or cot on wheels.

2. To _____ injured muscles, doctors often prescribe physical therapy.

3. Doctors sometimes perform _____ to repair damaged organs.

4. Medicines are sometimes given by _____ injection.

5. A _____ is a vial of medicine with a needle designed to penetrate a vein.

6. Drinking liquids and getting plenty of rest is _____ for the common cold.

7. A patient's _____ period after surgery is sometimes spent in the hospital.

8. The hospital stores medicines in the _____.

9. _____ is a medical specialty involving X-rays.

10. _____ is a medical specialty involving the health of children.

Lesson 23

The **list words** contain Greek roots that appear frequently in English words. Many English words are a combination of two Greek roots.

Greek Root	Meaning	English Word	Meaning
chronos	"time"	chronic	"lasting a long time"
thermos	"hot; heat"	thermostat	"device for regulating a heating system"
metron	"measure"	thermometer	"device for measuring heat level"
		chronometer	"an extremely accurate clock"
baros	"weight"	barometer	"device for measuring atmospheric pressure"

Vocabulary Development

Write the **list word** that matches each synonym or definition clue.

1. drugstore _____

2. eagerness _____

3. conversation _____

4. life story _____

5. short story _____

6. helpless inactivity _____

7. insulated bottle _____

8. eight-sided figure _____

9. recurring often _____

10. colorless gas _____

Dictionary Skills

Write the **list word** that comes between each pair of dictionary guide words.

1. parade/parallelogram _____

2. biohazard/biometry _____

3. geoid/geometry _____

4. thermoscope/thesaurus _____

5. humor/hydrogen _____

6. telephone/thermodynamic _____

7. geodesic/geologic _____

8. banner/beacon _____

9. aqua/aster _____

10. parameter/parboil _____

LIST WORDS

1. aristocrat
2. biography
3. thermostat
4. octagon
5. parasite
6. barometer
7. chronic
8. geographical
9. parallel
10. pharmacy
11. biological
12. dialogue
13. geological
14. parable
15. televise
16. hydrant
17. enthusiasm
18. neon
19. paralysis
20. thermos

Spelling Practice

DID YOU KNOW ?

Enthusiasm comes from the Greek words *en*, meaning "in or within" and *theos*, meaning "god." Poets and prophets long ago were thought to be inspired by a god. Today, *enthusiasm* usually means "a strong liking, excitement, or interest."

Word Analysis

Write the **list word** derived from the Greek roots given.

1. para ("beside") + **allelos** ("one another") _____

2. bios ("life") + **logos** ("word; thought") _____

3. geo ("earth") + **logos** ("word; thought") _____

4. bios ("life") + **graphe** ("writing") _____

5. para ("beside") + **sitos** ("food") _____

6. geo ("earth") + **graphe** ("writing") _____

7. para ("beside") + **lusis** ("disable; loosen") _____

8. thermos ("heat") + **statos** ("standing") _____

Analogies

Write a **list word** to complete each analogy.

1. Radio is to broadcast as television is to _____.

2. Food is to cooler as beverage is to _____.

3. Iron is to aluminum as helium is to _____.

4. Influenza is to virus as barnacle is to _____.

5. Dread is to apprehension as eagerness is to _____.

6. Fuel is to gas pump as water is to _____.

7. *Yield* is to triangle as *Stop* is to _____.

8. Dancer is to waltz as reader is to _____.

Word Application

Select a **list word** from the choices in parentheses to complete each sentence. Write the **list word** on the line.

1. The _____ of legendary cowboy Pecos Bill claims he rode a mountain lion and wielded a rattlesnake whip. (enthusiasm, biography)

2. The moral of the _____ is to treat others with kindness. (biography, parable)

3. The _____ was last seen greeting the princess. (thermostat, aristocrat)

4. _____ studies concern rocks and minerals. (geographical, geological)

5. A _____ is a device that measures pressure in the atmosphere. (barometer, thermostat)

LIST WORDS

aristocrat	barometer	octagon	hydrant
biography	enthusiasm	dialogue	chronic
thermostat	geographical	parallel	neon
biological	geological	parasite	parable
paralysis	pharmacy	televise	thermos

Syllables

Write each **list word** under the correct category.

Words with Two Syllables	Words with Four Syllables	Words with Five Syllables
1. _____	5. _____	9. _____
2. _____	6. _____	10. _____
3. _____	7. _____	11. _____
4. _____	8. _____	12. _____

Puzzle

Each clue is an example, or illustration, of a **list word**. Write the **list words** in the answer spaces. Then, transfer the numbered letters to the spaces below to answer the question.

1. She jumped for joy. ___ ___ ___ ___ ___ ___ ___ ___ ___ ___
                                                                    2   15

2. *The Life of Helen Keller* ___ ___ ___ ___ ___ ___ ___ ___ ___
                                   1   6   12

3. a stop sign ___ ___ ___ ___ ___ ___ ___
                    5   16

4. a long illness ___ ___ ___ ___ ___ ___ ___ ___ ___
                          11   8

5. "Who's there?" ___ ___ ___ ___ ___ ___ ___ ___
      "It's John."   13   3

6. ▬▬▬▬▬ ___ ___ ___ ___ ___ ___ ___ ___
                              10   4

7. Davidson's Drugstore ___ ___ ___ ___ ___ ___ ___ ___
                             9   14

8. to broadcast on a TV ___ ___ ___ ___ ___ ___ ___ ___
                            17   7

Question: What two **list words** could describe an elephant?

Answer: ___ ___ ___ ___ ___ ___ ___ ___ ___ ___
            1   2   3   4   5   6   7   8   9   10

___ ___ ___ ___ ___ ___ ___
11 12 13 14 15 16 17

Proofreading

Use the proofreading marks to correct the mistakes in the paragraph below. Then, write the misspelled **list words** correctly on the lines.

Proofreading Marks

⬭ spelling mistake   ℮ delete word

↲ add apostrophe   ⌃ add comma

Have you heard of Pecos Bill? He was a a legendary cowboy hero who personified the frontier virtues of strength, courage ingenuity and enthuziasm. His biographey comprises a series of superhuman feats that illustrate these virtues. Pecos Bill is said to have been born in Texas in the 1830s. According to legend, after falling out of his parents wagon near the Pecos River, he became lost and was raised by coyotes. As an adult, Bill created many new geografical and geolojical features throughout the West. During a cronic drought, he drained the Río Grande to water his ranch.

1. _____

2. _____

3. _____

4. _____

5. _____

Writing a Tall Tale

Have you ever felt as "hungry as a bear"? Such exaggerated expressions are called hyperboles. They are used in speech and literature to overstate reality, often for comic effect. Write a tall tale about a legendary character using an example of hyperbole to "stretch" the facts. Use as many **list words** as you can. After proofreading and revising, read your tall tale to the group.

BONUS WORDS

| mimicry | synonymous | sarcasm | euphemism | memoir |
| rhetoric | anachronism | paradox | epigram | epithet |

Write a **bonus word** to complete each sentence.

1. Words that are _____ have similar meanings.

2. "He passed away" is a _____ for he died.

3. "The child is father of the man" is an example of _____.

4. "Early Romans driving fancy sports cars" is an example of _____.

5. The title *Richard the Lion-Hearted* is an example of _____.

6. In a personal _____ , someone might recall important events in his or her life.

7. Edison's saying "Genius is 1% inspiration and 99% perspiration" is a famous _____.

8. To say, "Thanks a lot!" to a person who has not been helpful is to use _____.

9. To use eloquent "ten-dollar words" that do not communicate clearly is to use _____.

10. Onomatopoetic words, such as *honk, sputter, clatter,* and *buzz,* are examples of _____.

- The prefixes **co** and **syn** mean "together." Examples include <u>coauthor</u> and <u>synonym</u>. When added to a root beginning with **l**, **syn** changes to **syl**, as in <u>syllable</u>. It changes to **sym** when it is added to roots beginning with **b**, **m**, or **p**. Examples include <u>symbol</u>, <u>symmetry</u>, and <u>sympathy</u>.

- The prefixes **non**, **neg**, **in**, **im**, and **a** mean "not." Examples include <u>nonchalant</u>, <u>negligent</u>, <u>indecisive</u>, <u>impossible</u>, and <u>apolitical</u>. The prefix **a** becomes **an** when it is added to a root beginning with a vowel. Examples include <u>anarchy</u> and <u>anemia</u>.

- Many English words have Greek or Latin origins. Knowing the meanings of Greek and Latin prefixes and roots will help you to define and spell many unfamiliar words.

Prefix/Root	Source	Meaning	English Word	Meaning
ex + orbita	Latin	"out of track"	<u>exorbitant</u>	"excessive"
optio	Latin	"wish; desire"	<u>option</u>	"power to choose"
sub + urbs	Latin	"near;" "town"	<u>suburban</u>	"just outside a city"
ex + hilaris	Latin	"very;" "glad"	<u>exhilarated</u>	"cheerful; lively"
aēr + naus	Greek	"air;" "ship"	<u>aeronautics</u>	"the science of aircraft"
theo + logos	Greek	"god;" "words"	<u>theology</u>	"the study of religion"
okto + gonia	Greek	"eight;" "angles"	<u>octagon</u>	"eight-sided figure"

Lesson 19

List Words

coherent

coordinate

synchronize

symphonic

synagogue

symmetry

symptom

syntax

coincide

symbolize

_____

_____

Select a **list word** from the choices in parentheses to complete each sentence. Write the **list word** on the line.

1. A rash of small red dots is a _____ of measles. (syntax, symptom)

2. Let's _____ our watches. (synchronize, coincide)

3. In my poem, the sun will _____ power. (synagogue, symbolize)

4. Hal has been chosen to _____ the project. (coincide, coordinate)

5. He worships at a _____. (synagogue, symmetry)

6. This year, school vacation will _____ with my father's business trip to Argentina. (coincide, symbolize)

7. Mozart wrote many beautiful _____ works. (symphonic, coordinate)

8. We study grammar and _____. (syntax, coherent)

9. Maria got an A on her oral report because it was interesting and _____. (symphonic, coherent)

10. Pieces of art that are balanced have _____. (symmetry, synchronize)

List Words

anonymous

impersonate

inaccurate

negligent

nonexistent

immobilize

anemia

immaculate

incognito

anesthesia

_____

_____

Each of these sentences contains the wrong **list word**.
Cross out the word and write the correct **list word** on the line.

1. No one knew who sent the anesthesia note. _____

2. I'm afraid I was nonexistent, and forgot to feed the cat last night. _____

3. Don't let shyness immaculate you when new friends invite you to join them in a game. _____

4. To protect her privacy, the movie star decided to travel negligent. _____

5. The comedian will inaccurate a gorilla. _____

6. The doctor will administer anemia to the patient prior to surgery. _____

7. The city's plans to enlarge the library will be postponed because the funds are anonymous. _____

8. Honest people tend to avoid incognito facts. _____

9. Eat foods that are rich in iron to protect yourself from impersonate. _____

10. The players' immobilize uniforms became wet and grimy because the field was muddy. _____

List Words

auditor

exorbitant

exhilarated

juvenile

ordinance

quarantine

documentary

opulent

optician

molecular

_____

_____

Write a **list word** to answer each definition clue.

1. maker or seller of eyeglasses _____

2. of or relating to molecules _____

3. luscious; prosperous _____

4. too much; excessive _____

5. an informative film based on facts _____

6. the act of isolating a diseased person or animal _____

7. a child or young person _____

8. very happy and excited _____

9. an examiner of financial accounts _____

10. a regulation or rule _____

Write a **list word** to complete each sentence.

List Words

archaic

metropolis

architect

economical

democracy

analysis

archive

aeronautics

criticize

theology

_____

_____

1. _____ is the study of God and religious beliefs.

2. The _____ is the one who will design the building.

3. _____ was the form of government of ancient Greece.

4. New York City is the largest _____ in the United States.

5. To _____ a film is to describe its strengths and weaknesses.

6. A law firm might file source documents in its _____.

7. Something that is _____ to buy is considered a bargain.

8. _____ is the science, study, or design of aircraft.

9. The chemical _____ revealed a trace of iron in the compound.

10. One of the _____ laws that once existed in Arizona made hunting for camels illegal.

Use the **list words** to complete the crossword puzzle.

List Words

paralysis

enthusiasm

biological

dialogue

parallel

pharmacy

chronic

parable

geographical

thermostat

_____

_____

ACROSS

3. story that teaches a lesson
5. related to the study of living things
6. device to regulate heat level
7. related to the study of the Earth's surface
9. drugstore
10. inability to move

DOWN

1. at the same distance apart, at every point
2. intense or eager interest
4. conversation
8. enduring; continuous

Show What You Know

One word is misspelled in each set of **list words**. Fill in the circle next to the **list word** that is spelled incorrectly.

1. ○ coauthor ○ anesethesia ○ bureaucracy ○ dominion
2. ○ colateral ○ immobilize ○ juvenile ○ eclipse
3. ○ option ○ magnetic ○ impatiantly ○ copilot
4. ○ theology ○ indecisive ○ quaranteen ○ symptom
5. ○ negative ○ aristocrat ○ synagogue ○ verman
6. ○ exhilirated ○ immaculate ○ biography ○ anemia
7. ○ coexist ○ maximmum ○ coordinate ○ thermostat
8. ○ syllable ○ inaccurate ○ nonchalant ○ opulint
9. ○ regime ○ symetry ○ cooperative ○ octagon
10. ○ verdict ○ barometer ○ synchronize ○ parascite
11. ○ academy ○ coherant ○ anonymous ○ chronic
12. ○ archaive ○ invalid ○ geographical ○ impromptu
13. ○ inactive ○ symphonic ○ cosmapolitan ○ parallel
14. ○ pharmacy ○ neglect ○ economicle ○ synthesis
15. ○ syncopate ○ metropolis ○ nonexistent ○ biological
16. ○ dialogue ○ coincide ○ aironautics ○ auditor
17. ○ archaic ○ exorbitant ○ symbolise ○ hydrant
18. ○ molecular ○ televise ○ symposium ○ parabble
19. ○ criticise ○ syntax ○ Republican ○ elastic
20. ○ syllabus ○ democracy ○ geological ○ ordinence
21. ○ paralysis ○ anarchey ○ documentary ○ analysis
22. ○ insectiscide ○ architect ○ enthusiasm ○ imprudent
23. ○ crisis ○ optician ○ impersonaite ○ neon
24. ○ politics ○ incognito ○ cosmos ○ publcity
25. ○ neglegent ○ thermos ○ suburban ○ anagram

Words Ending in ize, ise, ent, ant

Words ending in **ize**, **ise**, **ent** and **ant** are easy to confuse. Listen for the ending sounds of underline{enterprise} and underline{apologize}. They sound alike but are spelled differently. Other sounds are also easy to confuse. The ends of underline{prudent} and underline{relevant} sound alike but have different spellings. You must memorize which words end in **ise** or **ize** and which end in **ent** or **ant**.

Vocabulary Development

Write the **list word** that matches each definition clue.

1. eternal _____
2. a business _____
3. joyful _____
4. showing good judgment _____
5. express regrets _____
6. save money _____
7. relying on another _____
8. agreeable or pleasing _____
9. able _____
10. watchful _____
11. direction hands of clock move _____
12. meaningful _____
13. list _____
14. usual _____

LIST WORDS

1. pleasant
2. competent
3. rationalize
4. jubilant
5. prevalent
6. enterprise
7. compromise
8. franchise
9. lengthwise
10. prudent
11. apologize
12. dependent
13. harmonize
14. observant
15. relevant
16. clockwise
17. economize
18. itemize
19. permanent
20. significant

Dictionary Skills

Write the **list word** that matches each sound-spelling.

1. (käm′prə mīz) _____
2. (pʉr′mə nənt) _____
3. (leŋkth′wīz) _____
4. (əb zʉr′vənt) _____
5. (rash′ən ə līz′) _____
6. (plez′n′t) _____
7. (här′mə nīz) _____
8. (rel′ə vənt) _____
9. (prev′ə lənt) _____
10. (fran′chīz) _____

DID YOU KNOW ?

Everyone knows that **clockwise** means "in the direction of the clock," but most people do not know where the word *clock* came from. The clock got its name from the bell that sounded its hours. It is derived from the Latin word, *clocca*, meaning "bell."

Spelling Practice

Word Analysis

Write each **list word** under its ending.

ise

1. _____
2. _____
3. _____
4. _____
5. _____

ant

6. _____
7. _____
8. _____
9. _____
10. _____

ize

11. _____
12. _____
13. _____
14. _____
15. _____

ent

16. _____
17. _____
18. _____
19. _____
20. _____

Write the **list word** that has the same root as each word given.

1. economy _____
2. please _____
3. rational _____
4. observe _____

5. items _____
6. dependable _____
7. prevail _____
8. unobserved _____

Word Application

Replace the underlined word or words in each sentence with a **list word**. Write the **list word** on the line.

1. On the round edges, paint <u>in the direction the clock hands turn</u>, but on the floor, paint <u>with the length</u>. _____ _____

2. Mrs. Flores is supervising the entire <u>job</u>, and she seems <u>delighted</u> with the results.

   _____ _____

3. It would be <u>wise</u> to try to <u>save money</u> on non-essential features.

   _____ _____

4. When their voices all <u>sing in agreement</u>, they make a <u>pleasing</u> sound.

   _____ _____

pleasant	enterprise	apologize	compromise
prudent	clockwise	dependent	economize
itemize	franchise	harmonize	rationalize
jubilant	significant	observant	permanent
relevant	competent	prevalent	lengthwise

Puzzle

Use the **list words** to complete the crossword puzzle.

ACROSS

3. in the direction of the length
5. a right given to sell something
7. to make conform to reason
8. to sing in harmony
10. lasting forever
12. meaningful to a certain situation or thing
15. careful; cautious
16. having the ability to do what is needed
18. full of meaning
19. to list each item

DOWN

1. a settling of an argument by both sides giving in
2. in the direction of the clock
4. be thrifty
6. relying on another
9. a business or undertaking
10. happening over a wide area
11. to say that one is sorry
13. joyful and proud
14. paying careful attention
17. nice; agreeable

Use the proofreading marks to correct the mistakes in the article below. Then, write the misspelled **list words** correctly on the lines.

⬭ spelling mistake / small letter
↗ add comma # add space

A franchize isa legal agreement. It allows an Entirprise or organization with a product theright to grant another business owner the opportunity to sell that product. This kind of agreement first became popular in the 1950s. Since then it has had a signifikant and permunent effect on the rise of small business owners in the American Economy. Many fastfood businesses that are prevelent throughout the country are run this way.

1. _____

2. _____

3. _____

4. _____

5. _____

Writing an Ad

Think like a business person and write an advertisement using simile for a product of your choice. Here's an example of a simile: *These fans will sell like hot cakes!* Use as many of the **list words** as you can in your ad. When finished, proofread and revise your ad, and then share it with classmates.

BONUS WORDS

| inflation | corporation | proprietary | mercantile | diversify |
| proxy | conglomerate | negotiation | securities | liquidate |

Write the **bonus word** that matches each clue given.

1. discussion to reach agreement

_____

2. authority to act for another

_____

3. more dollars buy less

_____

4. stocks and bonds, for example

_____

5. commercial

_____

6. give variety to

_____

7. a legal entity

_____

8. convert assets into cash

_____

9. many companies in one big one

_____

10. held under patent or trademark

_____

Noun-Forming Suffix ity

TIP

The suffix **ity** can form a noun from an adjective. For example, legal becomes legality. When the suffix is added to words ending in **ble**, the ending of the base word changes, as in visible/visibility. A few other words, such as generous and hospitable, change in different ways to become generosity and hospitality.

Vocabulary Development

Write the **list word** that matches each definition clue.

1. ability to be on time _____

2. ability to move _____

3. ability to be taken or purchased _____

4. singularity _____

5. following prescribed customs _____

6. abilities not yet developed _____

7. ability to be seen _____

8. state of being lesser _____

9. ability to bend _____

10. temperament _____

11. unselfish act _____

12. a possible event _____

LIST WORDS

1. punctuality
2. personality
3. liability
4. practicality
5. formality
6. individuality
7. technicality
8. availability
9. inferiority
10. mobility
11. visibility
12. hospitality
13. eligibility
14. capability
15. generosity
16. eventuality
17. superiority
18. legality
19. flexibility
20. similarity

Dictionary Skills

Rewrite each of the following **list words** to show how they are divided into syllables.

1. legality _____
2. similarity _____
3. eligibility _____
4. liability _____
5. formality _____
6. mobility _____
7. superiority _____
8. hospitality _____
9. practicality _____
10. technicality _____
11. capability _____
12. generosity _____

Spelling Practice

DID YOU KNOW ?

Technicality is formed from the word *technical* and the suffix *ity*. *Technical* comes from the Greek word *tekhnikos*, meaning "of art," which comes from the Greek word for "art," *tekhn*. It also shares the root **teks**, meaning "to weave" or "to fabricate," which is the basis for other English words such as *text*, *tissue*, *context*, *pretext*, *subtle*, *architect*, and *technology*.

Word Analysis

Form **list words** by adding the suffix **ity** to these adjectives to make nouns.

1. mobile _____
2. inferior _____
3. practical _____
4. formal _____
5. liable _____
6. personal _____
7. punctual _____
8. available _____
9. individual _____
10. technical _____

11. visible _____
12. similar _____
13. hospitable _____
14. eventual _____
15. superior _____
16. generous _____
17. capable _____
18. legal _____
19. flexible _____
20. eligible _____

Word Application

Select a **list word** from the choices in parentheses to complete each sentence. Write the **list word** on the line.

1. Due to his _____, Bill got to work on time. (punctuality, similarity)

2. This engine has the _____ to pull both boxcars. (formality, capability)

3. Bowing before the prince is merely a _____. (generosity, formality)

4. Tara called to let us know of her _____ for the job. (legality, availability)

5. Emily's clothing reflected her sense of _____. (eventuality, individuality)

6. The glass door's breaking was an _____. (availability, eventuality)

7. Our insurance company has _____ for the accident. (flexibility, liability)

8. _____ was why Rick chose a small dog. (practicality, visibility)

9. Some exercises increase the body's _____. (visibility, flexibility)

10. Crossing guards wear orange vests for _____. (punctuality, visibility)

11. Mark's and your voice have a great _____. (similarity, practicality)

12. Jan's wheelchair has greatly increased her _____. (mobility, liability)

13. The club thanked the donor for her _____. (individuality, generosity)

14. A lawyer researched the _____ of the situation. (mobility, legality)

LIST WORDS

visibility	individuality	punctuality	capability
mobility	technicality	hospitality	inferiority
liability	availability	practicality	eligibility
formality	personality	superiority	flexibility
legality	generosity	eventuality	similarity

Puzzle

Unscramble the **list words** using the blank spaces to the right. Then, transfer the numbered letters to the spaces below to solve the riddle.

1. lenittchcaiy   ___ ___ (15) ___ ___ (2) ___ ___ ___ ___ ___ ___

2. tivabyaiilla   ___ ___ ___ ___ (9) ___ ___ ___ ___ ___ ___ ___

3. cuttiypunal   ___ ___ (4) ___ ___ ___ ___ ___ ___ ___

4. pioyurerits   ___ ___ ___ ___ ___ (7) ___ ___ ___ ___

5. ernoitifiry   ___ ___ ___ (12) ___ ___ (18) ___ ___ ___

6. tyinegrose   ___ ___ ___ (3) ___ (17) ___ ___ ___

7. mitboily   ___ ___ (11) ___ ___ ___ ___ ___

8. tiallibiy   ___ ___ ___ ___ (5) ___ ___ ___

9. undidailyivit   ___ ___ ___ (10) ___ ___ ___ ___ ___ ___ ___ ___ (1) ___

10. spoalyernit   ___ ___ ___ ___ ___ (14) ___ ___ ___ (6) ___

11. sitopithaly   ___ ___ (13) ___ ___ ___ ___ ___ ___ ___

12. yuittneeval   ___ ___ ___ ___ ___ (8) ___ ___ ___ ___

13. mayrlfito   ___ (16) ___ ___ ___ ___ ___ (19) ___

RIDDLE: Why isn't your nose twelve inches long?

ANSWER: ___ ___ ___ ___ ___ ___ **W** ___ ___ ___ ___
            1   2   3   4   5   6   7   8   9   10

___ ___ ___ ___ ___ ___ ___ ___ ___
11 12   13 14 15   16 17 18 19

Proofreading

Use the proofreading marks to correct the mistakes in the following article. Then, write the misspelled **list words** correctly on the lines.

Good manners, such as punctualety when keeping an appointment, are always an admirable social asset. in the eventuallity that you travel to another country, it is always a good idea to read upon what is considered polite and impolite in the country you will be visiting After all, offending someone unknowingly canbe a definite lyeability! In japan, for example, it is impolite to eat something while walking down the street. Gift giving is very important in japan, but extravagant gifts require an equally extravagant gift in return It's best to avoid giving pricey gifts to repay a host's hospetality and genirosity.

Proofreading Marks

◯ spelling mistake   ⊙ add period
≡ capital letter   # add space

1. _____
2. _____
3. _____
4. _____
5. _____

Writing a Persuasive Paragraph

A metaphor compares two things without using the words <u>like</u> or <u>as</u>. For example, "Good manners are a paved road to success" is a metaphor. Write a short persuasive paragraph on why good manners are an asset, using one or two metaphors and as many **list words** as you can. Proofread and revise your paragraph, and then share it with the class.

BONUS WORDS

trigonometry	abacus	logarithm	correlation	statistical
geometric	finite	analytical	numerical	calculus

Write the **bonus word** that matches each clue.

1. not infinite _____

2. having lines, circles, or other forms _____

3. early kind of calculator _____

4. kind of exponent _____

5. a mutual relationship _____

6. able to analyze _____

7. based on numerical facts or data _____

8. math that deals with triangles _____

9. expressed by numbers _____

10. math dealing with changes _____

Words Ending in <u>ary</u>, <u>ory</u>

Lesson 27

TIP

Words ending in **ary** and **ory** sometimes sound alike. Listen for the ending sounds in <u>compulsory</u> and <u>infirmary</u>. They sound similar but are spelled differently. Study and memorize words that end with **ary** or **ory** carefully.

Vocabulary Development

Write the **list word** that matches each synonym or definition clue.

1. flattering _____
2. mythical _____
3. words of a language _____
4. modern _____
5. bringing radical change _____
6. meeting a need or wish _____
7. a safe place _____
8. a viewing place _____
9. first _____
10. health clinic _____
11. financial _____
12. tasty _____
13. remarkable _____
14. needed _____
15. required _____

LIST WORDS

1. advisory
2. extraordinary
3. mandatory
4. preliminary
5. satisfactory
6. compulsory
7. infirmary
8. monetary
9. primary
10. savory
11. complimentary
12. introductory
13. necessary
14. revolutionary
15. subsidiary
16. contemporary
17. legendary
18. observatory
19. sanctuary
20. vocabulary

Dictionary Skills

Write the **list word** that matches each sound-spelling.

1. (prī′mer′ē) _____
2. (səb sid′ē er′ē) _____
3. (nes′ə ser′ē) _____
4. (sā′vər ē) _____
5. (kəm pul′sər ē) _____
6. (man′də tôr′ē) _____
7. (sat′is fak′tər ē) _____
8. (in′trə duk′tər ē) _____
9. (ad vī′zər ē) _____
10. (vō kab′yə ler′ē) _____

Spelling Practice

DID YOU KNOW ?

In colonial days, a child's first reading book was called a primer, and today, the first grades of school are called the primary grades. **Primary** is taken from the Latin word, *primus*, which meant "first." Today, we use this same word to describe the first or the best of something, like the prime rib of beef.

Word Analysis

Write **list words** to answer the following questions.
Which **list word** contains the same root as the word given?

1. legend _____
2. infirm _____
3. compliment _____
4. observe _____
5. satisfy _____
6. prime _____

7. savor _____
8. advise _____
9. introduce _____
10. revolution _____
11. mandate _____
12. compel _____

Which **list words** end in **ory**?

13. _____
14. _____
15. _____
16. _____

17. _____
18. _____
19. _____

Word Application

Replace the underlined word or words in each phrase with a **list word**. Write the **list word** on the line.

1. a division of Worldwide <u>Manufacturers</u> _____
2. the <u>opening</u> round of competition _____
3. an artist who is <u>living and working today</u> _____
4. a free <u>preliminary</u> offer _____
5. a storm and hurricane <u>warning bulletin</u> _____
6. an <u>out of the ordinary</u> piece of music _____
7. a <u>famous</u> cartoon character _____
8. a national wildlife <u>protected place</u> for birds _____
9. many <u>money</u> considerations _____
10. the solar <u>viewing place</u> _____
11. medicines <u>essential</u> for the patient's recovery _____
12. the words on the English test _____
13. the <u>health clinic</u> where Dr. Jarvis works _____

LIST WORDS

contemporary	infirmary	satisfactory	mandatory
extraordinary	advisory	introductory	legendary
compulsory	monetary	observatory	necessary
revolutionary	primary	preliminary	sanctuary
complimentary	savory	vocabulary	subsidiary

Puzzle

This is a crossword puzzle without clues. Use the length and the spelling of each **list word** to complete the puzzle.

Proofreading

Use the proofreading marks to correct the mistakes in the article below. Then, write the misspelled **list words** correctly on the lines.

Proofreading Marks

⬭ spelling mistake ℓ delete word
☰ capital letter
? add question mark

Did you know the invention of banking actually took place before the invention of monetory units such as as coins and paper money Banking originated in in ancient mesopotamia where it was not only necesary, but mandutary that the royal palaces and temples provide a sankchuary for the safe-keeping of grain. Receipts came to be used for transfers if the farmer who deposited the grain needed to give some of it to someone else. Over time, keeping track of grain and other goods in this fashion came to be a a primmary function of priests in mesopotamia. They became the world's first bankers.

1. _____

2. _____

3. _____

4. _____

5. _____

Writing Sentences Using Alliteration

Alliteration is a literary device that employs two or more words with the same beginning sounds, such as "Sandy sang a simple song of sunny Sundays sailing." Write two sentences containing as much alliteration as possible on the topic of banking or U.S. or foreign currency, and try to use at least two **list words** in your sentences. After you proofread and revise your sentences, combine them with classmates' to create poems.

BONUS WORDS

| franc | mark | rupee | yen | guilder |
| peso | ruble | pound | lira | shekel |

Write the **bonus word** that is associated with each country given.

1. Netherlands _____

2. Mexico _____

3. India _____

4. Italy _____

5. Israel _____

6. England _____

7. Russia _____

8. France _____

9. Germany _____

10. Japan _____

Words of French Origin

 TIP

Several English words have French roots. For example, the English word porcelain comes from the French word *porcelaine*. The English word surgeon comes from the French word *cirurgien*.

Many other English words have been borrowed directly, in original form, from the French language. Examples include fiancée, bouillon, souvenir, and sauté. The spelling of such words can be tricky. Some, like sauté, contain accent marks. Others contain sounds spelled by letter combinations that are common to French words but rare to English words. For example, the letters **et** at the end of croquet and the **ee** at the end of fiancée stand for the long a sound.

Vocabulary Development

Write the **list word** that matches each synonym or definition.

1. manners _____

2. puppet _____

3. keepsake _____

4. shellfish _____

5. egg dish _____

6. broth _____

7. tennis equipment _____

8. to fry quickly _____

9. medical specialist _____

10. dinner choices _____

11. small bouquet _____

12. lawn game _____

Dictionary Skills

Write the **list word** that matches each sound-spelling.

1. (krō kā′) _____

2. (fē′än sā′) _____

3. (en′dīv) _____

4. (skav′in jər) _____

5. (pôr′s′l in) _____

6. (fi nes′) _____

7. (prōt′ə zhā) _____

8. (so͞o flā′) _____

9. (rez′o͞o mā′) _____

10. (ō pāk′) _____

11. (so͞o və nir′) _____

LIST WORDS

1. bouillon
2. fiancée
3. opaque
4. racquet
5. scallop
6. croquet
7. finesse
8. corsage
9. résumé
10. soufflé
11. endive
12. marionette
13. porcelain
14. sauté
15. souvenir
16. etiquette
17. menu
18. protégé
19. scavenger
20. surgeon

DID YOU KNOW ?

Etiquette is a French word that actually means "ticket," "label," or "list." It was first used on the lists of rules that were posted in a court or army camp. We might also say that etiquette can be a ticket that allows a person to enter polite society.

Spelling Practice

Word Analysis

Write **list words** to answer the following questions.

In which words does **et**, **é**, or **ée** spell the long **a** sound, as in <u>day</u>?

1. _____   3. _____   5. _____

2. _____   4. _____   6. _____

Which words contain the letter combination **que**?

7. _____   9. _____

8. _____   10. _____

Which words contain these double consonants?

11. **ss** _____   13. **tt** _____   15. **ll** _____

12. **tt** _____   14. **ff** _____   16. **ll** _____

Analogies

Write a **list word** to complete each analogy.

1. Bat is to baseball as _____ is to tennis.

2. Judge is to courtroom as _____ is to operating room.

3. Gems are to bracelet as flowers are to _____.

4. Fork is to silver as cup is to _____.

5. Flour is to bread as eggs are to _____.

6. Lion is to predator as buzzard is to _____.

7. Back is to forth as transparent is to _____.

8. Apple is to lemon as cabbage is to _____.

Word Application

Write a **list word** to complete each sentence.

1. Ellen kept the ticket stub as a _____ of her wonderful trip.

2. The waiter told us about the dinner specials that were not listed on the _____.

3. The magician fooled us with cleverness and _____.

4. It is considered to be poor _____ to talk with your mouth full of food.

5. Two weeks before the wedding, we had a party for Jeff and his _____, Josie.

6. Sara listed all of her summer jobs on her _____.

LIST WORDS

bouillon	croquet	etiquette	endive
fiancée	finesse	marionette	menu
opaque	corsage	porcelain	scallop
racquet	résumé	scavenger	sauté
protégé	surgeon	souvenir	soufflé

Classification

Write a **list word** to complete each series.

1. chowder, soup, _____

2. glass, china, _____

3. ball, _____, net

4. apprentice, student, _____

5. bake, boil, _____

6. style, cleverness, _____

Puzzle

Use the **list words** to complete the crossword puzzle.

ACROSS

1. egg dish
3. not transparent
6. doctor who operates
9. animal that feeds on decaying organic matter
10. list of jobs and related experiences
17. list of dinner selections
18. sporting equipment
19. game with mallets, balls, and wickets
20. engaged female

DOWN

2. skill; artfulness; craft
4. leafy green plant
5. ceramic material used for dishes
7. bouquet that is worn
8. stringed puppet
11. scrapbook item
12. clear soup or broth
13. to fry briefly
14. shellfish
15. code of acceptable manners
16. person who receives help or guidance from another

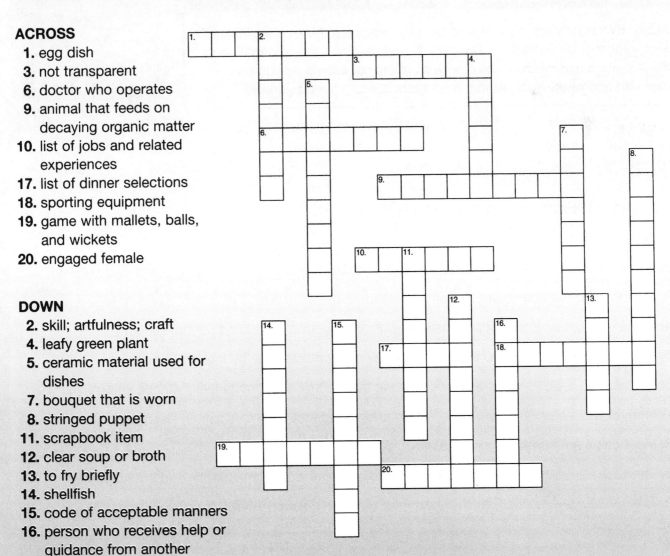

Proofreading

Use the proofreading marks to correct the mistakes in the article below. Then, write the misspelled **list words** correctly on the lines.

Proofreading Marks

⬭ spelling mistake ⊙ add period

¶ new paragraph ╱ small letter

Although, croquette and tennis do not look as if they would have anything in common, they have many striking similarities Both are thought to have originated in France—tennis, around the twelfth century, and croquet, perhaps around the thirteenth century. While one game is played with a mallet and the other is played with a racket, both require a great deal of finese. During the Nineteenth century, guidebooks of rules and playing etiquitte appeared.

Today, Tennis has become so popular that a soovenir from a tennis match such as Wimbledon can cost a great deal of money

1. _____

2. _____

3. _____

4. _____

5. _____

Writing a Comparison

Choose two sports you have played or enjoy watching. Make a list in which you compare and contrast the two sports, and then use this information to write a comparison of them. Try to use as many **list words** as you can. Proofread and revise your writing, then share it with your classmates.

| impurity | refraction | crystallize | turquoise | obsidian |
| facets | dispersion | amethyst | sapphire | diamond |

Write a **bonus word** to complete each sentence.

1. The _____ is a hard, black stone that is formed by the intense heat of volcanoes.

2. A tiny crack or _____, even if invisible to the eye, can make a gem's value plunge.

3. The polished surfaces of a cut gem are called _____.

4. The _____ of light reflecting off a cut gem can create a rainbow effect.

5. Due to _____ of light, you'll see a distorted image by looking through a cut gem.

6. The _____ is a colorless stone that is the hardest natural substance known.

7. The _____, which is named after the planet Saturn, is usually deep blue.

8. Most gems are formed when minerals _____.

9. The _____ is greenish-blue and contains aluminum, copper, and phosphorus.

10. The _____, which is purple or violet, is a variety of quartz or corundum.

Challenging Words

Many English words do not follow ordinary spelling rules. The best way to become familiar with these challenging words is to study, memorize, and practice using them.

Challenging Word	"Trick"
schedules	**d** = sound of **j**
emphatically	**ph** = sound of **f**
jeopardy	**eo** = sound of short **e**
accessory	**cc, ss**
	double consonants

Vocabulary Development

Write the **list word** that matches each synonym.

1. servant _____

2. pier _____

3. shabby _____

4. allowed _____

5. peaceful _____

6. danger _____

7. dictatorship _____

8. timetables _____

9. completed _____

10. intrigue _____

11. sensitive _____

12. terrible _____

Dictionary Skills

Write the **list word** that comes between each pair of dictionary guide words.

1. **scan/scene** _____

2. **wheat/zinc** _____

3. **instant/key** _____

4. **display/far** _____

5. **tyrant/vulgar** _____

6. **yellow/zoom** _____

7. **mystery/odd** _____

8. **over/python** _____

9. **dimple/embrace** _____

10. **able/alive** _____

LIST WORDS

1. accessory
2. emphatically
3. attendant
4. schedules
5. vulnerable
6. allotted
7. fascinate
8. notarize
9. tranquil
10. wharf
11. dilapidated
12. fulfilled
13. precinct
14. tyranny
15. yeast
16. disastrous
17. jeopardy
18. scarcity
19. umbrella
20. zinnia

Spelling Practice

DID YOU KNOW ?

In England during the sixteenth century, when a chess player was forced to make a move with which he could lose the game, his position was called *iuparti*. This term came from the French *jeu parti*, which meant "divided game." Today, we know the word as **jeopardy**, which can describe any situation in which winning or losing hangs in a delicate balance.

Word Analysis

Fill in the missing letters to form **list words**. Then, write the completed **list words** on the lines.

1. vuln___ ___ ___ble   _____
2. not___r___ ___e   _____
3. di___as___ ___ ___us   _____
4. a___ ___e___ ___ ___ry   _____
5. ___m___ ___atic___ ___ly   _____
6. fa___ ___inate   _____
7. t___r___ ___ny   _____
8. w___ ___ ___f   _____
9. tra___ ___ ___il   _____

Classification

Write a **list word** to complete each series.

1. waiter, valet, _____
2. charm, enchant, _____
3. calm, restful, _____
4. raincoat, boots, _____
5. trouble, danger, _____
6. scarf, pin, _____
7. witness, sign, _____
8. freighter, harbor, _____
9. marigold, petunia, _____
10. dough, bread, _____

Word Application

Replace each underlined word or words in the sentences with a **list word**. Write the **list word** on the line.

1. He <u>strongly</u> denied that he was responsible for the <u>ruinous</u> accident.

   _____   _____

2. The landlord <u>satisfied</u> his promise to repair the <u>run-down</u> apartment building.

   _____   _____

3. Due to the <u>shortage</u> of seats, each graduate was <u>given</u> only four tickets.

   _____   _____

4. The sergeant posted <u>lists of times</u> for officers assigned to his <u>division</u>.

   _____   _____

LIST WORDS

accessory	allotted	zinnia	disastrous
emphatically	scarcity	wharf	jeopardy
dilapidated	notarize	precinct	fascinate
schedules	tranquil	tyranny	umbrella
vulnerable	fulfilled	yeast	attendant

Puzzle

Use the **list words** to complete the crossword puzzle.

ACROSS

3. great danger or peril
6. something extra
7. free from disturbance
9. to witness a legal signing
11. a wooden structure in a harbor where ships load and unload goods
12. substance used in baking to make dough rise
13. a person who helps or serves someone
15. to have made happen; completed
17. having great destruction or misfortune
18. lists of arriving and departing trains and buses
19. very cruel and unjust use of power

DOWN

1. a portable covering to protect from rain
2. a showy garden flower
4. the district or area patrolled by police
5. open to harm or danger
8. distributed little by little
10. run down; in ruin
14. with force of expression
15. to delight or charm
16. a lacking or shortage of something

Proofreading

Use the proofreading marks to correct the mistakes in the article below. Then, write the misspelled **list words** correctly on the lines.

Proofreading Marks

⬭ spelling mistake

≡ capital letter   ⌗ add space

! add exclamation mark

If you are lucky enough to live where wolves are common, you may sometimes hear them howl. The howl is one important method wolves useto communicate with each other. It certainly is an eerie sound. Unfortunately, although wolves have always tended to fascinnate people, they have also been a source of fear. Asa result, there is a scarsity of wolves in the lower 48 states. For many years, wolves were vulneruble to hunters and ranchers who wanted to remove them from wilderness areas. Once in jepardy, wolves are now making a comeback in states like minnesota and maine, with atendant laws to protect them.

1. _____

2. _____

3. _____

4. _____

5. _____

Writing Sentences Using Onomatopoeia

Onomatopoeia is a word in which the sound gives the word meaning. "Plink, plink went the raindrops as they fell into the puddle" is an example. Write several sentences with onomatopoeia, using as many **list words** as you can. Proofread and revise your onomatopoeic sentences, then compare them with those of your classmates and discuss which ones work best.

BONUS WORDS

| vociferous | enunciate | strident | amplification | taciturn |
| reverberate | inaudible | timbre | intonation | reticent |

Write the **bonus word** that matches each clue given.

1. cause a sound to echo _____

2. cannot be heard _____

3. loud; noisy; vehement _____

4. say clearly and distinctly _____

5. making sound louder _____

6. harsh-sounding; shrill _____

Write the **bonus words** that are synonyms or near-synonyms for the phrases given.

distinguishing quality of a voice   almost always silent

7. _____   9. _____

8. _____   10. _____

- Understanding word endings can help you spell many words correctly. Some are easy to confuse, such as **ise** and **ize**, **ent** and **ant**, and **ary** and **ory**. Pay close attention to the spelling of words with similar endings. Here are several examples:

  preval**ent**, relev**ant**, franch**ise**, harmon**ize**, advis**ory**, prelimin**ary**

- The suffix **ity** forms a noun from an adjective, as when <u>formal</u> becomes <u>formality</u>. When this suffix is added to words ending in **ble**, an **i** is inserted before the **l**, so that words like <u>liable</u> become <u>liability</u>. In some words, the base word changes in different ways. For example, <u>hospitable</u> becomes <u>hospitality</u>.

- Many English words come from French and may contain letter combinations that are common in French words but unusual in English words, such as the ending of <u>finesse</u>. Other words from the French may contain accent marks, as in <u>sauté</u>.

- Our language also has words that do not follow the usual spelling rules. These may contain unusual spellings for certain sounds or unexpected double consonants. In the word <u>jeopardy</u>, for example, the vowel sound for short **e** is spelled **eo**. The word <u>allotted</u> has two pairs of double consonants.

- The best way to learn words with unusual spellings is to study them and use them.

Lesson 25

List Words

pleasant
apologize
compromise
dependent
observant
competent
economize
jubilant
enterprise
itemize
_____
_____

Replace the underlined word or words in each sentence with a **list word**. Write the **list word** on the line.

1. The swimmer was <u>very happy</u> when she won. _____
2. Make sure you go to a <u>skilled</u> mechanic. _____
3. An <u>aware</u> neighbor called the fire dept. _____
4. The breeze makes this room quite <u>nice</u>. _____
5. If you can <u>reach an agreement through negotiation</u>, you can both get what you want. _____
6. This <u>business</u> will not be sold! _____
7. We can <u>save money</u> by buying generic brands. _____
8. When we go camping, we are no longer <u>relying</u> on city facilities for entertainment. _____
9. I want to <u>say I'm sorry</u> for arriving late. _____
10. <u>Make a list of</u> the ingredients you need. _____

Write the **list word** with the same base word or root as the word given.

List Words

hospitality
availability
individuality
eligibility
similarity
flexibility
generosity
personality
capability
visibility

_____

_____

dissimilar

1. _____

individualized

2. _____

inhospitable

3. _____

inflexible

4. _____

incapable

5. _____

invisibly

6. _____

generously

7. _____

unavailable

8. _____

ineligible

9. _____

impersonate

10. _____

Write a **list word** to complete each sentence.

List Words

infirmary
legendary
mandatory
necessary
satisfactory
monetary
primary
sanctuary
extraordinary
complimentary

_____

_____

1. If people or animals are safe in a place, the place may be a

_____.

2. Financial plans affect a nation's _____ system.

3. If something is essential, it is _____.

4. If someone says that Seth looked wonderful, that person is making

a _____ statement.

5. The _____ pitcher was inducted into the Baseball
Hall of Fame.

6. If you feel sick, go to the _____.

7. Health is the _____ reason for exercising.

8. If you and your family are generally pleased, the carpenter did a

_____ job.

9. If a dancer's performance is truly outstanding, you might also call it

an _____ performance.

10. If seatbelts are required, they are _____.

Write **list words** to answer the questions. Some words will be used more than once.

List Words

- bouillon
- etiquette
- porcelain
- racquet
- souvenir
- surgeon
- opaque
- croquet
- marionette
- soufflé

_____

_____

Which words contain the vowel combination **ue**?

1. _____ 3. _____

2. _____ 4. _____

Which word contains the vowel combination **eo**?

5. _____

Which words contain the vowel combination **ou**?

6. _____ 8. _____

7. _____

Which word completes each series?

9. light blocking, nontransparent, _____

10. doll, puppet, _____

11. manners, conduct, _____

12. pediatrician, neurologist, _____

Use the **list words** to complete the crossword puzzle.

List Words

- accessory
- fascinate
- schedules
- vulnerable
- disastrous
- fulfilled
- scarcity
- tranquil
- wharf
- yeast

_____

_____

ACROSS

4. charm or bewitch
6. able to be hurt
7. causing great damage
9. lack or shortage
10. carried out

DOWN

1. pier or dock
2. timetables
3. bread ingredient
5. tie, scarf, or glove, for instance
8. serene

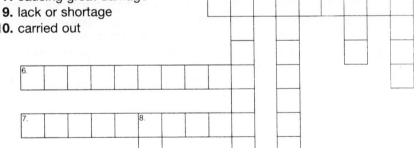

Show What You Know

One word is misspelled in each set of **list words**. Fill in the circle next to the **list word** that is spelled incorrectly.

1. ○ individuality ○ pleasent ○ introductory ○ etiquette
2. ○ technicality ○ necessary ○ compitent ○ menu
3. ○ revolutionary ○ availability ○ rationalise ○ protégé
4. ○ inferiority ○ subcidiary ○ contemporary ○ jubilant
5. ○ scavenger ○ prevalent ○ observatory ○ surgeaon
6. ○ enterprise ○ legendery ○ accessory ○ visibility
7. ○ compromize ○ hospitality ○ emphatically ○ mobility
8. ○ eligibility ○ franchise ○ sanctuary ○ attendent
9. ○ vocabulery ○ schedules ○ lengthwise ○ capability
10. ○ vulnerable ○ generosity ○ bouillion ○ prudent
11. ○ eventuality ○ fiancée ○ alloted ○ apologize
12. ○ dependent ○ opacque ○ superiority ○ fascinate
13. ○ notarize ○ flexability ○ harmonize ○ legality
14. ○ observent ○ tranquil ○ similarity ○ racquet
15. ○ scallop ○ relevant ○ dilapidatted ○ advisory
16. ○ clockwise ○ croquet ○ extrordinary ○ wharf
17. ○ economise ○ fulfilled ○ mandatory ○ finesse
18. ○ preliminary ○ corsage ○ precinct ○ itemise
19. ○ permanent ○ savory ○ résumé ○ tyranney
20. ○ compulsery ○ yeast ○ significant ○ soufflé
21. ○ disastrous ○ endive ○ punctuality ○ infirmery
22. ○ personality ○ monetary ○ marionette ○ jeopurdy
23. ○ porcelin ○ liability ○ scarcity ○ primary
24. ○ satisfactery ○ sauté ○ practicality ○ umbrella
25. ○ souvenir ○ zinia ○ complimentary ○ formality

Words from Science

TIP

The study of science involves the recognition and comprehension of many unfamiliar words. Words such as indigestion, microorganism, and respiration may seem complicated and difficult to spell. With practice, you can master these challenging words.

All the **list words** are from science. Memorize and practice spelling these words.

Classification

Write a **list word** to complete each series.

1. current, wattage, _____
2. air, lungs, _____
3. space, orbit, _____
4. esophagus, trachea, _____
5. inoculate, serum, _____
6. electron, proton, _____
7. mold, parasite, _____
8. annual, biennial, _____
9. mammals, birds, _____
10. microscope, bacteria, _____
11. pollen, sneezing, _____
12. mind, thought, _____

LIST WORDS

1. allergy
2. indigestion
3. physics
4. neutron
5. vaccinate
6. fungus
7. larynx
8. psychology
9. transmitter
10. voltage
11. diagnose
12. microorganism
13. satellite
14. transfusion
15. friction
16. iodine
17. perennial
18. respiration
19. turbine
20. zoology

Dictionary Skills

Write the **list word** that matches each sound-spelling.

1. (tʉr′bīn) _____
2. (ī′ə dīn) _____
3. (fiz′iks) _____
4. (frik′shən) _____
5. (al′ər jē) _____
6. (trans mit′ər) _____
7. (in′di jes′chən) _____
8. (trans fyo͞o′zhen) _____
9. (sī käl′ə jē) _____
10. (dī′əg nōs′) _____

DID YOU KNOW ?

A **turbine** is a rotary engine that generates power. It may have gotten its name from the Latin word *turb* meaning "spinning top," or from the Greek word *turb*, meaning "turmoil." Either is quite reasonable since a turbine must be turning in order to work. Indeed, if you were spinning about in a turbine, you would certainly be in a great deal of turmoil.

Word Analysis

Write each **list word** under the correct category.

Words with Two Syllables

1. _____
2. _____
3. _____
4. _____
5. _____
6. _____
7. _____

Words with Three Syllables

8. _____
9. _____
10. _____
11. _____
12. _____
13. _____
14. _____

Words with Four Syllables

15. _____
16. _____
17. _____
18. _____
19. _____

Word with Six Syllables

20. _____

Word Application

Underline the **list word** in each sentence that is used incorrectly. Write the correct **list word** on the line.

1. That voltage plant comes up year after year despite the cold weather. _____

2. The pneumonia in Kim's lungs had a severe effect on her vaccinate. _____

3. A bacteria is an example of a neutron. _____

4. High-respiration towers carry a tremendous amount of electrical power. _____

5. Sandy suffered from perennial after she ate some bad food. _____

6. Atoms have particles that include the electron, the proton, and the iodine.

_____

7. Be sure to larynx your pet so that it won't get the rabies virus. _____

8. My brother sneezes all the time due to his microorganism to dust. _____

9. The thyroid gland uses indigestion to help the body function properly. _____

10. Tom injured his allergy and couldn't talk for weeks. _____

LIST WORDS

allergy	vaccinate	indigestion	neutron
larynx	diagnose	microorganism	voltage
friction	satellite	psychology	physics
iodine	transmitter	transfusion	turbine
fungus	perennial	respiration	zoology

Puzzle

Use the **list words** to complete the crossword puzzle.

ACROSS

1. mold; mildew; mushroom
4. something that sends signals
6. the study of human behavior
9. discomfort caused by inability to digest foods properly
11. a sensitivity to a substance such as food or plants
13. science dealing with energy, matter, and movement
14. detect an illness
17. inject a serum to protect against a disease
18. upper part of the throat
19. returning or becoming active again and again

DOWN

2. uncharged particle of an atom
3. an object in orbit around the Earth
5. bacteria not visible to the human eye
7. the act of moving blood from one person to another
8. the study of animals and their behavior
10. reddish-colored disinfectant
12. breathing
15. the resistance to motion of two objects that touch
16. a steam engine
17. measurement of electrical current

Proofreading

Use the proofreading marks to correct the mistakes in the article. Then, write the misspelled **list words** correctly on the lines.

Proofreading Marks

◯ spelling mistake   ⌃ add comma
¶ new paragraph   ℓ delete word

The best way to prevent an alergy is to recognize that you have one. Many people diagnoze it as a cold or flu. Colds are short-lived and are passed from person to to person. Allergies are an immune-system reaction to a normally harmless substance, like pollen or fungis. Sneezing, watery eyes, or resperation trouble that lasts for more than 10 days without a a fever may actually be allergic symptoms.

Food allergies have different symptoms. They may cause indijestion. Whatever the cause however there are many treatments available for allergies today.

1. _____

2. _____

3. _____

4. _____

5. _____

Writing a Persuasive Speech

Which field of science interests you—zoology, biology, microbiology, or physics? Write a persuasive speech that tells why the field you're interested in should receive more grants for research than any other field. Use **list words** when possible. After proofreading and revising your speech, get together with others that wrote about the same field. Hold a class debate to decide which field of science merits more funding.

BONUS WORDS

fraternity	confederation	cartel	sorority	clique
syndicate	affiliation	guild	faction	troupe

Write the **bonus word** that matches each definition clue.

1. a small exclusive circle of people _____

2. a small group within an organization working against goals of the main body _____

3. a group of women or girls with similar interests _____

4. an alliance; a political union of states _____

5. an association that fixes prices and monopolizes an industry _____

6. connected with a particular group _____

7. a group of actors, singers, performers _____

8. a group of men or boys with similar interests _____

9. an association formed to transact a planned financial project _____

10. a trade union _____

Words from Occupations

Words that name occupations are usually another form of a word related to that occupation. The suffixes **or**, **er**, **an**, **ist**, or **ive** are added to make the word mean "one who does something." For example, a <u>librarian</u> is one who works in a library. Here are some other examples.

manicure — manicurist	announce — announcer
arbitrate — arbitrator	represent — representative

The **list words** name occupations. Notice the special spelling patterns of each word. Memorize and practice spelling them.

Classification

Write a **list word** to complete each series.

1. hammer, nails, _____

2. jokes, laughter, _____

3. prescription, drugstore, _____

4. books, catalogue cards, _____

5. animals, medicine, _____

6. microphone, radio, _____

7. dentist, teeth, _____

8. nail file, polish, _____

9. wiring, outlets, _____

10. laboratory, chemicals, _____

11. owner, manager, _____

Dictionary Skills

Rewrite each of the following **list words** to show how they are divided into syllables.

1. proprietor _____
2. researcher _____
3. arbitrator _____
4. therapist _____
5. representative _____
6. administrator _____
7. analyst _____
8. vendor _____
9. paramedic _____
10. technician _____

LIST WORDS

1. administrator
2. librarian
3. therapist
4. proprietor
5. electrician
6. arbitrator
7. vendor
8. paramedic
9. veterinarian
10. chemist
11. comedian
12. technician
13. representativ
14. announcer
15. pharmacist
16. hygienist
17. analyst
18. manicurist
19. carpenter
20. researcher

Spelling Practice

DID YOU KNOW?

The word **comedian** once referred to a person who wrote comedies, or humorous works. William Shakespeare was the first to use it to mean "a humorous actor" in his play *Twelfth Night*, and it has carried that meaning to this day.

Word Analysis

Fill in the missing letters to form **list words**. Then, write the completed **list words** on the lines.

1. ph___rm___c___st   _____

2. res___ ___rch___r   _____

3. lib___ ___ ___ ___an   _____

4. p___r___med___ ___   _____

5. rep___esen___ ___ ___ive   _____

6. ven___ ___r   _____

7. pr___p___ ___ ___t___r   _____

8. arb___t___ ___t___r   _____

9. a___ ___ounc___r   _____

10. man___c___r___st   _____

Vocabulary Development

Write the **list word** that matches each derivative given.

1. chemistry _____
2. electricity _____
3. therapy _____
4. technical _____
5. carpentry _____

6. analyze _____
7. comedy _____
8. administrate _____
9. hygiene _____
10. veterinary _____

Word Application

Write a **list word** to complete each sentence.

1. The _____ filled Grandpa's medicine prescription.

2. The _____ of the store listened to the customer's complaint.

3. Mr. Ortega is an _____ who settles disputes between labor and management.

4. Fatimah is a _____ trying to find new ways to recycle trash.

5. The _____ treated the injured people at the scene of the accident.

6. Kitty, our pet cat, was examined by Dr. Schwartz, the _____.

7. The _____ built new bookcases for the library.

vendor	arbitrator	administrator	paramedic
librarian	comedian	veterinarian	technician
therapist	hygienist	representative	manicurist
analyst	proprietor	announcer	carpenter
chemist	electrician	pharmacist	researcher

Puzzle

Use the **list words** to complete the crossword puzzle.

ACROSS

1. one who fixes fingernails
3. a specialist in physical or mental disorders
7. a doctor for animals
9. a person who installs electrical wiring
10. an expert in chemistry
12. a person who examines the details of something
13. one who assists a trained medical professional
14. a person who tells jokes and amusing stories
17. one who sells; a peddler
19. one who investigates in order to establish facts
20. one who manages or directs

DOWN

2. one who builds and repairs wooden things
4. one who dispenses medicines
5. a person skilled in the technicalities of a subject
6. one who speaks or acts for someone or something
8. one who introduces radio or television programs
11. a person who assists a dentist
15. one who settles disputes
16. one who owns and operates a business
18. a person who manages a library

Proofreading

Use the proofreading marks to correct the mistakes in the article. Write the misspelled **list words** correctly on the lines.

A representative at a job-counseling center can give you a variety of helpful tips when you're looking for that first career job. For example, it doesnt matter whether you are looking for a position that requires a great deal of specialized training—such as a Vetrinarian or a chemmist—or a job that requires less training, such as a manikurist or an anouncer Most Job Counselors will tell you to avoid ruling out excellent jobs on the basis of geographic preferences. You probably wont be at your first job forever and may need to apply for lots of jobs before getting one you really like.

Proofreading Marks

○ spelling mistake / small letter
∨ add apostrophe ⊙ add period

1. _____
2. _____
3. _____
4. _____
5. _____

Writing an Essay

Imagine that you have graduated from school and are looking for your first position. What would you pursue? Choose an occupation from one of the **list words** and write a short informative essay on why this kind of job would interest you. Use as many of the other **list words** in your essay as you can. When finished, proofread and revise your essay, and then share it with the class.

BONUS WORDS

| cholesterol | plaque | arthritis | stimulant | addiction |
| hypertension | enzyme | nicotine | depressant | tolerance |

Write the **bonus word** that matches each definition clue.

1. a complete dependence on a substance _____

2. poisonous substance found in tobacco leaves _____

3. organic compound that aids in digestion _____

4. high blood pressure _____

5. a waxy substance found in animal fats _____

6. the ability to resist the effects of stimuli _____

7. lowers the rate of nervous or muscular activity _____

8. increases the rate of brain-cell activity _____

9. inflammation of the joints _____

10. sticky film on teeth _____

Words from Literature

TIP

Like science and math, the field of literature and composition has a specific vocabulary of technical terms. Words like <u>fiction</u>, <u>sonnet</u>, and <u>prose</u> describe types of literature. Other words, including <u>simile</u>, <u>metaphor</u>, and <u>personification</u>, describe types of figurative language.

All of the **list words** are related to literature and composition. Knowing how to define and spell them will be of great benefit to you throughout your studies.

Vocabulary Development

Write the **list word** that matches each definition.

1. list of source materials for a nonfiction work _____

2. art or writing that exaggerates someone's features _____

3. false "pen" name used by a writer _____

4. poem of fourteen lines with one central theme _____

5. old, familiar saying that states a simple truth _____

6. repetition of the same beginning sound _____

7. symbolic story that teaches or explains _____

8. all literature that is not poetry _____

9. literature that explains true facts or events _____

10. two lines of poetry _____

Dictionary Skills

Write the **list words** in alphabetical order.

1. _____ 8. _____ 15. _____
2. _____ 9. _____ 16. _____
3. _____ 10. _____ 17. _____
4. _____ 11. _____ 18. _____
5. _____ 12. _____ 19. _____
6. _____ 13. _____ 20. _____
7. _____ 14. _____

LIST WORDS

1. alliteration
2. caricature
3. literature
4. parody
5. proverb
6. allegory
7. couplet
8. narrative
9. personification
10. pseudonym
11. analogy
12. exposition
13. fiction
14. poetic
15. simile
16. bibliography
17. idiom
18. prose
19. stanza
20. sonnet

Spelling Practice

DID YOU KNOW ?

The word **allegory** comes from two words in Greek, one meaning "different" or "other" and the second meaning "to speak openly" or "to speak publicly." Allegories are stories with hidden meanings, or meanings different from the ones at the surface of the story.

Word Analysis

Write the **list word** that has the same base word or root as the word given.

1. verb _____
2. personally _____
3. sonic _____
4. narrate _____
5. analogous _____

6. stand _____
7. ode _____
8. couple _____
9. similar _____
10. expose _____

Word Application

Select a **list word** from the choices in parentheses to complete each sentence. Write the **list word** on the line.

1. _____ lines contain rhythm, meter, and often rhyme. (poetic, simile)

2. _____, a general class of literature, includes novels and plays. (exposition, fiction)

3. Through _____, the relationships between words are analyzed. (allegory, analogy)

4. "The shifting sands of summer" is an example of _____. (simile, alliteration)

5. A section of a poem, usually four or more lines in length, is a _____. (stanza, couplet)

6. An example of _____ is "My dog voted to sample my lunch." (personification, allegory)

7. Stories, nonfiction articles, and plays are _____. (exposition, literature)

8. The movie was a _____ of old science-fiction films. (bibliography, parody)

9. The _____ "I heard it through the grapevine" means "I heard it through gossip." (idiom, proverb)

10. The cartoonist drew a _____ of the president. (narrative, caricature)

11. Entries are alphabetized, by author's last name, in the _____. (exposition, bibliography)

12. All literature that is not poetry is called _____. (narrative, prose)

13. A story about a character overcoming a dragon named "Greed" is an _____. (allegory, analogy)

14. John was thinking of writing a _____ history of skateboarding. (pseudonym, narrative)

LIST WORDS

allegory	alliteration	proverb	simile
caricature	exposition	couplet	fiction
literature	bibliography	stanza	prose
narrative	personification	parody	idiom
analogy	pseudonym	sonnet	poetic

Puzzle

Each of the clues below is an example of a literary term defined by a **list word**. Write your answers in the spaces. Then, transfer the numbered letters to the spaces below to answer the question.

1. "A stitch in time saves nine."
—Ben Franklin

__ __ __ __ __ __ __
1   15   11

2. "I shall be as secret as the grave."
—Miguel de Cervantes

__ __ __ __ __ __
10   9   12

3. "A little Madness in the Spring is wholesome even for the King."
—Emily Dickinson

__ __ __ __ __ __ __
       4   18

4. "Go put your creed into your deed, Nor speak with double tongue."
—Ralph Waldo Emerson

__ __ __ __ __
5

5. "Hail, Columbia! happy land! Hail, ye heroes! heaven-born band!"
—Joseph Hopkinson

__ __ __ __ __ __ __ __ __ __
       19   16   7

6. "Thy head is as full of quarrels as an egg is full of meat."
—William Shakespeare

__ __ __ __ __ __ __
20   8

7. "Hunger is the handmaid of genius."
—Mark Twain

__ __ __ __ __ __ __ __ __ __
2   14   17

8. "A young man named Ernest Hemingway lives in Paris, writes for the *Transatlantic Review,* and has a brilliant future."
—F. Scott Fitzgerald

__ __ __ __ __ __ __ __ __
3   6   13

Question: Who was Mrs. Silence Dogwood?

Answer: one of many __ __ __ __ __ __ __ __ __ __ used by
                          1 2 3 4 5 6 7 8 9 10

__ __ __ __ __ __ __ K __ __ __
11 12 13 14 15 16 17   18 19 20

Proofreading

Use the proofreading marks to correct the mistakes in the article below. Then, write the misspelled **list words** correctly on the lines.

Proofreading Marks

○ spelling mistake   ‿ delete word

∨∨ add quotation mark

? add question mark

Like jazz, science fictoin is a a native 20th-century art form, and it boasts an impressive track record. Did you know that atom bombs, spaceships, cloning—even credit cards—all appeared in works of this genre before they became reality. Still, for many years, it was not considered "real literachure. Some authors in in the field even took to writing under a psudonym because there was such a lack of respect for the genre. Today, however, writers who use their imaginations to conceive what the future might be like, or to picture other worlds, are as respected as a poet who labors over his couplit or sonet.

1. _____

2. _____

3. _____

4. _____

5. _____

Writing a Science-Fiction Story

Most science fiction is set in the future. It builds on today's established facts, stretching them to imagine new technologies or areas of exploration. Write a science-fiction story that includes a new invention, alien creature, and/or bold exploration. Use as many **list words** as you can. Proofread and revise your story, then share it with others.

BONUS WORDS

nebula	module	luminosity	planetarium	centrifugal force
inertia	relativity	celestial	momentum	encapsulate

Write a **bonus word** to complete each sentence.

1. You can view stars and constellations at a _____.

2. The planet Saturn is a _____ body surrounded by rings.

3. A _____ is a cloud of interstellar gas or dust.

4. According to Einstein's theory of _____, no energy can travel faster than light.

5. The tendency for a being at rest to stay at rest is called _____.

6. When something orbits around a central core, _____ pulls it outward.

7. To calculate the _____ of a moving object, physicists multiply mass times speed.

8. The moon's _____ is created by reflected light from the sun.

9. Astronauts _____ themselves in suits equipped with oxygen supplies.

10. In 1969, the first lunar _____ to be piloted by humans landed on the moon.

Words from Language Arts

 TIP

You are probably familiar with many words that refer to English usage and language arts. Many of these common words, such as grammar, preposition, capitalization, and homonym are often misspelled.

All the **list words** name words from language arts. Study the spelling patterns of each word. Memorize and practice spelling them.

Vocabulary Development

Write the **list word** that matches each definition clue.

1. shows surprise _____

2. an incomplete sentence _____

3. the mark used in a contraction _____

4. a word's meaning _____

5. a joining word _____

6. the use of upper-case letters _____

7. changing the meaning of _____

8. word formed from beginnings of other words _____

9. verb used as a noun, ending in **ing** _____

10. verb that takes a direct object _____

11. curved line used for explanations _____

Dictionary Skills

Write the **list words** that come between each pair of dictionary guide words. Write the words in alphabetical order.

gesture/interrupt

1. _____

2. _____

3. _____

4. _____

5. _____

parade/press

6. _____

7. _____

8. _____

9. _____

10. _____

LIST WORDS

1. acronym
2. conjunction
3. gerund
4. modifying
5. parenthesis
6. apostrophe
7. exclamation
8. grammar
9. glossary
10. preposition
11. predicate
12. definition
13. homonym
14. paraphrase
15. transitive
16. capitalization
17. fragment
18. infinitive
19. participle
20. interrogative

Spelling Practice

DID YOU KNOW?

The word **acronym** means "tip of the name," and is a word made up of the beginnings of other words. Although acronyms have been in use for a long time, the word *acronym* was made up in 1943, when many acronyms were created by the military during World War II.

Word Analysis

Write the **list words** to answer the following questions.

Which words contain the letter combination **nym**?

1. _____   2. _____

Which words contain the following double consonants?

3. **rr** _____   5. **mm** _____

4. **ss** _____

Word Application

Write a **list word** to complete each sentence.

1. A word's first _____ listed in the dictionary is its most common meaning.

2. Adjectives are usually found _____ a noun or another adjective.

3. *Soar* is a _____ for the word *sore*.

4. A sentence _____ is a part of a sentence missing a subject or a predicate.

5. A comma and a _____ can join two complete sentences.

6. A verb that ends with **ing** and is used as a noun is called a _____.

7. The complete _____ includes the verb and all its modifiers in a sentence.

8. Look up the word in the _____ at the end of your reading textbook.

9. When you repeat something in different words, you _____ it.

10. *Radar* is an _____ for "radio detecting and ranging."

11. In the phrase "to the store," *store* is the object of the _____.

12. _____ is the study of English usage.

13. A _____ verb shows action and takes a direct object.

Word Application

Write the **list word** that matches each clue.

1. (_____   5. Why? _____

2. Wow! _____   6. Washington _____

3. Mary's _____ 7. in, for, at _____

4. to go _____   8. The boy to the store _____

LIST WORDS

acronym	participle	conjunction	capitalization
predicate	fragment	modifying	exclamation
gerund	grammar	homonym	parenthesis
definition	glossary	paraphrase	apostrophe
infinitive	transitive	preposition	interrogative

Puzzle

Unscramble the **list words** to complete the crossword puzzle.

ACROSS

2. CMINELAOTAX
4. PPRAEAHASR
5. REPPIOISNTO
8. OAYLSGSR
9. NERIOITEARGTV
12. MOMOYHN
14. EUDRGN
15. TAEFGRMN
16. PAIACIANTILZTO
17. FNEINIIITV

DOWN

1. FNDIINIETO
3. IAIERNSTTV
4. EIEPADRCT
5. RPETEASNHSI
6. DIYMOGFIN
7. RCNOMAY
8. RMRMAGA
10. POTESPAROH
11. ONCCJINUNTO
13. ACIERPTIPL

Proofreading

Use the proofreading marks to correct mistakes in the article. Write the misspelled **list words** correctly on the lines.

Proofreading Marks

⬯ spelling mistake ⌃ add comma
¶ new paragraph ⊙ add period

The most beautiful thoughts in the world will move no one unless the writer who expresses them uses proper grammer For example, an infinetive and a participal are both capable of conveying the idea of action in time so it is important to observe the appropriate tense sequence when using them. Pay close attention to the rules of capitalisation and to the proper use of an apostrofe to indicate a contraction.

Also, providing a transition between ideas is something many writers neglect. You may be able to go from one idea to another but your readers may need stepping stones—a cunjunction such as *and, but,* or *nevertheless*

1. _____

2. _____

3. _____

4. _____

5. _____

6. _____

Writing Survey Questions and a Summary

How do students feel about the importance of using proper grammar? Write a questionnaire to conduct a survey to find out. Include at least six questions. Try to use **list words** in your questions. After proofreading and revising, conduct the survey in your classroom or among your friends. Tally and write a summary of the results, then present your findings.

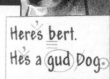

Here's bert. He's a gud Dog⊙

| intramural | participation | tournament | facility | skiing |
| volleyball | interscholastic | racquetball | lacrosse | rugby |

Write the **bonus word** that matches each definition clue.

1. sport similar to handball played with a small racquet _____

2. among or between schools _____

3. a form of football _____

4. a series of games played to determine a championship _____

5. a winter snow sport _____

6. between teams of the same school _____

7. a place or building where sporting events are held _____

8. playing an active role _____

9. sport in which two teams are separated by a net _____

10. team sport played with long-handled, pouched sticks _____

Challenging Words

 TIP

Some words are especially difficult to spell because they contain silent letters, such as the **h** in <u>scheme</u> and the **i** in <u>marriage</u>. Other challenging words contain the schwa sound in unstressed syllables. Although /ə/ sounds like short **u**, or the sound of **uh**, it may be spelled with any of the vowels. Examples include the first **o** in <u>oppose</u>, the **a** and final **e** in <u>equivalent</u>, and the **o** and **io** in <u>solution</u>.

Vocabulary Development

Write the **list word** that matches each synonym or definition.

1. many _____
2. hopeful _____
3. problem _____
4. wedding _____
5. equal _____
6. answer _____
7. tiny _____
8. show _____
9. contraption _____
10. strange or cold _____
11. disagree with _____
12. urban _____
13. chances _____
14. circumstances _____
15. testing room _____
16. simple; rough _____

Dictionary Skills

Write the **list word** that comes between each pair of dictionary guide words.

1. **oat/open** _____
2. **pebble/pray** _____
3. **zebra/zoo** _____
4. **say/scratch** _____
5. **private/prune** _____
6. **mauve/mince** _____
7. **prime/probe** _____
8. **mace/meter** _____
9. **eon/ether** _____
10. **opposite/option** _____

LIST WORDS

1. device
2. laboratory
3. obstacle
4. primitive
5. situation
6. dilemma
7. marriage
8. opportunities
9. procedure
10. solution
11. equivalent
12. metropolitan
13. oppose
14. scheme
15. peculiar
16. exhibit
17. miniature
18. optimistic
19. several
20. zinc

Spelling Practice

DID YOU KNOW ?

One of the meanings of **miniature** is "a small painting," from the Latin root *miniare*, meaning "to paint with red lead." In the Middle Ages, manuscripts were created by hand, and paintings called miniatures were placed on the pages. Because of their small size, the word *miniature* now also means "a copy of reduced size."

Word Analysis

Write the **list word** containing the same root as the word given.

1. primates _____

2. dissolve _____

3. unequal _____

4. unopposed _____

5. obstruction _____

6. inopportune _____

7. pessimistic _____

8. politician _____

Analogies

Write a **list word** to complete each analogy.

1. Kitchen is to chef as _____ is to scientist.

2. Gate is to go as _____ is to stop.

3. Performance is to drama as _____ is to photograph.

4. Gigantic is to redwood as _____ is to bonzai.

5. Wood is to oak as metal is to _____.

6. Memories are to past as _____ are to future.

7. "Yes" is to agree as "no" is to _____.

8. Three is to few as eight is to _____.

Word Application

Select a **list word** from the choices in parentheses to complete each sentence. Write the **list word** on the line.

1. John was hopeful that his _____ would work. (optimistic, scheme)

2. The _____ became chaotic during the reconstruction. (solution, situation)

3. The paint roller is a clever, time-saving _____. (device, dilemma)

4. Many friendships have led to _____. (dilemma, marriage)

5. Will you accept the terms or will you _____ them? (scheme, oppose)

6. His quirky sense of humor is very _____. (peculiar, procedure)

7. We used to have just one bunny, but now we have _____. (situation, several)

8. The stone tools are very _____, but they work. (primitive, metropolitan)

9. Many of _____ New York's buildings are giant, steel skyscrapers. (metropolitan, laboratory)

10. An _____ person looks at the bright side of life. (obstacle, optimistic)

LIST WORDS

device	dilemma	equivalent	primitive
zinc	marriage	metropolitan	miniature
oppose	obstacle	opportunities	optimistic
exhibit	scheme	procedure	situation
several	solution	laboratory	peculiar

Classification

Write a **list word** to complete each series.

1. invention, machine, _____

2. chances, occasions, _____

3. _____, average, enormous

4. ancient, simple, _____

5. hurdle, sand trap, _____

6. gallery, museum, _____

7. many, a lot, _____

8. plot, plan, _____

9. copper, aluminum, _____

10. sum, remainder, _____

Puzzle

Use the **list words** to complete the crossword puzzle.

ACROSS

2. a place for experiments
7. chances
8. a metallic element
9. something that gets in the way
11. pertaining to a large city
13. position or circumstances
15. ancient; simple; rough
17. the answer to a problem
18. many; more than a few
19. a difficult problem

DOWN

1. union; wedding
3. to disagree or work against
4. a tool or machine
5. a method of doing something
6. strange; unusual; rare
10. tiny
12. equal
14. hopeful
16. a public show
18. a plan or system

Proofreading

Use the proofreading marks to correct the mistakes in the article. Write the misspelled **list words** correctly on the lines.

Proofreading Marks

⬭ spelling mistake   ⌗ add space
≡ capital letter   ℒ delete word

The first primetive computer, a calculating divice called the Difference Engine, was designed in 1822 by by the English mathematician, Charles babbage. In 1833, he started designing the Analytical Engine, a more sophisticated machine. The programming procidure for this this invention was developed by Ada byron Lovelace. Opprtunities for women were few in the early nineteenthcentury, but lovelace became an expert in sevarel subjects, including math and foreignlanguages. She translated and added extensive notes to a paper on Babbage's Engines written in French by an Italian engineer. Her document was the best contemporary description of of the engines.

1. _____

2. _____

3. _____

4. _____

5. _____

Writing a Description

Thomas Edison changed the world when he invented the electric light bulb. Now it's your turn. Invent a machine. Draw a diagram of it, labeling its parts. Then, write a description of what it does, how it works, and why it will "change the world," using as many **list words** as you can. Proofread and revise your work, then display it. Discuss which inventions might really work.

| hydraulic | implement | electromagnetic | combustion | conduit |
| fabricate | ventilator | mechanical | incinerator | lathe |

Write a **bonus word** to complete each sentence.

1. Rubbish can be burned in the _____.

2. A _____ allows for the passage and circulation of fresh air.

3. _____ is synonymous with _tool_.

4. A stapler is a _____ device for attaching sheets of paper together.

5. _____ brakes are operated by the movement and force of brake fluid.

6. A _____ is a carpentry device that can turn square timbers into cylindrical poles.

7. In a _____ engine, fuel mixes with oxygen and is then ignited to create energy.

8. Workers on that assembly line manufacture, or _____, automobiles.

9. Current passes through wire, creating _____ energy to run the motor.

10. The electric wires are encased in a protective _____ to avoid fires and shocks.

Lessons 31–35 · Review

- Knowing how to define and spell words from various fields of study is an advantage to any student. In this unit, you learned many words related to specific subjects. Practice using and spelling these words.

- Here are examples of words from science.

  <u>physics</u>, <u>psychology</u>, <u>zoology</u>

- Pay special attention to the endings of words that name occupations.

  <u>librarian</u>, <u>paramedic</u>, <u>chemist</u>

- The field of literature has its technical terms.

  <u>caricature</u>, <u>parody</u>, <u>exposition</u>

- Words from language arts are familiar but often difficult to spell.

  <u>exclamation</u>, <u>transitive</u>, <u>capitalization</u>

- Some words have unexpected spellings, with irregular spelling patterns. These words are especially difficult to spell because they do not follow normal spelling rules. Memorize and practice spelling these challenging words.

  <u>device</u>, <u>dilemma</u>, <u>metropolitan</u>, <u>several</u>

Lesson 31

List Words

allergy

neutron

vaccinate

larynx

voltage

diagnose

microorganism

satellite

iodine

respiration

_____

_____

Write the **list word** that matches each definition.

1. the measure of electrical force _____

2. inhaling and exhaling air _____

3. a hypersensitivity to a specific substance _____

4. muscle and cartilage in the throat _____

5. to inject a serum in an attempt to ward off a disease _____

6. to decide the nature of a disease after careful examination _____

7. a man-made object rocketed into orbit around the Earth _____

8. an uncharged elementary particle of an atom with the same mass as a proton _____

9. a chemical element used as an antiseptic _____

10. any microscopic animal or vegetable organism _____

List Words

hygienist
proprietor
vendor
analyst
comedian
technician
representative
pharmacist
administrator
veterinarian

_____
_____

Write a **list word** to complete each sentence.

1. If you are fascinated by radios, televisions, and computers, be an electronics _____.
2. If people talk to you about money problems, you are a financial _____.
3. If you purchase a store, you are the _____.
4. If you clean people's teeth, you are a dental _____.
5. If you practice medicine dealing with diseases in animals, you are a _____.
6. If you stand on a corner selling trinkets, you are a street _____.
7. To speak for the voters, be a state _____.
8. If you can make people laugh, be a _____.
9. To share medical expertise about prescriptions, be a _____.
10. To manage or direct a business or office, be an _____.

List Words

alliteration
allegory
couplet
narrative
bibliography
pseudonym
poetic
simile
personification
idiom

_____
_____

Write **list words** to answer the questions.

Which words contain the vowel combination **io**?

1. _____ 3. _____
2. _____ 4. _____

Which words contain the following vowel combinations?

5. oe _____ 7. eu _____
6. ou _____

Which word contains the double consonant **rr**?

8. _____

Which word begins with the Latin root **sim** meaning "alike"?

9. _____

Which word contains letters in the same order as these four words: <u>all</u>, <u>leg</u>, <u>ego</u>, <u>gory</u>?

10. _____

Write the **list words** that come between each pair of dictionary guide words. Write the words in alphabetical order.

List Words

- paraphrase
- conjunction
- parenthesis
- apostrophe
- interrogative
- definition
- homonym
- acronym
- fragment
- grammar

abhor/friction

1. _____
2. _____
3. _____
4. _____
5. _____

gradual/partial

6. _____
7. _____
8. _____
9. _____
10. _____

Unscramble the **list words** to complete the crossword puzzle.

List Words

- laboratory
- obstacle
- solution
- equivalent
- oppose
- scheme
- peculiar
- exhibit
- miniature
- optimistic

ACROSS
2. MESHEC
3. BOATLECS
4. LEANVIQUET
5. PEOSPO
7. IRATEMUNI
8. PUREILCA

DOWN
1. BOATROARYL
2. LOUSONIT
5. MITTPICSOI
6. BIXHITE

Show What You Know

One word is misspelled in each set of **list words**. Fill in the circle next to the **list word** that is spelled incorrectly.

1. ○ pseudonym   ○ apostrophe   ○ arbitrater   ○ allergy
2. ○ exclamaition   ○ vendor   ○ indigestion   ○ analogy
3. ○ paramedic   ○ grammer   ○ exposition   ○ physics
4. ○ nutron   ○ fiction   ○ veterinarian   ○ glossary
5. ○ predicate   ○ vacinate   ○ preposition   ○ chemist
6. ○ homonym   ○ comedian   ○ metropolitan   ○ fungas
7. ○ tecknician   ○ larynx   ○ paraphrase   ○ transitive
8. ○ pyschology   ○ fragment   ○ representative   ○ zinc
9. ○ several   ○ announcer   ○ transmittor   ○ optimistic
10. ○ pharmacist   ○ infinnitive   ○ capitalization   ○ voltage
11. ○ participal   ○ diagnose   ○ hygienist   ○ miniature
12. ○ peculiar   ○ exhibit   ○ microrganism   ○ analyst
13. ○ satellite   ○ manicurist   ○ interogative   ○ scheme
14. ○ poetic   ○ definition   ○ transfusion   ○ carpentor
15. ○ oppose   ○ friction   ○ researcher   ○ similie
16. ○ situation   ○ equivilent   ○ alliteration   ○ iodine
17. ○ perennial   ○ caricature   ○ opportunitites   ○ idiom
18. ○ literature   ○ proze   ○ respiration   ○ marriage
19. ○ stanza   ○ turbine   ○ bibiliography   ○ parody
20. ○ sonet   ○ proverb   ○ procedure   ○ zoology
21. ○ solution   ○ acronym   ○ administrater   ○ allegory
22. ○ primitive   ○ librarien   ○ conjunction   ○ obstacle
23. ○ therapist   ○ couplet   ○ labrotory   ○ gerund
24. ○ dilemma   ○ proprieter   ○ modifying   ○ narrative
25. ○ parenthesis   ○ electrician   ○ personifcation   ○ device

Writing and Proofreading Guide

1. Select a topic to write about.

2. Write your first draft without worrying about mistakes.

3. Now organize your writing so that it makes sense.

4. Use the proofreading marks to revise your work.

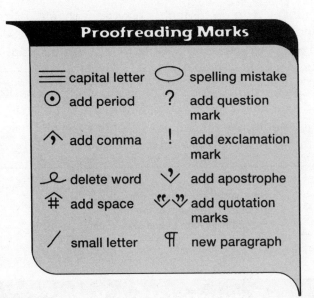

Proofreading Marks

≡	capital letter	⬭	spelling mistake
⊙	add period	?	add question mark
^,	add comma	!	add exclamation mark
ℓ	delete word	∨'	add apostrophe
^#	add space	∨" ∨"	add quotation marks
/	small letter	¶	new paragraph

I had been wandering for what seemd like ours, trying to find my way way out of the Jungle⊙Why was i walking incircles?All of a sudden I heard a voice saying, "Why dont you use your compass?" In my quandry, I had forgotten all about my backpack containing food, a flashlight, and my compass.

5. Write your final copy.

I had been wandering for what seemed like hours, trying to find my way out of the jungle. Why was I walking in circles? All of a sudden I heard a voice saying, "Why don't you use your compass?" In my quandry, I had forgotten all about my backpack containing food, a flashlight, and my compass.

Using Your Dictionary

The *Spelling Workout* Dictionary shows you many things about your spelling words.

The **entry word** listed in alphabetical order is the word you are looking up.

The **sound-spelling** or **respelling** tells how to pronounce the word.

The **part of speech** is given as an abbreviation.

The **definition** tells what the word means.

re·hearse (ri hurs′) *v.* **1** to go through a play, speech, etc. for practice, before giving it in public **2** to repeat in detail [They *rehearsed* all their troubles to me.] —**re·hearsed′, re·hears′ing** —**re·hears′al** *n.*

Rehearse comes from an old French word which means "to harrow again." The harrow is a device used after plowing to break up land and make it smooth. We rehearse a speech or play to make it smooth the way a farmer harrows the land.

Other **forms** of the word are given.

The **etymology** is the history of the word. It appears in the tinted area following the definitions.

Sample sentences or phrases show how to use the word.

Pronunciation Key

SYMBOL	KEY WORDS	SYMBOL	KEY WORDS	SYMBOL	KEY WORDS	SYMBOL	KEY WORDS
a	ask, fat	o͞o	look, pull	b	bed, dub	t	top, hat
ā	ape, date	yo͞o	unite, cure	d	did, had	v	vat, have
ä	car, lot	o͞o	ooze, tool	f	fall, off	w	will, always
		yo͞o	cute, few	g	get, dog	y	yet, yard
e	elf, ten	ou	out, crowd	h	he, ahead	z	zebra, haze
er	berry, care			j	joy, jump		
ē	even, meet	u	up, cut	k	kill, bake	ch	chin, arch
		u	fur, fern	l	let, ball	ŋ	ring, singer
i	is, hit			m	met, trim	sh	she, dash
ir	mirror, here	ə	a in ago	n	not, ton	th	thin, truth
ī	ice, fire		e in agent	p	put, tap	*th*	then, father
			e in father	r	red, dear	zh	s in pleasure
ō	open, go		i in unity	s	sell, pass		
ô	law, horn		o in collect				
oi	oil, point		u in focus				

An Americanism is a word or usage of a word that was born in this country. An open star (☆) before an entry word or definition means that the word or definition is an Americanism.

ab·a·cus (ab′ə kəs) *n.* a frame with groups of beads sliding back and forth on wires: the abacus is used for doing arithmetic quickly without writing —*pl.* **ab´a·cus·es**

a·ban·don (ə ban′dən) *v.* **1** to give up completely [Don't *abandon* hope of being saved.] **2** to leave, desert [The crew *abandoned* the burning ship.] ◆*n.* freedom of actions or feelings, with no control [to dance with wild *abandon*] —**a·ban´don·ment**

ab·hor (əb hôr′) *v.* to feel great fear, disgust, or hatred for; hate very much [Frank *abhors* fighting.] —**ab·horred´, ab·hor´ring**

a·bol·ish (ə bäl′ish) *v.* to do away with completely; get rid of [Congress may *abolish* a law.]

a·brupt (ə brupt′) *adj.* **1** coming or happening suddenly, without warning [to make an *abrupt* stop] **2** very blunt or gruff [He answered with an *abrupt* "No!"] —**a·brupt´ly** *adv.* —**a·brupt´ness** *n.*

ab·solve (əb zälv′) *v.* **1** to say that a person is free of guilt or blame or will not be punished for sin [I was *absolved* of the crime. The priest *absolved* the sinner.] **2** to make someone free from a duty or promise —**ab·solved´, ab·solv´ing**

ab·stain (əb stān′) *v.* to do without willingly; hold oneself back [to *abstain* from meat during Lent]

ab·stract (ab strakt′ *or* ab′strakt) *adj.* **1** thought of apart from a particular act or thing [A just trial is a fair one, but justice itself is an *abstract* idea.] **2** hard to understand [That explanation is too *abstract*.] **3** formed with designs taken from real things, but not actually like any real object or being [an *abstract* painting]

ab·surd (əb sʉrd′ *or* ab zʉrd′) *adj.* so clearly untrue or unreasonable as to be something to laugh at or make fun of [It is *absurd* to eat peas with a knife.] —**ab·surd´ly** *adv.*

a·cad·e·my (ə kad′ə mē) *n.* **1** a private high school **2** any school for special training, as in music, art, or military science **3** a society of scholars, writers, artists, etc. working in the interests of the arts or sciences —*pl.* **a·cad´e·mies**

Academy comes from the Greek name for a grove of trees near Athens. Plato, an ancient Greek philosopher and teacher, taught his students in that grove. The Greeks thought that it had once belonged to a hero in Greek legend named *Akademos.*

a·cap·pel·la (ä′kə pel′ə) *adv., adj.* singing without the accompaniment of musical instruments

ac·cept·ance (ək sep′təns) *n.* **1** an accepting or being accepted [the *acceptance* of an award] **2** approval or belief [That theory now has the *acceptance* of most scientists.]

ac·ces·so·ry (ək ses′ər ē) *n.* **1** something extra; thing added, as for convenience, comfort, or decoration [A radio and air conditioner are *accessories* on a car. A purse and gloves are *accessories* to an outfit.] **2** a person who helps another to break the law, although absent at the time of the crime [The doorkeeper became an *accessory* by helping the murderer escape.] —*pl.* **ac·ces´so·ries** ◆*adj.* being something extra or added to help the more important thing [The vacuum cleaner has *accessory* attachments.]

ac·ci·den·tal (ak′sə den′t'l) *adj.* happening by chance [Goodyear's discovery of how to vulcanize rubber was *accidental*.] —**ac´ci·den´tal·ly** *adv.*

ac·quit (ə kwit′) *v.* to rule that a person accused of something is not guilty [The judge *acquitted* the suspect.] —**ac·quit´ted, ac·quit´ting**

☆**ac·ro·nym** (ak′rə nim) *n.* a word that is formed from the first letters, or first syllables, of two or more words ["Comsat" is an *acronym* formed from "communication satellite."]

ad·dict (ad′ikt) *n.* a person who has a habit so strong that he cannot easily give it up [a drug *addict*] ◆*v.* (ə dikt′) to give oneself up to some strong habit [Some people are *addicted* to watching television.] —**ad·dic´tion**

ad·jec·tive (aj′ik tiv) *n.* a word used with a noun or pronoun to tell which, what kind of, how many, or whose [In the sentence "Every egg was fresh," the words "every" and "fresh" are *adjectives*.] —**ad·jec·ti·val** (aj′ik tī′v'l) *adj.*

ad-lib (ad′lib′) *v.* to make up and put in words, gestures, etc. not in the script as one is performing; *used only in everyday talk* [Good actors learn to *ad-lib* when they forget their lines.] —**ad´-libbed´, ad´-lib´bing**

Ad-lib is a shortened form of a Latin phrase *ad libitum*, meaning "as one pleases," that is used in music to mark a part that performers can change or leave out as they please.

ad·min·is·tra·tor (əd min′ə strāt′ər) *n.* a person who administers or directs something; executive; manager

ad·mit (əd mit′) *v.* **1** to permit or give the right to enter [One ticket *admits* two persons.] **2** to have room for [The hall *admits* 500 people.] **3** to take or accept as being true; confess [Lucy will not *admit* her mistake.] —**ad·mit´ted, ad·mit´ting**

a	ask, fat
ā	ape, date
ä	car, lot
e	elf, ten
er	berry, care
ē	even, meet
i	is, hit
ir	mirror, here
ī	ice, fire
ō	open, go
ô	law, horn
oi	oil, point
oo	look, pull
ᴏ̄ᴏ̄	ooze, tool
yoo	unite, cure
yᴏ̄ᴏ̄	cute, few
ou	out, crowd
u	up, cut
ʉ	fur, fern
ə	a in ago
	e in agent
	e in father
	i in unity
	o in collect
	u in focus
ch	chin, arch
ŋ	ring, singer
sh	she, dash
th	thin, truth
th	then, father
zh	s in pleasure
′	as in (ā b'l)

151

ad·verb (ad′vʉrb) *n.* a word used with a verb, adjective, or another adverb to tell when, where, how, and what kind, or how much: *quickly* tells how in "run *quickly*"; *always* tells when in "*always* sad"; *bright* tells what kind in "*bright* red dress"; *very* tells how much in "run *very* quickly." —**ad·ver·bi·al** (ad vʉr′bē əl) *adj.*

ad·vi·so·ry (əd vī′zər ē) *adj.* advising or able to advise [*advisory* experts] ◆*n.* a warning that bad weather is on the way —*pl.* **ad·vi·so·ries**

ad·vo·cate (ad′və kāt) *v.* to speak or write in support of; be in favor of [The senator *advocated* a new housing bill.] —**ad′vo·cat·ed, ad′vo·cat·ing** ◆*n.* (ad′və kit *or* ad′və kāt) **1** a person who speaks or writes in favor of something **2** a person who argues another's case; especially, a lawyer

aer·o·nau·tics (er′ə nô′tiks) *pl. n.* the science of making and flying aircraft; *used with a singular verb* —**aer′o·nau′ti·cal** *or* **aer′o·nau′tic** *adj.*

af·fa·ble (af′ə b'l) *adj.* pleasant and easy to talk to; friendly —**af·fa·bil′i·ty** *n.* —**af′fa·bly** *adv.*

af·fi·da·vit (af′ə dā′vit) *n.* a statement written by a person who swears that it is the truth [He signed an *affidavit* saying that he had paid the debt.]

af·fil·i·ate (ə fil′ē āt) *v.* to take in or be taken in as a member or another part; join [Our store has become *affiliated* with a large supermarket chain.] —**af·fil′i·at·ed, af·fil′i·at·ing** ◆*n.* (ə fil′ē it) an affiliated person or organization [a local *affiliate* of a national group] —**af·fil′i·a′tion**

Affiliate comes from a Latin verb meaning "to adopt as a son." When people become affiliated with a group, it is as though they are being adopted.

af·firm·a·tive (ə fʉr′mə tiv) *adj.* saying that something is true; answering "yes" [an *affirmative* reply] ◆*n.* **1** a word, phrase, or action showing that one approves or agrees [She nodded her head in the *affirmative*.] **2** the side that favors or agrees with the point being debated [There were more votes in the negative than in the *affirmative*.]

af·flu·ent (af′loo wənt *or now also* af loo′ənt) *adj.* having much money or property; prosperous; rich

ag·gra·vate (ag′rə vāt) *v.* **1** to make worse; make more troublesome [You will *aggravate* your sprained ankle by walking.] **2** to make impatient; annoy; bother; *used only in everyday talk* [The talking in the audience began to *aggravate* us.] —**ag′gra·vat·ed, ag′gra·vat·ing** —**ag′gra·va′tion** *n.*

Aggravate comes from a Latin word which means "to make heavier" and is related to the word **gravity**. When a problem is aggravated, it is made heavier or greater than it was.

ag·gres·sive (ə gres′iv) *adj.* **1** ready to start fights or quarrels [an *aggressive* bully] **2** bold and active; full of energy and ideas [an *aggressive* leader] —**ag·gres′sive·ly** *adv.* —**ag·gres′sive·ness** *n.*

al·le·go·ry (al′ə gôr′ē) *n.* a story used to teach or explain an idea or moral rule: in allegories people, animals, and things have hidden meanings beside the ones that are easily seen [Aesop's fables are short *allegories*.] —*pl.* **al′le·go′ries** —**al′le·gor′i·cal** *adj.*

☆**al·ler·gy** (al′ər jē) *n.* a condition in which one becomes sick, gets a rash, etc. by breathing in, touching, eating, or drinking something that is not harmful to most people [Hay fever is usually caused by an *allergy* to certain pollens.] —*pl.* **al′ler·gies**

al·li·ga·tor (al′ə gāt′ər) *n.* **1** a large lizard like the crocodile, found in warm rivers and marshes of the United States and China **2** a scaly leather made from its hide

al·lit·er·a·tion (ə lit′ə rā′shən) *n.* a repeating of the same sound at the beginning of two or more words, as in a line of poetry [There is an *alliteration* of *s* in "Sing a song of sixpence."]

al·lot (ə lät′) *v.* **1** to divide or give out in shares or by lot [The land was *allotted* equally to the settlers.] **2** to give to a person as a share [Each speaker is *allotted* five minutes.] —**al·lot′ted, al·lot′ting**

al·lu·vi·al (ə loo′vē əl) *adj.* made up of the sand or clay washed down by flowing water [*alluvial* deposits at the mouth of the river]

al·tru·is·tic (al′troo is′tik) *adj.* putting the good of others ahead of one's own interests; unselfish —**al′tru·is′ti·cal·ly** *adv.*

am·bas·sa·dor (am bas′ə dər) *n.* **1** an official of highest rank sent by a country to represent it in another country **2** any person sent as a representative or messenger [the U.S. *ambassador* to the United Nations]

am·e·thyst (am′ə thist) *n.* **1** a purple stone, especially a kind of quartz, that is used as a jewel **2** purple or violet

Amethyst comes from a Greek word meaning "not drunk." The ancient Greeks believed that someone wearing an amethyst would not get drunk from drinking alcoholic liquor.

am·phib·i·ous (am fib′ē əs) *adj.* **1** that can live both on land and in water [an *amphibious* plant] **2** that can operate or travel on both land and water [an *amphibious* truck]

am·phi·the·a·ter *or* **am·phi·the·a·tre** (am′fə thē′ə tər) *n.* a round or oval building having rising rows of seats around an open space in which sports events, plays, etc. are held

am·pli·fi·ca·tion (am′plə fi kā′shən) *n.* **1** an amplifying, or making larger or stronger; increase **2** more details [Your report needs *amplification*.]

am·pli·fi·er (am′plə fī′ər) *n.* **1** a person or thing that amplifies **2** a device, especially one with vacuum tubes or semiconductors, used to make electric or radio waves stronger before they are changed into sounds, as in a phonograph or radio

a·nach·ro·nism (ə nak′rə niz′m) *n.* **1** the connecting of a person, thing, or happening with another that came later in history [Shakespeare was guilty of an *anachronism* when he had a clock striking in a play about ancient Rome.] **2** anything that is or seems to be out of its proper time in history [A horse on a city street is an *anachronism* today.]

an·a·gram (an′ə gram) *n.* **1** a word or phrase made from another word or phrase by changing the order of the letters ["Dare" is an *anagram* of "read."] **2 anagrams,** *pl.* a game played by forming words from letters picked from a pile

a·nal·o·gy (ə nal′ə jē) *n.* likeness in some ways between things that are otherwise unlike; resemblance in part [How a jet airplane flies can be explained by showing an *analogy* with air escaping fast from a toy balloon.] —*pl.* **a·nal′o·gies**

a·nal·y·sis (ə nal′ə sis) *n.* a separating or breaking up of something into its parts so as to examine them and see how they fit together [A chemical *analysis* of a substance will tell what elements are in it. The *analysis* of a problem will help tell what caused it.] —*pl.* **a·nal·y·ses** (ə nal′ə sēz)

an·a·lyst (an′ə list) *n.* **1** a person who analyzes **2** *a shorter form of* **psychoanalyst**

an·a·lyt·i·cal (an′ə lit′i k′l) or **an·a·lyt·ic** (an′ə lit′ik) *adj.* **1** having to do with analysis [an *analytical* process] **2** good at analyzing [an *analytical* person] —**an′a·lyt′i·cal·ly** *adv.*

an·arch·y (an′ər kē) *n.* **1** the complete absence of government and law **2** a condition of disorder or confusion —**an·ar·chic** (an är′kik) *adj.*

an·ces·tor (an′ses tər) *n.* **1** a person who comes before one in a family line, especially someone earlier than a grandparent; forefather [Their *ancestors* came from Poland.] **2** an early kind of animal from which later kinds have developed [The *ancestor* of the elephant was the mammoth.]

an·chor (aŋ′kər) *n.* **1** a heavy object let down into the water by a chain to keep a ship from drifting: it is usually a metal piece with hooks that grip the ground at the bottom of the water **2** anything that keeps something else steady or firm [In time of trouble, faith was the old folks′ *anchor*.] ◆*v.* **1** to keep from drifting or coming loose by using an anchor **2** to attach or fix firmly [The shelves are *anchored* to the wall.]

a·ne·mi·a (ə nē′mē ə) *n.* a condition in which a person′s blood does not have enough red corpuscles or hemoglobin so that it does not carry a normal amount of oxygen: the person becomes pale and tired

an·es·the·sia (an′əs thē′zhə) *n.* a condition in which one has no feeling of pain, heat, touch, etc. in all or part of the body

an·gu·lar (aŋ′gyə lər) *adj.* **1** having angles or sharp corners [an *angular* building] **2** measured by an angle [the *angular* motion of a pendulum] **3** with bones that jut out; gaunt [an *angular* face]

an·nex (ə neks′) *v.* to add on or attach a smaller thing to a larger one [Texas was *annexed* to the Union in 1845.] ◆*n.* (an′eks) something added on; especially, an extra part built on or near a building to give more space —**an′nex·a′tion**

an·ni·hi·late (ə nī′ə lāt) *v.* to destroy completely; wipe out [An atomic bomb can *annihilate* a city.] —**an·ni′hi·lat·ed, an·ni′hi·lat·ing** —**an·ni′hi·la′tion** *n.*

an·no·tate (an′ə tāt) *v.* to add notes that explain something or give one′s opinions [Scholars *annotate* the plays of Shakespeare.] —**an′no·tat·ed, an′no·tat·ing**

an·nounce·ment (ə nouns′mənt) *n.* **1** an announcing of something that has happened or will happen **2** something announced, often in the form of a written or printed notice [The wedding *announcements* are here.]

an·nounc·er (ə nouns′ər) *n.* a person who announces; especially, one who introduces radio or television programs, reads commercials, etc.

an·nul (ə nul′) *v.* to do away with; put an end to; make no longer binding under the law; cancel [The marriage was *annulled* after a week.] —**an·nulled′, an·nul′ling** —**an·nul′ment** *n.*

a·non·y·mous (ə nän′ə məs) *adj.* **1** whose name is not known [an *anonymous* writer] **2** written, given, etc. by a person whose name is kept secret [an *anonymous* gift] —**a·non′y·mous·ly** *adv.*

an·te·ced·ent (an′tə sēd′ənt) *adj.* coming or happening before; previous [The pilot told of the storm *antecedent* to the crash.] ◆*n.* **1** a thing or happening coming before something else **2** one′s ancestry, past life, etc. **3** the word or group of words to which a pronoun refers [In "the guide who led us," "guide" is the *antecedent* of "who."]

an·te·ri·or (an tir′ē ər) *adj.* **1** at or toward the front; forward **2** coming before; earlier

an·te·room (an′ti rōōm) *n.* a room leading to a larger or more important room; waiting room

a	ask, fat
ā	ape, date
ä	car, lot
e	elf, ten
er	berry, care
ē	even, meet
i	is, hit
ir	mirror, here
ī	ice, fire
ō	open, go
ô	law, horn
oi	oil, point
ōō	look, pull
ōō	ooze, tool
yōō	unite, cure
yōō	cute, few
ou	out, crowd
u	up, cut
ʉ	fur, fern
ə	a in ago
	e in agent
	e in father
	i in unity
	o in collect
	u in focus
ch	chin, arch
ŋ	ring, singer
sh	she, dash
th	thin, truth
th	then, father
zh	s in pleasure
′	as in (ā b′l)

153

☆**an·ti·bi·ot·ic** (an'ti bī ät'ik) *n.* a chemical substance produced by bacteria, fungi, etc., that can kill, or stop the growth of, germs: antibiotics, such as penicillin, are used in treating diseases

an·ti·his·ta·mine (an'ti his'tə mēn) *n.* a medicine used to relieve asthma, hay fever, and, sometimes, the common cold

an·ti·so·cial (an'ti sō'shəl) *adj.* 1 not liking to be with other people [Are you so *antisocial* that you never have visitors?] 2 harmful to society in general [All crimes are *antisocial* acts.]

anx·i·e·ty (aŋ zī'ə tē) *n.* 1 the condition of feeling uneasy or worried about what may happen; concern [She waited with *anxiety* to hear what the doctor would say.] 2 an eager but often uneasy desire [He fumbled the ball in his *anxiety* to do well.] —*pl.* **anx·i·e·ties**

a·pol·o·gize (ə päl'ə jīz) *v.* to make an apology; say that one is sorry for doing something wrong or being at fault [They *apologized* for being late.] —**a·pol'o·gized, a·pol'o·giz·ing**

a·pos·tro·phe (ə päs'trə fē) *n.* the mark (') used: 1 in a shortened word or phrase to show that a letter or letters have been left out [ne'er for *never*; I'll for *I will*] 2 to show the possessive case [the *soldier's* uniform; the *teachers'* lounge] 3 to form certain plurals [five *6's*; to dot the *i's*]

ap·pe·tite (ap'ə tīt) *n.* 1 a desire or wish for food [Exercise gave her a strong *appetite*.] 2 any strong desire [He has an *appetite* for good books.]

ap·pli·ca·ble (ap'li kə b'l) *adj.* that can be applied or used; suitable [Your suggestion is not *applicable* to the problem.] —**ap'pli·ca·bil'i·ty** *n.*

aq·ua·ma·rine (ak'wə mə rēn') *n.* 1 a clear, pale blue-green mineral, used in jewelry 2 a pale blue-green color ◆*adj.* blue-green

a·quar·i·um (ə kwer'ē əm) *n.* 1 a glass tank or bowl in which living fishes, water animals, and water plants are kept 2 a building where collections of such animals and plants are shown to the public —*pl.* **a·quar'i·ums** or **a·quar·i·a** (ə kwer'ē ə)

a·quat·ic (ə kwät'ik *or* ə kwat'ik) *adj.* 1 growing or living in or upon water [*aquatic* plants] 2 done in or upon the water [*aquatic* sports]

ar·bi·tra·tor (är'bə trāt'ər) *n.* a person chosen to judge a dispute

ar·cade (är kād') *n.* 1 a covered passageway, as through a building, often with an arched roof; especially, such a passage with small shops on both sides 2 a row of arches supported by columns

ar·cha·ic (är kā'ik) *adj.* 1 belonging to an earlier time; ancient or old-fashioned [a yard with an *archaic* iron fence] 2 that is now seldom used except in poetry, the Bible, etc. ["Thou art" is an *archaic* form of "you are."]

ar·chi·tect (är'kə tekt) *n.* a person who works out the plans for buildings, bridges, etc. and sees that these plans are carried out by the builders

ar·chive (är'kīv) *n.* usually **archives**, *pl.* 1 a place where old public records or papers of historical interest are kept 2 such records or papers

ar·du·ous (är'jōō wəs) *adj.* 1 hard to do; difficult [*arduous* work] 2 using much energy; strenuous [*arduous* efforts] —**ar'du·ous·ly** *adv.*

a·ris·to·crat (ə ris'tə krat) *n.* 1 a member of the aristocracy, or upper class 2 a person who acts, thinks, or believes like people of the upper class

ar·thri·tis (är thrīt'is) *n.* a disease in which the joints of the body swell up and become sore and stiff —**ar·thrit·ic** (är thrit'ik) *adj.*

ar·tic·u·late (är tik'yə lit) *adj.* 1 spoken in such a way that all the sounds and words are clear and distinct [an *articulate* reply] 2 able to speak in this way; also, able to tell one's thoughts clearly so they are understood [an *articulate* speaker] ◆*v.* (är tik'yə lāt) to say in a clear, distinct way —**ar·tic'u·lat·ed, ar·tic'u·lat·ing**

ar·ti·fi·cial (är'tə fish'əl) *adj.* 1 made by a human being, not by nature; not natural [*artificial* flowers made of plastic] 2 put on just for an effect; not sincere; false [an *artificial* smile] —**ar·ti·fi·ci·al·i·ty** (är'tə fish'ē al'ə tē) *n.* —**ar'ti·fi'cial·ly** *adv.*

as·cer·tain (as'ər tān) *v.* to find out in such a way as to be sure [We *ascertained* the facts about the case by reading through old newspapers.] —**as'cer·tain'a·ble** *adj.* —**as'cer·tain'ment** *n.*

as·sist·ance (ə sis'təns) *n.* help; aid

at·oll (a'tôl *or* a'täl) *n.* a coral island that is shaped like a ring around a lagoon

at·tend·ant (ə ten'dənt) *adj.* 1 attending or taking care [an *attendant* nurse] 2 that goes along; joined with; accompanying [Every job has its *attendant* problems.] ◆*n.* a person who attends, or serves; servant, keeper, etc. [an *attendant* at the zoo; the queen and her *attendants*]

attorney general (ə tʉr'nē jen'ər əl) *n.* the chief law officer of a country or state [The U.S. *Attorney General* is the head of the Justice Department.] —*pl.* **attorneys general** or **attorney generals**

au·di·tion (ô dish'ən) *n.* a hearing in which an actor or musician who is being tested for a job gives a short performance ◆*v.* 1 to give an audition to 2 to perform in an audition

au·di·tor (ô'də tər) *n.* 1 a listener or hearer 2 a person whose work is auditing accounts

☆**au·to·mo·bile** (ôt'ə mə bēl' *or* ôt'ə mə bēl') *n.* a car moved by an engine that is part of it, used for traveling on streets or roads; motorcar

auxiliary verb (ôg zil′yər ē vʉrb) *n.* a verb that is used to form tenses, moods, or voices of other verbs

Have, be, may, can, must, do, shall, will are used as **auxiliary verbs**. In the sentence "He will be late, but she may not be," *will* and *may* are auxiliary verbs.

a·vail·a·ble (ə vā′lə b'l) *adj.* that can be got, used, or reached [This style is *available* in three colors.] —**a·vail′a·bil′i·ty** *n.*

av·a·lanche (av′ə lanch) *n.* 1 a large mass of snow, ice, rocks, etc. sliding swiftly down a mountain 2 anything that comes suddenly and in large numbers [an *avalanche* of mail; an *avalanche* of blows]

Bb

bank·rupt (baŋk′rupt) *adj.* 1 not able to pay one's debts and freed by law from the need for doing so [Any property a *bankrupt* person may still have is usually divided among those to whom the person owes money.] 2 that has failed completely [The school's policy on this matter seems *bankrupt*.] ◆*n.* a person who is bankrupt ◆*v.* to make bankrupt

Bankrupt comes from two Italian words meaning "broken bench." Moneylenders used to carry on their business at a bench or table. They would be put out of business if the bench were broken, just as nowadays people are put out of business if they cannot pay their debts.

bar·be·cue (bär′bə kyo͞o) *n.* 1 a hog, ox, etc. roasted whole on a spit over an open fire 2 any meat roasted over an open fire ☆3 a picnic or party at which such meat is served 4 a stove or pit for cooking outdoors ◆*v.* 1 to roast on a spit over an open fire 2 to broil or roast meat or fish in a highly seasoned sauce (called **barbecue sauce**) —**bar′be·cued, bar′be·cu·ing**

ba·rom·e·ter (bə räm′ə tər) *n.* 1 an instrument that measures the pressure of the air around us: it is used in forecasting changes in the weather and finding the height above sea level 2 anything that shows changes in conditions [The stock market is a *barometer* of business.] —**bar·o·met·ric** (bar′ə met′rik) *adj.*

ben·e·fac·tor (ben′ə fak′tər) *n.* a person who has given money or other help to someone in need

ben·e·fit (ben′ə fit) *n.* 1 help or advantage; also, anything that helps [Speak louder for the *benefit* of those in the rear.] 2 *often* **benefits**, *pl.* money paid by an insurance company, the government, etc. as during old age or sickness, or for death 3 any public event put on to raise money for a certain person, group, or cause [The show is a *benefit* for crippled children.] ◆*v.* 1 to do good for; aid; help [The new tax law *benefits* big businesses.] 2 to be helped; profit [You'll *benefit* from exercise.]

be·nign (bi nīn′) *adj.* 1 good-natured; kindly [a *benign* smile] 2 doing good; helpful [The sickly child was taken to a more *benign* climate.] 3 doing little or no harm; not likely to cause death [a *benign* tumor] —**be·nign′ly** *adv.*

bib·li·og·ra·phy (bib′lē äg′rə fē) *n.* a list of writings about a certain subject or by a certain author —*pl.* **bib′li·og′ra·phies** —**bib·li·o·graph·i·cal** (bib′lē ə graf′i k'l) *adj.*

bi·og·ra·phy (bī äg′rə fē) *n.* the story of a person's life written by another person —*pl.* **bi·og′ra·phies** —**bi·o·graph·i·cal** (bī′ə graf′i k'l) *adj.*

bi·o·log·i·cal (bī′ə läj′i k'l) *adj.* having to do with biology —**bi·o·log′i·cal·ly** *adv.*

biv·ou·ac (biv′wak *or* biv′o͞o wak′) *n.* a camp of soldiers outdoors with little or no shelter, set up for a short time ◆*v.* to camp outdoors —**biv′ou·acked, biv′ou·ack·ing**

bois·ter·ous (bois′tər əs) *adj.* 1 rough and stormy 2 noisy and lively [a *boisterous* party]

bor·ough (bʉr′ō) *n.* 1 a town or village that has a charter to govern itself 2 one of the five main divisions of New York City

bouil·lon (bo͞ol′yän) *n.* a clear soup

boy·cott (boi′kät) *v.* to join together in refusing to buy, sell, or use something or to have any dealings with someone [We all *boycotted* the ice-cream store because it was dirty.] ◆☆*n.* the act of boycotting a business, etc.

The word **boycott** comes from the name of Captain Charles C. Boycott, who collected rent for a landlord in Ireland. After he raised the rents of his neighbors in 1880, they had no more to do with him. They wouldn't even sell him groceries.

broad·cast (brôd′kast) *v.* 1 to send over the air by means of radio or television [to *broadcast* a program] —**broad′cast** or **broad′cast·ed, broad′cast·ing** 2 to scatter or spread widely —**broad′cast, broad′cast·ing** ◆*n.* 1 the act of broadcasting 2 a radio or television program [the six o'clock news *broadcast*] ◆*adv.* scattered about; far and wide [Seed may be sown *broadcast* or in rows.]

bu·reauc·ra·cy (byo͞o rä′krə sē) *n.* 1 government by appointed officials who follow all rules without question and without exceptions 2 such officials, as a group, or the way they govern —*pl.* **bu·reauc′ra·cies**

but·tress (but′ris) *n.* 1 a support built against a wall to make it strong 2 any support or prop ◆*v.* to prop up or support [to *buttress* a wall; to *buttress* an argument]

a	ask, fat
ā	ape, date
ä	car, lot
e	elf, ten
er	berry, care
ē	even, meet
i	is, hit
ir	mirror, here
ī	ice, fire
ō	open, go
ô	law, horn
oi	oil, point
o͝o	look, pull
o͞o	ooze, tool
yo͞o	unite, cure
yo͞o	cute, few
ou	out, crowd
u	up, cut
ʉ	fur, fern
ə	a in ago
	e in agent
	e in father
	i in unity
	o in collect
	u in focus
ch	chin, arch
ŋ	ring, singer
sh	she, dash
th	thin, truth
th	then, father
zh	s in pleasure
′	as in (ā b'l)

ca·dence (kād′′ns) *n.* **1** flow or rhythm with a regular beat [to march in fast *cadence*; the *cadence* of waves breaking on the shore] **2** the rise or fall of the voice or the tone of the voice in speaking **3** the final chords or other ending of a section of music

cal·cu·lus (kal′kyə ləs) *n.* a kind of mathematics used to solve hard problems in science and statistics

Calculus is a Latin word meaning "pebble." The early Romans used little stones for counting or "calculating" in doing arithmetic.

can·cel·la·tion (kan′s′l ā′shən) *n.* **1** the act of canceling **2** something canceled **3** a mark that cancels, as on a postage stamp

can·o·py (kan′ə pē) *n.* **1** a cloth or other covering fastened as a roof above a throne, bed, etc., or held on poles over a person or sacred thing **2** anything that seems to cover like a canopy [We walked through the woods beneath a *canopy* of leaves.] —*pl.* **can′o·pies** ✦*v.* to put or form a canopy over —**can′o·pied, can′o·py·ing**

ca·pa·bil·i·ty (kā′pə bil′ə tē) *n.* the power to do something; ability [She has the *capability* to become a lawyer.] —*pl.* **ca′pa·bil′i·ties**

cap·i·tal·i·za·tion (kap′ə t′l ə zā′shən) *n.* **1** the act of capitalizing **2** the stocks and bonds that stand for the total capital of a business

car·i·ca·ture (kar′ə kə chər) *n.* **1** a picture or imitation of a person or thing in which certain features or parts are exaggerated in a joking or mocking way **2** the skill or work of making such pictures, etc. ✦*v.* to make or be a caricature of [Cartoonists often *caricature* the President.] —**car′i·ca·tured, car′i·ca·tur·ing** —**car′i·ca·tur·ist** *n.*

car·pen·ter (kär′pən tər) *n.* a worker who builds and repairs wooden things, especially the wooden parts of buildings, ships, etc.

car·tel (kär tel′) *n.* a group of companies joined together to have complete control over the production and prices of certain products; trust or monopoly [an international *cartel* of oil producers]

ce·les·tial (sə les′chəl) *adj.* **1** of the heavens or sky [The stars are *celestial* bodies.] **2** of the finest or highest kind; perfect [*celestial* bliss]

Cel·si·us (sel′sē əs) *adj.* of or describing a thermometer on which the freezing point of pure water is 0° and the boiling point is 100°: *also called* **centigrade**

cen·sor (sen′sər) *n.* an official who has the power to examine books, news stories, mail, movies, etc. and to remove or change anything the government does not wish people to see or hear ✦*v.* to examine books, letters, movies, etc. and to remove or hold back anything thought not right for people to see or hear —**cen′sor·ship** *n.*

cen·ti·grade (sen′tə grād) *adj., n. same as* **Celsius**

cen·ti·me·ter (sen′tə mēt′ər) *n.* a unit of measure, equal to 1/100 meter

cen·tral·ize (sen′trə līz) *v.* to bring or come to a center; especially, to bring under one control [All government powers were *centralized* under a dictator.] —**cen′tral·ized, cen′tral·iz·ing** —**cen′tral·i·za′tion** *n.*

cen·trif·u·gal force (sen trif′yə gəl) *n.* the force that pulls a thing outward when it is spinning rapidly around a center

cer·e·bral (ser′ə brəl *or* sə rē′brəl) *adj.* having to do with the brain or with the cerebrum

chan·de·lier (shan də lir′) *n.* a lighting fixture hanging from the ceiling with branches for several lights

chem·ist (kem′ist) *n.* an expert in chemistry

Chil·e (chil′ē) a country on the southwestern coast of South America —**Chil′e·an** *adj., n.*

☆**chi·ro·prac·tor** (kī′rə prak′tər) *n.* a person who practices a system of treating diseases by pressing and moving the spine and the joints of the body with the hands

cho·les·ter·ol (kə les′tə rōl) *n.* a waxy substance found in the body and in certain foods: when there is much of it in the blood, it is thought to cause hardening of the arteries

chron·ic (krän′ik) *adj.* **1** going on for a long time or coming back again and again [a *chronic* disease] **2** having been one for a long time; constant or habitual [a *chronic* complainer; a *chronic* invalid] —**chron′i·cal·ly** *adv.*

cin·e·ma (sin′ə mə) *n.* **1** a movie; motion picture **2** a movie theater **3** the art or business of making movies

clas·si·cal (klas′i k′l) *adj.* describing a kind of music that is not simple in form and that requires much study and training to write and perform [Symphonies, concertos, sonatas, etc. are called *classical* music.] —**clas′si·cal·ly** *adv.*

clause (klôz) *n.* **1** a group of words that includes a subject and verb, but that forms only part of a sentence [In the sentence "She will visit us if she can," *She will visit us* is a *clause* that could be a complete sentence, and *if she can* is a *clause* that depends on the first *clause*.] **2** any of the separate points or articles in a law, contract, treaty, etc.

cli·ché (klē shā′) *n.* an expression or idea that has become stale from too much use ["As old as the hills" is a *cliché*.]

clique (klēk *or* klik) *n.* a small group of people who are friendly only with one another and have little to do with outsiders

clock·wise (kläk′wīz) *adv., adj.* in the direction in which the hands of a clock move [When you turn the knob *clockwise*, the radio goes on.]

closed circuit (klōzd sʉr′kit) *n.* a system of sending television signals by cable to just a certain number of receiving sets for some special purpose

co·au·thor (kō ô′thər) *n.* an author who works with another author in writing something, as a book

co·ex·ist (kō′ig zist′) *v.* 1 to go on living or existing together at the same time 2 to live together in a peaceful way even though there are political or other differences —**co′ex·ist′ence** *n.*

co·her·ent (kō hir′ənt) *adj.* 1 sticking together [a *coherent* blob of jelly] 2 having all parts connected in a proper way; clear [She told a rambling story that was not very *coherent*.] 3 speaking or thinking in a way that makes sense [He was terrified and no longer *coherent*.] —**co·her′ence** *n.* —**co·her′ent·ly** *adv.*

co·in·cide (kō′in sīd′) *v.* 1 to be exactly alike in shape and size [If one circle fits exactly over another, they *coincide*.] 2 to happen at the same time [Our birthdays *coincide*.] 3 to agree; be the same [Our interests do not *coincide*.] —**co′in·cid′ed, co′in·cid′ing**

col·i·se·um (käl′ə sē′əm) *n.* a large building or stadium for sports events, shows, etc.

col·lab·o·rate (kə lab′ə rāt) *v.* 1 to work together in preparing something [Charles and Mary Lamb *collaborated* in writing "Tales from Shakespeare."] 2 to help or work with an enemy that has invaded one's country —**col·lab′o·rat·ed, col·lab′o·rat·ing** —**col·lab′o·ra′tion, col·lab′o·ra′tor** *n.*

col·lat·er·al (kə lat′ər əl) *adj.* that goes along with the main thing, but in a less important way; additional or secondary [*collateral* evidence] ◆☆*n.* stocks, bonds, or other property that is given to a lender of money to hold as a pledge that the loan will be repaid

col·league (käl′ēg) *n.* a person who works in the same office, the same profession, etc.; fellow worker

col·lec·tion (kə lek′shən) *n.* 1 the act of gathering [Rubbish *collection* is on Friday.] 2 things collected [a *collection* of coins] 3 something gathered into a mass or pile [a *collection* of dust] 4 money collected [a *collection* for a church]

col·li·sion (kə lizh′ən) *n.* 1 the act of coming together with force; crash [an automobile *collision*] 2 a clash of ideas, interests, etc.

col·lo·qui·al (kə lō′kwē əl) *adj.* being or containing the words and phrases that are used only in everyday talk ["My buddy flunked the exam" is a *colloquial* way of saying "My close friend failed the examination."] —**col·lo′qui·al·ly** *adv.*

col·on·nade (käl ə nād′) *n.* a row of columns as along the side of a building

col·o·ny (käl′ə nē) *n.* 1 a group of people who settle in a distant land but are still under the rule of the country from which they came 2 the place where they settle [the Pilgrim *colony* at Plymouth] 3 a land that is ruled by a country some distance away [Java was once a Dutch *colony*.] —*pl.* **col′o·nies**

co·los·sal (kə läs′'l) *adj.* very large or very great; enormous or immense

com·bus·tion (kəm bus′chən) *n.* the act or process of burning [An internal-*combustion* engine is one in which the fuel is burned within the engine itself.]

co·me·di·an (kə mē′dē ən) *n.* an actor who plays comic parts, or one who tells jokes and does funny things to make people laugh

com·mem·o·rate (kə mem′ə rāt) *v.* to honor or keep alive the memory of [The Washington Monument *commemorates* our first president.] —**com·mem′o·rat·ed, com·mem′o·rat·ing**

com·mence·ment (kə mens′mənt) *n.* 1 a beginning or start 2 the graduation ceremony of a school or college, when graduates receive their degrees or diplomas

com·ment (käm′ent) *n.* a remark or note that explains or gives an opinion [The teacher's *comments* on the poem helped us to understand it.] ◆*v.* to make comments or remarks [Doctors should not *comment* on their patients to others.]

com·men·tar·y (käm′ən ter′ē) *n.* 1 a series of comments or notes on a book, play, etc. [You need to read *commentaries* in order to understand Shakespeare's plays.] 2 something serving like a comment or illustration [This political scandal is a *commentary* on our corrupt society.] —*pl.* **com′men·tar′ies**

com·merce (käm′ərs) *n.* the buying and selling of goods, especially when done on a large scale between cities, states, or countries; trade

com·mis·sion·er (kə mish′ə nər) *n.* 1 a member of a commission 2 the head of a government commission or department [a water *commissioner*]

com·mit·ment (kə mit′mənt) *n.* 1 a committing or being committed 2 a promise; pledge

a	ask, fat
ā	ape, date
ä	car, lot
e	elf, ten
er	berry, care
ē	even, meet
i	is, hit
ir	mirror, here
ī	ice, fire
ō	open, go
ô	law, horn
oi	oil, point
σο	look, pull
σο	ooze, tool
yσο	unite, cure
yσο	cute, few
ou	out, crowd
u	up, cut
ʉ	fur, fern
ə	a in ago
	e in agent
	e in father
	i in unity
	o in collect
	u in focus
ch	chin, arch
ŋ	ring, singer
sh	she, dash
th	thin, truth
th	then, father
zh	s in pleasure
′	as in (ā b'l)

com·mod·i·ty (kə mäd′ə tē) *n.* anything that is bought and sold; article of trade or commerce —*pl.* **com·mod′i·ties**

com·mon·wealth (käm′ən welth) *n.* **1** the people of a nation or state **2** a nation or state in which the people hold the ruling power; democracy or republic ☆**3** sometimes, any State of the United States

com·mu·nal (käm′yoon 'l *or* kə myoon′l) *adj.* **1** of or belonging to the community; public [This park is *communal* property.] **2** of a commune —**com·mu′nal·ly** *adv.*

com·mune (käm′yoon) *n.* **1** the smallest district that has a local government in France, Belgium, and some other countries in Europe ☆**2** a small group of people living together and sharing their earnings, the work to be done, etc.

com·mute (kə myoot′) *v.* ☆**1** to travel as a commuter **2** to change a punishment, duty, etc. to one that is less harsh [to *commute* a prisoner's sentence from five to three years] —**com·mut′ed, com·mut′ing** —**com·mu·ta·tion** (käm′yə tā′shən) *n.*

com·pe·tent (käm′pə tənt) *adj.* having enough ability to do what is needed; capable [a *competent* typist] —**com′pe·tent·ly** *adv.*

com·plex (kəm pleks′ *or* käm′pleks) *adj.* made up of different parts connected in a way that is hard to understand; not simple; intricate [A computer is a *complex* machine. Unemployment is a *complex* problem.] ◆*n.* (käm′pleks) **1** a group of connected ideas, things, etc. that form a single whole [the *complex* of roads in a state] **2** a mixed-up feeling about something that makes one show fear, dislike, etc. [an inferiority *complex*; a *complex* about traveling in airplanes]

com·pli·ca·tion (käm′plə kā′shən) *n.* **1** a complicated or mixed-up condition; confusion or intricacy **2** a happening that makes something more complicated or involved [the *complications* of a plot; a disease with *complications*]

com·pli·men·ta·ry (käm′plə men′tər ē) *adj.* **1** paying a compliment; giving praise or admiring [*complimentary* remarks] **2** given free [a *complimentary* ticket to a play]

com·pro·mise (käm′prə mīz) *n.* a settling of an argument or dispute in which each side gives up part of what it wants ◆*v.* **1** to settle by a compromise [They *compromised* by taking turns on the bicycle.] **2** to put in danger of being criticized or disgraced [Do not *compromise* your reputation by cheating.] —**com′pro·mised, com′pro·mis·ing**

com·pul·so·ry (kəm pul′sər ē) *adj.* that must be done; required [*compulsory* training]

con·cen·tric (kən sen′trik) *adj.* having the same center [*concentric* circles]

con·duit (kän′dit *or* kän′doo wit) *n.* **1** a pipe or passage for carrying fluids, as a gas pipe, gutter, or sewer **2** a tube for protecting electric wires or cables

con·fed·er·a·tion (kən fed′ə rā′shən) *n.* **1** a uniting or being united in a league or alliance **2** nations or states joined in a league, as for defense; alliance

con·fer (kən fur′) *v.* **1** to give or grant [They *conferred* a medal upon the hero.] **2** to meet for a discussion; have a talk [The mayor will *confer* with the city council.] —**con·ferred′, con·fer′ring**

con·fron·ta·tion (kän′frən tā′shən) *n.* a face-to-face meeting, as of two persons who hold opposite views on some matter

con·glom·er·ate (kən gläm′ə rāt) *v.* to form or collect into a rounded mass —**con·glom′er·at·ed, con·glom′er·at·ing** ◆*adj.* (kən gläm′ər it) made up of separate parts or materials formed into one mass [A *conglomerate* rock is made up of pebbles and stones cemented together in hard clay and sand.] ◆*n.* (kən gläm′ər it) ☆**2** a large corporation made up of a number of companies dealing in different products or services —**con·glom′er·a′tion**

con·junc·tion (kən junk′shən) *n.* **1** a joining together; combination [High winds, in *conjunction* with rain, made travel difficult.] **2** a word used to join other words, phrases, or clauses [*And, but, or, if*, etc. are *conjunctions*.]

con·quer (käŋ′kər) *v.* **1** to get or gain by using force, as by winning a war [The Spaniards *conquered* Mexico.] **2** to overcome by trying hard; get the better of; defeat [She *conquered* her bad habits.] —**con′quer·or** *n.*

con·ser·va·to·ry (kən sur′və tôr′e) *n.* a school of music, art, etc. —*pl.* **con·ser′va·to′ries**

con·sol·i·date (kən säl′ə dāt) *v.* **1** to join together into one; unite; merge [The corporation was formed by *consolidating* many companies.] **2** to make or become strong or firm [The troops *consolidated* their positions by bringing up heavy guns.] —**con·sol′i·dat·ed, con·sol′i·dat·ing** —**con·sol′i·da′tion** *n.*

con·spir·a·cy (kən spir′ə sē) *n.* **1** a secret plan by two or more people to do something bad or unlawful; plot [a *conspiracy* to kill the king] **2** a working or joining together [A *conspiracy* of events kept me from the party.] —*pl.* **con·spir′a·cies**

con·tem·po·rar·y (kən tem′pə rer′e) *adj.* existing or happening in the same period of time ◆*n.* a person living in the same period as another [The painters Mary Cassatt and Edgar Degas were *contemporaries*.] —*pl.* **con·tem′po·rar′ies**

con·tra·band (kän′trə band) *n.* things that it is against the law to bring into or take out of a country; smuggled goods

con·tra·dict (kän trə dikt′) *v.* **1** to say the opposite of; deny the things said by someone [The witness *contradicted* the story told by the suspect. Stop *contradicting* me.] **2** to be opposite to or different from; go against [The facts *contradict* your theory.]

Contradict comes from a Latin word that means "to speak against." In English to contradict someone means "to deny what someone else has said," which is one way of speaking against that person.

con·trar·y (kän′trer ē) *adj.* **1** opposite; completely different [to hold *contrary* opinions] **2** opposed; being or acting against [*contrary* to the rules] **3** (*often* kən trer′ē) opposing in a stubborn way; perverse [such a *contrary* child, always saying "No!"] ➧*n.* the opposite [Just the *contrary* of what you say is true.]

con·trast (kən trast′) *v.* **1** to compare in a way that shows the differences [to *contrast* France and England] **2** to show differences when compared [Golf *contrasts* sharply with tennis as a sport.] ➧*n.* (kän′trast) **1** a difference between things being compared [the *contrast* between air and rail travel] **2** something showing differences when compared with something else [Reading a novel is quite a *contrast* to seeing a movie based on the novel.]

con·trol·ler (kən trōl′ər) *n.* **1** a person in charge of spending, as for a company or government **2** a person or thing that controls

con·tro·ver·sial (kän′trə vʉr′shəl) *adj.* that is or can be much argued about; debatable [a *controversial* book] —**con′tro·ver′sial·ly** *adv.*

con·va·les·cent (kän′və les″nt) *adj.* getting back health and strength after illness ➧*n.* a convalescent person

co·op·er·a·tive (kō äp′ər ə tiv *or* kō äp′rə tiv) *adj.* **1** willing to cooperate; helpful **2** that is or belongs to a group whose members produce goods together or sell them and share the profits [Local farmers have started a *cooperative* store.] ➧*n.* a cooperative group, store, etc.

co·or·di·nate (kō ôr′də nāt) *v.* to bring together in the proper relation; make work well together [She was able to *coordinate* the efforts of dozens of volunteers.] —**co·or′di·nat·ed, co·or′di·nat·ing**

co·pi·lot (kō′pī lət) *n.* the assistant pilot of an airplane

cor·dial (kôr′jel) *adj.* deeply felt; hearty; sincere [a *cordial* welcome] ➧*n.* a sweet and rather thick alcoholic drink —**cor′dial·ly** *adv.*

Co·rin·thi·an (kə rin′thē ən) *adj.* **1** of Corinth **2** describing a highly decorated style of ancient Greek architecture in which the columns have fancy carvings of leaves at the top

cor·o·ner (kôr′ə nər) *n.* an official whose duty is to find out the cause of any death that does not seem to be due to natural causes

cor·po·ra·tion (kôr′pə rā′shən) *n.* a group of people who get a charter that gives the group some of the legal powers and rights that one person has [Cities and colleges, as well as businesses, can be organized as *corporations*.]

cor·re·la·tion (kôr′ə lā′shən) *n.* the relation or connection between things [the high *correlation* between ignorance and prejudice]

cor·rupt (kə rupt′) *adj.* changed from good to bad; having become evil, rotten, dishonest, incorrect, etc. [*corrupt* officials; *corrupt* business practices; a *corrupt* version of a book] ➧*v.* to make or become corrupt —**cor·rupt′ly** *adv.*

☆**cor·sage** (kôr säzh′ *or* kôr säj′) *n.* a small bunch of flowers for a woman to wear, as at the wrist or shoulder

cos·mo·pol·i·tan (käz′mə päl′ə t′n) *adj.* **1** having to do with the world as a whole **2** interested in and liking the people and cultures of all countries; feeling at home anywhere ➧*n.* a cosmopolitan person

cos·mos (käz′məs) *n.* **1** the universe as a system with order **2** any whole system with order

cou·plet (kup′lit) *n.* two lines of poetry that go together and are usually rhymed *Example*: He that fights and runs away May live to fight another day.

cou·ri·er (koor′ē ər *or* kur′ē ər) *n.* a messenger sent in a hurry with an important message

cour·te·sy (kur′tə sē) *n.* **1** courteous or polite behavior; good manners [Thank you for your *courtesy* in writing to me.] **2** a polite act or remark —*pl.* **cour′te·sies**

cre·scen·do (krə shen′dō) *adj., adv.* gradually becoming louder or stronger; *a direction in music shown by the sign* < ➧*n.* a gradual increase in loudness —*pl.* **cre·scen′dos**

cre·vasse (kri vas′) *n.* a deep crack or crevice, especially in a glacier

crim·i·nal (krim′ə n′l) *adj.* **1** being a crime; that is a crime [a *criminal* act] **2** having to do with crime [*criminal* law] ➧*n.* a person guilty of a crime —**crim′i·nal·ly** *adv.*

cri·sis (krī′sis) *n.* **1** any turning point, as in history **2** a time of great danger or trouble —*pl.* **cri·ses** (krī′sez)

crit·i·cize (krit′ə sīz) *v.* **1** to judge as a critic **2** to find fault with; disapprove of [The boss *criticizes* everything I do.] —**crit′i·cized, crit′i·ciz·ing**

cri·tique (kri tēk′) *n.* a piece of writing that gives a careful judgment of a book, play, etc.

cro·quet (krō kā′) *n.* an outdoor game in which the players use mallets to drive a wooden ball through hoops in the ground

a	ask, fat
ā	ape, date
ä	car, lot
e	elf, ten
er	berry, care
ē	even, meet
i	is, hit
ir	mirror, here
ī	ice, fire
ō	open, go
ô	law, horn
oi	oil, point
oo	look, pull
o͞o	ooze, tool
yoo	unite, cure
yo͞o	cute, few
ou	out, crowd
u	up, cut
ʉ	fur, fern
ə	a in ago
	e in agent
	e in father
	i in unity
	o in collect
	u in focus
ch	chin, arch
ŋ	ring, singer
sh	she, dash
th	thin, truth
th	then, father
zh	s in pleasure
′	as in (ā b′l)

159

cru·el (kr $\overline{oo}$ ′əl) *adj.* **1** liking to make others suffer; having no mercy or pity [The *cruel* Pharaoh made slaves of the Israelites.] **2** causing pain and suffering [*cruel* insults; a *cruel* winter] —**cru′el·ly** *adv.*

crys·tal·lize (kris′tə līz) *v.* **1** to form crystals [Boil the maple syrup until it *crystallizes.*] **2** to take on or give a definite form [Their customs were *crystallized* into law.] —**crys′tal·lized, crys′tal·liz·ing** —**crys′tal·li·za′tion** *n.*

cu·ri·os·i·ty (kyoor′ē äs′ə tē) *n.* **1** a strong feeling of wanting to know or learn [*Curiosity* is a child's best teacher.] **2** such a feeling about something that is not one's business [Control your *curiosity*; don't ask how much they paid for it.] **3** a strange or unusual thing [A fire engine pulled by horses is now a *curiosity.*] —*pl.* **cu′ri·os′i·ties**

cus·tom·ar·y (kus′tə mer′ē) *adj.* in keeping with custom; usual [It is *customary* to tip a waiter or waitress.] —**cus′tom·ar′i·ly** *adv.*

cus·tom·er (kus′tə mər) *n.* a person who buys, especially one who buys regularly [I have been a *customer* of that shop for many years.]

daunt·less (dônt′lis) *adj.* that cannot be frightened or discouraged; fearless [The *dauntless* rebels fought on.] —**daunt′less·ly** *adv.*

☆**dav·en·port** (dav′ən pôrt) *n.* a large sofa

dec·ade (dek′ād) *n.* a period of ten years

de·cant·er (di kan′tər) *n.* a decorative glass bottle for serving wine or liquor

de·ceased (di sēst′) *adj.* dead

de·cep·tion (di sep′shən) *n.* **1** a deceiving or fooling **2** something that fools, as a fraud

dec·i·li·ter (des′ə lēt′ər) *n.* a unit of volume, equal to 1/10 liter

dec·i·mal (des′ə m'l) *adj.* of or based upon the number ten; counted by tens [The metric system of measure is a *decimal* system.] ➧*n.* a fraction with a denominator of 10, or of 100 or 1,000, etc.: it is shown by a point (**decimal point**) before the numerator, as .5 (5/10) or .63 (63/100)

dec·i·me·ter (des′ə mēt′ər) *n.* **1** a measure of length, equal to 1/10 meter

de·ci·sion (di sizh′ən) *n.* **1** the act of deciding or settling something, or the opinion or choice decided on [The *decision* of the judges will be final.] **2** firmness of mind; determination [a person of *decision*]

de·cline (di klīn′) *v.* **1** to bend or slope downward [The lawn *declines* to the sidewalk.] **2** to become less, as in health, power, or value; decay [A person's strength usually *declines* in old age.] **3** to refuse something, especially in a polite way [I am sorry I must *decline* your invitation.] —**de·clined′, de·clin′ing** *n.* a becoming less, smaller, or weaker; decay [a *decline* in prices]

de·com·pose (dē kəm pōz′) *v.* **1** to rot or decay **2** to break up into its separate basic parts [Water can be *decomposed* into hydrogen and oxygen.] —**de·com·posed′, de·com·pos′ing** —**de·com·po·si·tion** (dē′käm pə zish′ən) *n.*

de·cre·scen·do (dē′krə shen′dō) *adj., adv.* gradually becoming softer; *a direction in music usually shown by the sign* > ➧*n.* a decrease in loudness —*pl.* **de′cre·scen′dos**

de·fense·less (di fens′lis) *adj.* having no defense; not able to protect oneself

de·fer (di fur′) *v.* to put off until a later time; postpone [The judge *deferred* the trial until the following week.] —**de·ferred′, de·fer′ring** —**de·fer′ment** *n.*

def·i·ni·tion (def′ə nish′ən) *n.* **1** a defining or being defined **2** a statement that tells what a thing is or what a word means **3** the clearness or sharpness of an outline

de·moc·ra·cy (di mäk′rə sē) *n.* **1** government in which the people hold the ruling power, usually giving it over to representatives whom they elect to make the laws and run the government **2** a country, state, etc. with such government **3** equal rights, opportunity, and treatment for all [The student council wants more *democracy* in our school.] —*pl.* **de·moc′ra·cies**

☆**dental hygienist** (den′t'l hī′jē ə nist) *n.* a dentist's assistant, who cleans teeth, takes X-rays of the teeth, etc.

de·pend·ent (di pen′dənt) *adj.* **1** controlled or decided by something else [The size of my allowance was *dependent* on our family income.] **2** relying on another for help or support [A baby is completely *dependent* on its parents.] ➧*n.* a person who depends on someone else for support

de·plete (di plēt′) *v.* to empty or use up; exhaust [Lack of rain will soon *deplete* our water supply. My energy was *depleted.*] —**de·plet′ed, de·plet′ing** —**de·ple·tion** *n.*

de·pres·sant (di pres′ənt) *adj.* lowering the rate of activities in the body ➧*n.* a drug that reduces physical activity or excitability

de·pres·sion (di presh′ən) *n.* **1** sadness; gloominess [to suffer from a fit of *depression*] **2** a hollow or low place [Water collected in the *depressions* in the ground.] ☆**3** a period during which there is less business and many people lose their jobs

de·scend·ant (di sen′dənt) *n.* a person who is descended from a certain ancestor

des·per·a·tion (des′pə rā′shən) *n.* **1** the condition of being desperate **2** recklessness that comes from despair [In *desperation* the hunted deer leaped across the chasm.]

de·struc·tion (di struk′shən) *n.* the act of destroying or the condition of being destroyed; ruin [The forest fire caused much *destruction*.]

de·ter (di tʉr′) *v.* to keep a person from doing something through fear, doubt, etc.; discourage [Does the death penalty *deter* crime?] —**de·terred′, de·ter′ring**

de·ter·mine (di tʉr′mən) *v.* **1** to settle or decide on [I haven't *determined* whether to go to college.] **2** to set one's mind on something; resolve [She is *determined* to be a lawyer.] **3** to find out exactly [First *determine* the area of the floor.] **4** to be the thing that decides; have an important effect on [One's hobbies often *determine* what one chooses to do for a living.] —**de·ter′mined, de·ter′min·ing**

de·tour (dē′tŏŏr) *n.* **1** a turning aside from the direct or regular route **2** a route used when the regular route is closed to traffic ◆*v.* to go or send by a detour

de·vice (di vīs′) *n.* something made or invented for some special use; tool, machine, etc. [A windmill is a *device* for putting wind power to work.]

di·ag·nose (dī əg nōs′) *v.* to make a diagnosis of —**di·ag·nosed′, di·ag·nos′ing**

di·ag·no·sis (dī′əg nō′sis) *n.* **1** the act or practice of examining a patient and studying the symptoms to find out what disease the patient has **2** a careful examination of all the facts in a situation to find out how it has been brought about [a *diagnosis* of the last election] —*pl.* **di·ag·no·ses** (dī′əg nō′sēz)

di·a·logue or **di·a·log** (dī′ə lôg) *n.* **1** a talking together, especially an open exchange of ideas, as in an effort to understand each other's views **2** the parts of a play, novel, radio or television program, etc. that are conversation

di·a·mond (dī′mənd *or* dī′ə mənd) *n.* **1** a very precious stone, usually colorless, formed of nearly pure carbon: it is the hardest known mineral and is used as a gem, as the tip of a phonograph needle, and in the cutting edge of tools **2** a figure shaped like this: ◇

☆**di·e·ti·tian** or **di·e·ti·cian** (dī′ə tish′ən) *n.* a person whose work is planning diets that will give people the kinds and amounts of food that they need

di·lap·i·dat·ed (di lap′ə dāt′id) *adj.* falling to pieces; broken down; shabby and neglected [a *dilapidated* barn]

di·lem·ma (di lem′ə) *n.* a situation in which one must choose between things that are equally unpleasant or dangerous; difficult choice

di·min·ish (də min′ish) *v.* to make or become smaller in size or less in force, importance, etc. [Overpopulation *diminishes* the world food supply. Danger of frost *diminishes* in April.]

dis·ad·van·tage (dis′əd van′tij) *n.* **1** anything that stands in the way of success; handicap; drawback [A trick knee is a *disadvantage* to a baseball player.] **2** loss or harm [This decision will work to your *disadvantage*.] —**dis·ad·van·ta·geous** (dis ad′vən tā′jəs) *adj.*

dis·as·ter (di zas′tər) *n.* a happening that causes much damage or suffering, as a flood or earthquake; catastrophe —**dis·as′trous** *adj.*

dis·mal (diz′m'l) *adj.* **1** causing gloom or misery; sad [a *dismal* story] **2** dark and gloomy [a *dismal* room] —**dis′mal·ly** *adv.*

Dismal comes from two Latin words meaning "evil days." In the Middle Ages certain days of the year were thought to be unlucky or evil. These "evil days" made people sad. In time, anything that made people sad could be called dismal.

dis·pen·sa·ry (dis pen′sə rē) *n.* a room or place, as in a school, where a person can get medicines or first-aid treatment —*pl.* **dis·pen′sa·ries**

dis·perse (dis pʉrs′) *v.* to break up and scatter; spread in all directions [The crowd began to *disperse* after the game was over. The wind *dispersed* the clouds.] —**dis·persed′, dis·pers′ing** —**dis·per′sal** or **dis·per′sion** *n.*

dis·pute (dis pyōōt′) *v.* **1** to argue or discuss a question; debate or quarrel **2** to question or deny the truth of [The United States *disputed* Spain's claim to Cuba.] —**dis·put′ed, dis·put′ing** ◆*n.* a disputing; argument, debate, etc.

dis·re·spect (dis′ri spekt′) *n.* lack of respect or politeness; rudeness —**dis′re·spect′ful** *adj.* —**dis′re·spect′ful·ly** *adv.*

dis·rupt (dis rupt′) *v.* **1** to break apart **2** to disturb the orderly course of [A few noisy members *disrupted* the meeting.] —**dis·rup′tion** *n.*

dis·sat·is·fac·tion (dis sat′is fak′shən) *n.* the condition of being dissatisfied; discontent

dis·sim·i·lar (di sim′ə lər) *adj.* not alike; different —**dis·sim·i·lar·i·ty** (di sim′ə lar′ə tē) *n.*

dis·solve (di zälv′) *v.* **1** to make or become liquid, as by melting in a liquid [to *dissolve* sugar in coffee] **2** to break up and disappear or make disappear [Our courage *dissolved* in the face of danger.] **3** to bring or come to an end; finish [They *dissolved* their partnership.] —**dis·solved′, dis·solv′ing**

a	ask, fat
ā	ape, date
ä	car, lot
e	elf, ten
er	berry, care
ē	even, meet
i	is, hit
ir	mirror, here
ī	ice, fire
ō	open, go
ô	law, horn
oi	oil, point
ŏŏ	look, pull
ōō	ooze, tool
yŏŏ	unite, cure
yōō	cute, few
ou	out, crowd
u	up, cut
ʉ	fur, fern
ə	a in ago
	e in agent
	e in father
	i in unity
	o in collect
	u in focus
ch	chin, arch
ŋ	ring, singer
sh	she, dash
th	thin, truth
th	then, father
zh	s in pleasure
′	as in (ā b'l)

dis·tort (dis tôrt′) **v.** **1** to twist out of its usual shape or look [The old mirror gave a *distorted* reflection.] **2** to change so as to give a false idea [The facts were *distorted*.] **3** to make a sound or signal sound different when reproduced [The sound of music is *distorted* on my new radio.] —**dis·tor′tion n.**

dis·tri·bu·tion (dis′trə byo͞o′shən) **n.** the act or way of distributing something [a *distribution* of funds; a fair *distribution*] —**dis·trib·u·tive** (dis trib′yo͞o tiv) **adj.**

di·ver·si·ty (də vur′sə tē) **n.** **1** the condition of being different or varied; difference [The male and female cardinal show a *diversity* in plumage.] **2** variety [a *diversity* of opinions] —*pl.* **di·ver′si·ties**

doc·u·men·ta·ry (däk′yə men′tə rē) **adj.** **1** made up of documents [You must show *documentary* proof of age.] **2** that shows or presents news events, social conditions, etc. in a story based mainly on facts [a *documentary* film] ◆**n.** a documentary film, TV show, etc. —*pl.* **doc′u·men·ta·ries**

dom·i·nate (däm′ə nāt) **v.** **1** to control or rule; be most important or powerful [A desire to win *dominates* all her actions. The colonies were *dominated* by the mother country.] **2** to tower over; rise high above [These tall buildings *dominate* the city.] —**dom′i·nat·ed, dom′i·nat·ing** —**dom′i·na·tion n.**

Dominate comes from the Latin word for "master," *dominus*, and so do the words **domineer** and **dominion.**

do·min·ion (də min′yən) **n.** **1** the power of governing; rule **2** a territory or country ruled over

Dor·ic (dôr′ik) **adj.** describing the oldest and plainest style of Greek architecture: the columns have no fancy carving at the top

drap·er·y (drā′pər ē) **n.** a curtain or other cloth hanging in loose folds —*pl.* **drap′er·ies**

driz·zle (driz′l) **v.** to rain lightly in fine drops —**driz′zled, driz′zling** —**driz′zly adj.**

du·et (do͞o et′ *or* dyo͞o et′) **n.** **1** a piece of music for two voices or two instruments **2** the two people who sing or play it

du·plex (doo′pleks *or* dyoo′pleks) **adj.** having two parts or units; double [a *duplex* house] ◆☆**n.** *a shorter form of* **duplex house**

du·pli·cate (do͞o′plə kit *or* dyo͞o′plə kit) **adj.** **1** exactly like another or like each other [*duplicate* keys] **2** double ◆**n.** a thing exactly like another; an exact copy [The typist made a *duplicate* of the letter.] ◆**v.** (do͞o′plə kāt *or* dyo͞o′plə kāt) to make an exact copy or copies of —**du′pli·cat·ed, du′pli·cat·ing** —**du′pli·ca′tion n.**

dy·nam·ic (dī nam′ik) **adj.** **1** having to do with energy or force in action **2** full of energy or power; forceful; vigorous [a *dynamic* person] —**dy·nam′i·cal·ly adv.**

ec·cen·tric (ik sen′trik) **adj.** not usual or normal in the way one behaves; odd or queer [an *eccentric* old hermit] ◆**n.** an eccentric person —**ec·cen′tri·cal·ly adv.**

e·clipse (i klips′) **n.** **1** a hiding of all or part of the sun by the moon when it passes between the sun and the earth (called a **solar eclipse**); also, a hiding of the moon by the earth's shadow (called a **lunar eclipse**) **2** a becoming dim or less brilliant [Her fame went into an *eclipse*.] ◆**v.** to cause an eclipse of; darken —**e·clipsed′, e·clips′ing**

e·co·nom·i·cal (ē′kə näm′i k'l *or* ek′ə näm′i k'l) **adj.** not wasting money, time, material, etc; thrifty [an *economical* person; an *economical* car] —**e′co·nom′i·cal·ly adv.**

e·con·o·mize (i kän′ə mīz) **v.** to be economical or to cut down on expenses [She *economized* by riding a bus to work.] —**e·con′o·mized, e·con′o·miz·ing**

ed·i·to·ri·al (ed′ə tôr′ē əl) **adj.** of or by an editor [*editorial* offices] ◆☆**n.** an article in a newspaper or magazine, or a talk on radio or TV, that openly gives the opinion of the editor, publisher, or owner —**ed′i·to′ri·al·ly adv.**

e·las·tic (i las′tik) **adj.** **1** able to spring back into shape or position after being stretched or squeezed; springy [an *elastic* rubber ball] **2** that can easily be changed to fit conditions; adaptable [*elastic* rules] ◆**n.** any cloth or tape with rubber or rubberlike threads running through it to make it elastic —**e·las′ti·cal·ly adv.**

☆**e·lec·tri·cian** (i lek′trish′ən) **n.** a person whose work is setting up or fixing electrical equipment

The word **electrician** was made up by Benjamin Franklin, who was one of the first people to study and experiment with electricity.

e·lec·tro·mag·net (i lek′trō mag′nit) **n.** a piece of soft iron with a coil of wire around it, that becomes a magnet when an electric current passes through the wire —**e·lec·tro·mag·net·ic** (i lek′trō mag net′ik) **adj.**

el·i·gi·ble (el′i jə b'l) **adj.** having the qualities or conditions that are required; qualified [Is the caretaker *eligible* for a pension?] —**el′i·gi·bil′i·ty n.**

el·o·quent (el′ə kwənt) *adj.* **1** having eloquence; stirring people's feelings or having an effect on how they think [an *eloquent* plea to a jury] **2** showing much feeling [an *eloquent* sigh of relief] —**el′o·quent·ly** *adv.*

El Sal·va·dor (el sal′və dôr) a country in western Central America

em·bry·o (em′brē ō) *n.* **1** an animal in the first stages of its growth, while it is in the egg or in the uterus **2** the part of a seed from which a plant develops —*pl.* **em′bry·os**

em·i·nent (em′ə nənt) *adj.* standing above most others in rank, worth, fame, etc.; very famous [an *eminent* scientist] —**em′i·nent·ly** *adv.*

em·phat·ic (im fat′ik) *adj.* **1** said or done with emphasis, or special force [She agreed with an *emphatic* nod.] **2** without doubt; definite [an *emphatic* defeat] —**em·phat′i·cal·ly** *adv.*

en·cap·su·late (in kap′sə lāt *or* in kap′syoo lāt) *v.* to enclose in a capsule or in something like a capsule —**en·cap′su·lat·ed, en·cap′su·lat·ing**

en·dive (en′dīv *or* än′dēv) *n.* a plant with ragged, curly leaves that are used in salads

en·ter·prise (en′tər prīz) *n.* **1** any business or undertaking, especially one that takes daring and energy **2** willingness to undertake new or risky projects [They succeeded because of their *enterprise*.]

en·thu·si·asm (in thoo′zē az′m) *n.* a strong liking or interest [an *enthusiasm* for baseball]

Enthusiasm comes from a Greek word meaning "inspired by a god." Poets and prophets long ago were thought to be inspired by a god. The earliest meaning of *enthusiasm* was "the inspiration of a poet or prophet."

en·tire (in tīr′) *adj.* **1** including all the parts; whole; complete [I've read the *entire* book.] **2** not broken, not weakened, not lessened, etc. [We have his *entire* support.] —**en·tire′ly** *adv.*

e·nun·ci·ate (i nun′sē āt) *v.* **1** to speak or pronounce words [A telephone operator must *enunciate* clearly.] **2** to state clearly; announce [to *enunciate* a theory] —**e·nun′ci·at·ed, e·nun′ci·at·ing** —**e·nun′ci·a′tion** *n.*

en·zyme (en′zīm) *n.* a substance produced in plant and animal cells that causes a chemical change in other substances but is not changed itself [Pepsin is an *enzyme* in the stomach that helps to digest food.]

ep·i·der·mis (ep′ə dur′mis) *n.* the outer layer of the skin of animals: it has no blood vessels

ep·i·gram (ep′ə gram) *n.* a short saying that makes its point in a witty or clever way ["Experience is the name everyone gives to his mistakes" is an *epigram*.] —**ep·i·gram·mat·ic** (ep′i grə mat′ik) *adj.*

ep·i·logue or **ep·i·log** (ep′ə lôg) *n.* a part added at the end of a play, novel, etc., in which the author makes some comment; especially, a closing speech to the audience by one of the actors in a play

ep·i·sode (ep′ə sōd) *n.* any happening or incident that forms part of a whole story, life, history, etc. [The surrender at Appomattox was the last *episode* of the Civil War.]

e·pis·tle (i pis′l) *n.* **1** a letter: *now used in a joking way* **2 Epistle**, any of the letters written by the Apostles and included as books of the New Testament

ep·i·taph (ep′ə taf) *n.* words carved on a tomb in memory of the person buried there

ep·i·thet (ep′ə thet) *n.* a word or phrase that describes a person or thing by naming some quality or feature, as America *the Beautiful*

Epithet comes from a Greek word meaning "something that is put on, or added." An epithet is a description that is added to the regular name.

e·qual (ē′kwəl) *adj.* **1** of the same amount, size, or value [The horses were of *equal* height.] **2** having the same rights, ability, or position [All persons are *equal* in a court of law in a just society.] ◆*n.* any person or thing that is equal [As a sculptor, she has few *equals*.] ◆*v.* **1** to be equal to; match [His long jump *equaled* the school record. Six minus two *equals* four.] **2** to do or make something equal to [You can *equal* my score easily.] —**e′qualed** or **e′qualled, e′qual·ing** or **e′qual·ling** —**e′qual·ly** *adv.*

e·quiv·a·lent (i kwiv′ə lənt) *adj.* equal or the same in amount, value, meaning, etc. ◆*n.* something that is equal or the same [Three teaspoonfuls are the *equivalent* of one tablespoonful.] —**e·quiv′a·lence** *n.*

e·ro·sion (i rō′zhən) *n.* an eroding or wearing away [the *erosion* of soil by water and wind]

es·ca·pade (es′kə pād) *n.* a daring or reckless adventure or prank

es·pe·cial·ly (ə spesh′əl ē) *adv.* mainly; in particular; specially [I like all fruit, but I am *especially* fond of pears.]

et·i·quette (et′i kət *or* et′i ket) *n.* rules that society has set up for the proper way to behave in dealing with other people; good manners [The best *etiquette* is based on being kind and polite to other people.]

Etiquette is a French word that actually means "ticket," "label," or "list." It was first used of the lists of rules that were posted in a court or army camp. We might also say that **etiquette** can be a "ticket" that allows a person to enter polite society.

eu·lo·gy (yoo′lə jē) *n.* a speech or writing praising a person or thing; often, a formal speech praising a person who has just died —*pl.* **eu′lo·gies**

a	ask, fat
ā	ape, date
ä	car, lot
e	elf, ten
er	berry, care
ē	even, meet
i	is, hit
ir	mirror, here
ī	ice, fire
ō	open, go
ô	law, horn
oi	oil, point
oo	look, pull
oo	ooze, tool
yoo	unite, cure
yoo	cute, few
ou	out, crowd
u	up, cut
u	fur, fern
ə	a in ago
	e in agent
	e in father
	i in unity
	o in collect
	u in focus
ch	chin, arch
ŋ	ring, singer
sh	she, dash
th	thin, truth
th	then, father
zh	s in pleasure
′	as in (ā b'l)

eu·phe·mism (yōō'fə miz'm) *n.* **1** a word or phrase that is used in place of another that is thought to be too strong or unpleasant ["Remains" is a *euphemism* for "corpse."] **2** the use of such words or phrases —**eu'phe·mis'tic** *adj.*

eu·pho·ri·a (yōō fôr'ē ə) *n.* a feeling of joy and excitement —**eu·phor'ic** *adj.*

e·ven·tu·al·i·ty (i ven'chōō wal'ə tē) *n.* a possible happening [Be prepared for any *eventuality.*] —*pl.* **e·ven'tu·al'i·ties**

ex·cess (ik ses' *or* ek'ses) *n.* **1** more than what is needed or proper; too much [Eating an *excess* of candy will harm the teeth.] **2** the amount by which one quantity is greater than another [After paying all my bills, I had an *excess* of $50 last month.] ◆*adj.* (*usually* ek'ses) more than the usual limit; extra [Airlines charge for *excess* luggage.] —**in excess of**, more than —**to excess**, too much [to eat *to excess*]

ex·cit·a·ble (ik sīt'ə b'l) *adj.* easily excited —**ex·cit'a·bil'i·ty** *n.*

ex·cla·ma·tion (eks'klə mā'shən) *n.* **1** the act of exclaiming **2** a word or phrase that is exclaimed to show strong feeling; interjection ["Oh!" and "Help!" are *exclamations.*]

ex·clude (iks klōōd') *v.* to keep out or shut out; refuse to let in, think about, include, etc.; bar. [They *excluded* John from their club. Don't *exclude* the possibility of defeat.] —**ex·clud'ed, ex·clud'ing**

ex·clu·sive (iks klōō'siv) *adj.* **1** given or belonging to no other; not shared; sole [That store has the *exclusive* right to sell this Swedish glassware.] **2** keeping out certain people, especially those who are not wealthy or against whom there is prejudice; not open to the public [an *exclusive* club] **3** shutting out all other interests, thoughts, activities, etc. [an *exclusive* interest in sports] —**exclusive of**, not including; leaving out [The workers get two weeks of vacation, *exclusive of* holidays.] —**ex·clu'sive·ly** *adv.*

ex·hib·it (ig zib'it) *v.* **1** to show or display to the public [to *exhibit* stamp collections] **2** to show or reveal [Such an act *exhibits* great courage.] ◆*n.* **1** something exhibited to the public [an art *exhibit*] **2** something shown as evidence in a court of law

ex·hil·a·rate (ig zil'ə rāt) *v.* to make feel cheerful and lively [I was *exhilarated* by the fresh air.] —**ex·hil'a·rat·ed, ex·hil'a·rat·ing** —**ex·hil'a·ra'tion** *n.*

ex·or·bi·tant (ig zôr'bə tənt) *adj.* too much or too great; not reasonable or not fair [an *exorbitant* price] —**ex·or'bi·tance** *n.*

ex·pec·ta·tion (ek'spek tā'shən) *n.* **1** the act of expecting, or looking forward to something [He sat on the edge of his seat in *expectation.*] **2** *often* **expectations**, *pl.* something expected, or looked forward to, especially with good reason [She has *expectations* of being promoted to a better job.]

ex·pel (ik spel') *v.* **1** to drive out or throw out with force; eject [a tea kettle *expelling* steam through its spout] **2** to send away or make leave as a punishment [Paul was *expelled* from the club because he failed to pay his dues.] —**ex·pelled', ex·pel'ling**

ex·pense (ik spens') *n.* **1** the act of spending money, time, etc. **2** *also* **expenses**, *pl.* the amount of money spent; often, money spent or needed for carrying out a job [Many salespersons are paid a salary, plus traveling *expenses.*] **3** something that causes spending [Owning a car is a great *expense.*] **4** loss or sacrifice [The battle was won at terrible *expense.*]

ex·per·i·men·tal (ik sper'ə ment't'l) *adj.* **1** based on or having to do with experiment [an *experimental* science] **2** being an experiment; testing; trial [a baby's first, *experimental* steps] —**ex·per'i·men'tal·ly** *adv.*

ex·pire (ik spīr') *v.* **1** to come to an end; stop [The lease *expires* next month.] **2** to die **3** to breathe out —**ex·pired', ex·pir'ing**

ex·po·si·tion (eks'pə zish'ən) *n.* **1** a large show or fair that is open to the public [Chicago held a great *exposition* in 1893.] **2** explanation, or some writing or speaking that explains something [Your *exposition* of the play was helpful.]

ex·po·sure (ik spō'zhər) *n.* **1** the act of exposing [the *exposure* of a plot] **2** the act of being exposed [tanned by *exposure* to the sun] **3** the position of a house, etc., described by the direction from which it is exposed to sun and wind [Our kitchen has a southern *exposure.*] **4** the time during which film in a camera is exposed to light; also, a section of film that can be made into one picture [Give this film a short *exposure.* There are twelve *exposures* on this film.]

ex·ter·mi·nate (ik stur'mə nāt) *v.* to kill or destroy completely; wipe out [That company's work is *exterminating* rats.] —**ex·ter'mi·nat·ed, ex·ter'mi·nat·ing** —**ex·ter'mi·na'tion, ex·ter'mi·na·tor** *n.*

ex·traor·di·nar·y (ik strôr'd'n er'ē) *adj.* much different from the ordinary; very unusual; remarkable [*extraordinary* skill] —**ex·traor'di·nar'i·ly** *adv.*

Ff

fab·ri·cate (fab′rə kāt) **v.** **1** to make or build by putting parts together; manufacture **2** to make up; invent [He *fabricated* an excuse for being late. In other words, he told a lie.] —**fab′ri·cat·ed, fab′ri·cat·ing** —**fab′ri·ca′tion, fab′ri·ca′tor n.**

fa·çade or **fa·cade** (fə säd′) **n.** **1** the front of a building **2** a grand or fine front that is meant to conceal something not at all grand

fac·et (fas′it) **n.** **1** any of the many polished sides of a cut gem, as a diamond **2** any of the various sides or appearances [the many *facets* of someone's personality]

fa·cil·i·ty (fə sil′ə tē) **n.** **1** ease or skill in working or acting [She reads French with great *facility*.] **2** *usually* **facilities,** *pl.* a thing that helps one do something [The apartment has its own laundry *facilities*.] **3** a building or room for some activity [This added wing is a new *facility* for the nursery school.] —*pl.* **fa·cil′i·ties**

fac·tion (fak′shən) **n.** **1** a group of people inside a political party, club, government, etc. working together against other such groups for its own ideas or goals **2** an arguing or quarreling among the members of a group [bitter *faction* in the Senate over taxes] —**fac′tion·al adj.**

fal·la·cy (fal′ə sē) **n.** **1** a false or mistaken idea, opinion, etc. **2** false reasoning —*pl.* **fal′la·cies**

fas·ci·nate (fas′ə nāt) **v.** to hold the attention of by being interesting or delightful; charm [The puppet show *fascinated* the children.] —**fas′ci·nat·ed, fas′ci·nat·ing** —**fas′ci·na′tion n.**

fer·til·ize (fur′t'l īz) **v.** **1** to make fertile, especially by adding fertilizer to [*Fertilize* your lawn in the spring.] **2** to bring a male germ cell to a female egg cell so as to cause a new animal or plant to develop [Bees *fertilize* flowers by carrying pollen from one to another.] —**fer′til·ized, fer′til·iz·ing** —**fer′til·i·za′tion n.**

fe·tus (fēt′əs) **n.** a human being or an animal in the later stages of its growth inside the uterus or egg —*pl.* **fe′tus·es**

fi·an·cée (fē′än sā′) **n.** the woman who is engaged to marry a certain man

fic·tion (fik′shən) **n.** **1** a piece of writing about imaginary people and happenings, as a novel, play, or story; also, such writings as a group **2** something made up or imagined [What she said about her uncle is just a *fiction*.] —**fic′tion·al adj.**

fi·nesse (fi nes′) **n.** **1** skill in taking care of difficult or touchy problems without causing anger [to show *finesse* in dealing with customers] **2** delicate or skillful work [the *finesse* with which the artist drew a portrait]

fi·nite (fī′nīt) **adj.** having definite limits; that can be measured [*finite* distances]

fis·cal (fis′kəl) **adj.** having to do with money matters; financial —**fis′cal·ly adv.**

flex·i·ble (flek′sə b'l) **adj.** **1** that bends easily without breaking [a *flexible* rubber hose] **2** easily changed or managed [Our doctor has *flexible* office hours.] —**flex′i·bil′i·ty n.**

for·bid (fər bid′) **v.** to order that something not be done; not allow; prohibit [The law *forbids* you to park your car there. Talking out loud is *forbidden* in the library.] —**for·bade** or **for·bad** (fər bad′), **for·bid′den, for·bid′ding**

for·mal·i·ty (fôr mal′ə tē) **n.** **1** the condition of being formal; especially, the following of rules or customs in an exact way **2** a formal act or ceremony [the *formalities* of graduation exercises] —*pl.* **for·mal′i·ties**

frag·ment (frag′mənt) **n.** **1** a piece of something that has broken; a part broken away [*fragments* of a broken cup] **2** a part taken from a whole [a *fragment* of a song]

franc (fraŋk) **n.** the basic unit of money in France, and also in Belgium, Switzerland, etc.

fran·chise (fran′chīz) **n.** **1** a special right or permission given by a government [One must get a *franchise* from the Federal government to operate a TV station.] **2** the right given to a dealer to sell the products of a certain company

fra·ter·nal (frə tur′n'l) **adj.** of or like brothers; brotherly

fra·ter·ni·ty (frə tur′nə tē) **n.** **1** the close tie among brothers; brotherly feeling **2** a club of men or boys, especially a social club, as in a college: fraternities usually have letters of the Greek alphabet for their name **3** a group of people with the same work, interests, beliefs, etc. [Doctors are often called the medical *fraternity*.] —*pl.* **fra·ter′ni·ties**

fre·quen·cy (frē′kwən sē) **n.** **1** the fact of being frequent, or happening often **2** the number of times something is repeated in a certain period [a *frequency* of 1,000 vibrations per second]: the frequency of radio waves is measured in hertz —*pl.* **fre′quen·cies**

fric·tion (frik′shən) **n.** **1** a rubbing of one thing against another **2** arguments or quarrels caused by differences of opinions **3** the force that slows down the motion of surfaces that touch [Ball bearings lessen *friction* in machines.]

a	ask, fat
ā	ape, date
ä	car, lot
e	elf, ten
er	berry, care
ē	even, meet
i	is, hit
ir	mirror, here
ī	ice, fire
ō	open, go
ô	law, horn
oi	oil, point
oo	look, pull
oo	ooze, tool
yoo	unite, cure
yoo	cute, few
ou	out, crowd
u	up, cut
ʉ	fur, fern
ə	a in ago
	e in agent
	e in father
	i in unity
	o in collect
	u in focus
ch	chin, arch
ŋ	ring, singer
sh	she, dash
th	thin, truth
th	then, father
zh	s in pleasure
′	as in (ā b'l)

frieze (frēz) *n.* a band of designs, drawings, or carvings used as a decoration along a wall or around a room

ful·fill or **ful·fil** (fŏŏl fil') *v.* to make happen; carry out, perform, do, complete, etc. [to *fulfill* a promise, a duty, a purpose, a mission] —**ful·filled´, ful·fill´ing** —**ful·fill´ment** or **ful·fil´ment** *n.*

fun·gus (fuŋ'gəs) *n.* a plant that has no leaves, flowers, or green color: mildews, molds, mushrooms, and toadstools are forms of fungus —*pl.* **fun·gi** (fun'jī *or* fuŋ'gī) or **fun´gus·es**

gar·goyle (gär'goil) *n.* a decoration on a building in the form of a strange, imaginary creature: it usually has a channel to let rainwater run off through its mouth

☆**gas·o·line** or **gas·o·lene** (gas ə lēn' *or* gas'ə lēn) *n.* a pale liquid that burns very easily and is used mainly as a motor fuel: it is made from petroleum

gen·er·os·i·ty (jen'ə räs'ə tē) *n.* **1** the quality of being generous **2** a generous or unselfish act —*pl.* **gen´er·os´i·ties**

ge·net·ics (jə net'iks) *pl. n.* the study of the way animals and plants pass on to their offspring such characteristics as size, color, etc.; science of heredity: *used with a singular verb* —**ge·net´ic** *adj.*

☆**ge·o·des·ic** (jē'ə des'ik *or* jē'ə dē'sik) *adj.* having a strong surface made of short, straight bars joined together in a framework [a *geodesic* dome]

ge·o·graph·i·cal (jē'ə graf'i k'l) or **ge·o·graph·ic** (je'e graf'ik) *adj.* having to do with geography —**ge´o·graph´i·cal·ly** *adv.*

ge·o·log·ic (jē'ə läj'ik) or **ge·o·log·i·cal** (jē'ə läj'i k'l) *adj.* having to do with geology —**ge´o·log·´i·cal·ly** *adv.*

ge·om·e·tric (jē'ə met'rik) or **ge·o·met·ri·cal** *adj.* **1** having to do with geometry **2** formed of straight lines, triangles, circles, etc. [a *geometric* pattern]

ger·und (jer'ənd) *n.* a verb ending in -*ing* that is used as a noun: a gerund can take an object [In "Playing golf is my only exercise," the word "playing" is a *gerund*.]

gey·ser (gī'zər) *n.* a spring that shoots streams of boiling water and steam up into the air from time to time

gla·cier (glā'shər) *n.* a large mass of ice and snow that moves very slowly down a mountain or across land until it melts: icebergs are pieces of a glacier that have broken away into the sea

glad·i·a·tor (glad'ē ät'ər) *n.* a man, usually a slave or prisoner, who fought against animals or other men in the arenas of ancient Rome, for the entertainment of the public

glos·sa·ry (gläs'ə rē *or* glôs'ə rē) *n.* a list of hard words with their meanings, often printed at the end of a book —*pl.* **glos´sa·ries**

Glossary comes from a Greek word meaning "tongue." And since the tongue is so important in forming words when we speak, it is easy to see the connection between that old Greek word and our modern term for a list of words.

gram·mar (gram'ər) *n.* **1** the study of the forms of words and of the way they are arranged in phrases and sentences **2** a system of rules for speaking and writing a particular language **3** a book containing such rules **4** the way a person speaks or writes, as judged by these rules [His *grammar* is poor.]

grat·i·tude (grat'ə tŏŏd *or* grat'ə tyŏŏd) *n.* the condition of being grateful for some favor; thankfulness

guard·i·an (gär'dē ən) *n.* **1** a person chosen by a court to take charge of a child or of someone else who cannot take care of his or her own affairs **2** a person who guards or protects; custodian [A sexton is a *guardian* of church property.] —**guard´i·an·ship´**

Gua·te·ma·la (gwä'tə mä'lə) a country in Central America, south and east of Mexico

guild (gild) *n.* **1** in the Middle Ages, a union of men in the same craft or trade to keep the quality of work high and to protect the members **2** any group of people joined together in some work or for some purpose [The Ladies' *Guild* of the church is planning a supper.]

guil·der (gil'dər) *n.* the basic unit of money in the Netherlands

gur·ney (gur'nē) *n.* a stretcher or cot on wheels, used in hospitals to move people who are sick or hurt —*pl.* **gur´neys**

hand·i·cap (han'dē kap) *n.* **1** a race or other contest in which things are made harder for some or easier for others so that all have an equal chance **2** something that holds a person back or makes things harder; hindrance [Lack of education can be a great *handicap*.] ◆*v.* to be or give a handicap; make things harder for —**hand´i·capped, hand´i·cap·ping**

har·mo·nize (här′mə nīz) **v. 1** to be, sing, or play in harmony [Those colors *harmonize* well. The voices *harmonized* in a quartet.] **2** to bring into harmony [to *harmonize* the colors in a room; to *harmonize* a melody]
—**har′mo·nized, har′mo·niz·ing**

har·row·ing (har′ō ing) **adj.** causing pain, fear, or discomfort [The fire was a *harrowing* experience.]

he·red·i·ty (hə red′ə tē) **n. 1** the passing on of certain characteristics from parent to offspring by means of genes in the chromosomes [The color of one's hair is determined by *heredity*.] **2** all the characteristics passed on in this way [Their good health is due to their *heredity*.]

hom·o·nym (häm′ə nim) **n.** a word that is pronounced like another word but that has a different meaning and is usually spelled differently ["Bore" and "boar" are *homonyms*.]

hor·ti·cul·ture (hôr′tə kul′chər) **n.** the science of growing flowers, fruits, and vegetables —**hor′ti·cul′tur·al adj.**
—**hor′ti·cul′tur·ist n.**

hos·pice (häs′pis) **n. 1** a kind of inn where travelers can stop for rest and food, especially one run by monks **2** a place with a homelike feeling where patients who are dying of some disease are taken care of and made comfortable

hos·pi·tal·i·ty (häs′pə tal′ə tē) **n.** a friendly and generous way of treating guests

hos·pi·tal·ize (häs′pi t'l īz′) **v.** to put in a hospital [I was *hospitalized* for a week when I broke my leg.] —**hos′pi·tal·ized′, hos′pi·tal·iz′ing**

hos·tage (häs′tij) **n.** a person given to or taken by an enemy and held prisoner until certain things are done

hos·tel (häs′t'l) **n.** an inn or other place for staying overnight; now often, a shelter for use by hikers

hos·tile (häs′t'l) **adj. 1** of or like an enemy; warlike [*hostile* tribes] **2** having or showing hate or dislike; unfriendly [a *hostile* look]
—**hos′tile·ly adv.**

☆**hy·drant** (hī′drənt) **n.** a closed pipe at a street curb, with a spout that can be opened up so as to draw water from a main waterline; fireplug

hy·drau·lic (hī drô′lik) **adj. 1** worked by the force of a moving liquid [*hydraulic* brakes] **2** hardening under water [*hydraulic* cement] **3** having to do with hydraulics —**hy·drau′li·cal·ly adv.**

hy·dro·plane (hī′drə plān) **n. 1** a small motorboat that skims along on the back of its hull at high speeds **2** *another name for* **seaplane**

hy·gi·en·ist (hī′jē ə nist *or* hī jē′nist) **n.** an expert in hygiene, or the rules of health

hy·per·ten·sion (hī′pər ten′shən) **n.** blood pressure that is much higher than normal

hys·ter·i·cal (his ter′i k'l) **adj. 1** of or like hysteria **2** having or likely to have wild fits of laughing, crying, etc. **3** very funny or comical: *also* **hys·ter′ic**
—**hys·ter′i·cal·ly adv.**

i·den·ti·cal (ī den′ti k'l) **adj. 1** the very same [This is the *identical* house where I was born.] **2** exactly alike [These two pictures are *identical*.] —**i·den′ti·cal·ly adv.**

id·i·om (id′ē em) **n. 1** a phrase or expression that has a meaning different from what the words suggest in their usual meaning ["To catch one's eye," meaning "to get one's attention," is an *idiom*.] **2** the way in which a certain people, writer, group, etc. puts words together to express meaning [the Italian *idiom*; the *idiom* of Shakespeare] —**id·i·o·mat·ic** (id′ē ə mat′ik) **adj.** —**id′i·o·mat′i·cal·ly adv.**

ig·ne·ous (ig′nē əs) **adj.** formed by fire or great heat, especially by the action of volcanoes [Granite is an *igneous* rock.]

im·mac·u·late (i mak′yə lit) **adj. 1** perfectly clean; spotless [an *immaculate* kitchen] **2** without sin; pure [the *immaculate* life of a saint] —**im·mac′u·late·ly adv.**

im·mense (i mens′) **adj.** very large; huge; vast [an *immense* territory] —**im·mense′ly adv.**

im·mi·grate (im′ə grāt) **v.** to come into a foreign country to make one's home [Over 15 million persons *immigrated* into the United States from 1900 to 1955.]
—**im′mi·grat·ed, im′mi·grat·ing**
—**im′mi·gra′tion n.**

im·mo·bi·lize (i mō′bə līz) **v.** to make immobile; keep from moving
—**im·mo′bi·lized, im·mo′bi·liz·ing**

im·pa·tient (im pā′shənt) **adj. 1** not patient; not willing to put up with delay, annoyance, etc. [Some parents become *impatient* when their children cry.] **2** eager to do something or for something to happen [Rita is *impatient* to go swimming.]
—**im·pa′tient·ly adv.**

im·pend (im pend′) **v.** to be about to happen; threaten [Disaster seemed to be *impending*.]

im·per·son·ate (im pʉr′sə nāt) **v. 1** to imitate or mimic in fun [The students *impersonated* their teachers in the school play.] **2** to pretend to be in order to cheat or trick [He was arrested for *impersonating* a police officer.] —**im·per′son·at·ed, im·per′son·at·ing** —**im·per′son·a′tion, im·per′son·a′tor n.**

a	ask, fat
ā	ape, date
ä	car, lot
e	elf, ten
er	berry, care
ē	even, meet
i	is, hit
ir	mirror, here
ī	ice, fire
ō	open, go
ô	law, horn
σi	oil, point
σσ	look, pull
σσ̄	ooze, tool
yσσ	unite, cure
yσσ̄	cute, few
ou	out, crowd
u	up, cut
ʉ	fur, fern
ə	a in ago
	e in agent
	e in father
	i in unity
	o in collect
	u in focus
ch	chin, arch
ŋ	ring, singer
sh	she, dash
th	thin, truth
th	then, father
zh	s in pleasure
′	as in (ā b'l)

im·ple·ment (im′plə mənt) *n.* something used in doing some work; tool or instrument [A plow is a farm *implement*.]
◆*v.* (im′plə ment) to carry out; put into effect [to *implement* a plan]

im·pli·cate (im′plə kāt) *v.* to show that someone has had a part, especially in something bad; involve [Her confession *implicated* Gordon in the crime.] —**im′pli·cat·ed, im′pli·cat·ing**

im·pos·tor (im päs′tər) *n.* a person who cheats or tricks people, especially by pretending to be someone else or a different sort of person

im·promp·tu (im prämp′tōō *or* im prämp′tyōō) *adj., adv.* without preparation or thought ahead of time; offhand [After winning the prize, she gave an *impromptu* speech.]

im·pru·dent (im prōōd′′nt) *adj.* not prudent or careful; rash or indiscreet —**im·pru′dence *n.* —im·pru′dent·ly *adv.***

im·pu·ri·ty (im pyōōr′ə tē) *n.* **1** the condition of being impure [a high level of *impurity*] **2** something mixed in that makes another thing impure [Strain the oil to remove *impurities*.] —*pl.* **im·pu′ri·ties**

in·ac·cu·rate (in ak′yər it) *adj.* not accurate or exact; in error; wrong [an *inaccurate* clock] —**in·ac′cu·rate·ly *adv.***

in·ac·tive (in ak′tiv) *adj.* not active; idle —**in·ac′tive·ly *adv.* —in′ac·tiv′i·ty *n.***

in·au·di·ble (in ô′də b'l) *adj.* not audible; that cannot be heard —**in·au′di·bly *adv.***

in·cin·er·a·tor (in sin′ə rāt′ər) *n.* a furnace for burning trash

in·clude (in klōōd′) *v.* to have or take in as part of a whole; contain [Prices *include* taxes.] —**in·clud′ed, in·clud′ing**

in·cog·ni·to (in′käg nēt′ō *or* in käg′ni tō′) *adv., adj.* using a false name [The king traveled *incognito*.]

in·cu·ba·tor (iŋ′kyə bāt′ər) *n.* **1** a container that is kept warm for hatching eggs **2** a container in which babies who are born too soon are kept warm and protected for a time

in·cur (in kur′) *v.* to bring something bad or unpleasant upon oneself [He *incurred* debts when he was out of work.] —**in·curred′, in·cur′ring**

in·de·ci·sive (in′di sī′siv) *adj.* **1** not able to decide or make up one's mind; hesitating **2** not deciding or settling anything [an *indecisive* reply] —**in′de·ci′sive·ly *adv.***

in·de·pend·ent (in′di pen′dənt) *adj.* **1** not ruled or controlled by another; self-governing [Many colonies became *independent* countries after World War II.] **2** not connected with others; separate [an *independent* grocer] **3** not influenced by others; thinking for oneself [an *independent* voter] ◆*n.* an independent person; especially, ☆a voter who is not a member of any political party —**in′de·pend′ent·ly *adv.***

in·dict (in dīt′) *v.* to accuse of having committed a crime; especially, to order that a suspect be put on trial after being charged with some crime [A grand jury can *indict* a person if it decides there is enough evidence to do so.] —**in·dict′ment *n.***

in·di·ges·tion (in′di jes′chən) *n.* **1** difficulty in digesting food **2** the discomfort caused by this

in·di·vid·u·al·i·ty (in′di vij′ōō wal′ə tē) *n.* **1** the qualities that make a person different from all others [Her unusual use of color shows her *individuality* as an artist.] **2** the condition of being different from others [Houses in the suburbs often have no *individuality*.] —*pl.* **in′di·vid′u·al′i·ties**

In·do·ne·sia (in′də nē′zhə) a country in the Malay Archipelago made up of Java, Sumatra, most of Borneo, and other islands

in·er·tia (in ur′shə) *n.* **1** the natural force in matter that makes it stay at rest or keep on moving in a fixed direction unless it is acted on by an outside force **2** a feeling that keeps one from wanting to do things, make changes, etc. [*Inertia* kept her from looking for a new job.]

Inertia comes from a Latin word meaning "having no skill" or "idle." A person who does not know how to do a certain thing tends to be idle and not do anything. Inertia keeps such a person from moving or acting.

in·ex·pli·ca·ble (in eks′pli kə b'l *or* in′ik splik′ə b'l) *adj.* that cannot be explained or understood —**in·ex′pli·ca·bly *adv.***

in·fe·ri·or·i·ty (in fir′ē ôr′ə tē) *n.* the condition of being inferior

in·fin·i·tive (in fin′ə tiv) *n.* a form of a verb that does not show person, number, or tense, and is usually used with "to" [In "I need to eat" and "I must eat," "eat" is an *infinitive*.]

in·fir·ma·ry (in fur′mə rē) *n.* a room or building where people who are sick or injured are cared for, especially at a school or other institution —*pl.* **in·fir′ma·ries**

in·fla·tion (in flā′shən) *n.* **1** an inflating or being inflated ☆**2** an increase in the amount of money in circulation: it makes the money less valuable and brings prices up

in·sec·ti·cide (in sek′tə sīd) *n.* any poison used to kill insects

in·spect (in spekt′) *v.* **1** to look at carefully; examine [You should *inspect* the bicycle before you buy it.] **2** to examine officially; review [The major will *inspect* Company B.] —**in·spec′tion *n.***

in·spi·ra·tion (in′spə rā′shən) *n.* **1** an inspiring or being inspired [Our cheers gave *inspiration* to the team.] **2** something that inspires thought or action [The ocean was an *inspiration* to the artist.] **3** an inspired idea, action, etc. [Your bringing the camera was an *inspiration*.] **4** a breathing in; inhaling —**in′spi·ra′tion·al** *adj.*

in·stall (in stôl′) *v.* **1** to place in an office or position with a ceremony [We saw the new governor *installed*.] **2** to fix in position for use [to *install* a gas stove] **3** to put or settle in a place [The cat *installed* itself in the big chair.] —**in·stal·la·tion** (in′stə lā′shən) *n.*

in·struc·tion (in struk′shən) *n.* **1** the act of teaching; education [The philosopher spent a lifetime in the *instruction* of others.] **2** something taught; lesson [swimming *instruction*] **3 instructions,** *pl.* orders or directions [*instructions* for a test]

in·te·gral (in′tə grəl) *adj.* **1** necessary to something to make it complete; essential [Wheels are *integral* parts of automobiles.] **2** having to do with integers

in·ter·jec·tion (in′tər jek′shən) *n.* **1** the act of interjecting **2** a word or phrase that is exclaimed to show strong feeling; exclamation ["Oh!" and "Good grief!" are *interjections*.] **3** a remark, question, etc. interjected

in·ter·rog·a·tive (in′tə räg′ə tiv) *adj.* that asks a question [an *interrogative* sentence]

in·ter·rupt (in tə rupt′) *v.* **1** to break in on talk, action, etc. or on a person who is talking, working, etc. [We *interrupt* this program with a news bulletin. Don't *interrupt* me!] **2** to make a break in; cut off [A strike *interrupted* steel production.]

in·ter·scho·las·tic (in′tər skə las′tik) *adj.* between or among schools [*interscholastic* sports]

in·to·na·tion (in′tə nā′shən) *n.* **1** the way of singing or playing notes with regard to correct pitch **2** the way the voice of a person who is talking rises and falls in pitch

in·tra·mur·al (in′trə myoor′əl) *adj.* between or among members of the same school, college, etc. [*intramural* sports]

in·tra·ve·nous (in′trə vē′nəs) *adj.* directly into a vein [an *intravenous* injection]

in·trep·id (in trep′id) *adj.* very brave; fearless; bold —**in·trep′id·ly** *adv.*

in·tro·duc·to·ry (in′trə duk′tər ē) *adj.* that introduces or begins something; preliminary [an *introductory* course in science]

in·va·lid¹ (in′və lid) *n.* a person who is sick or injured, especially one who is likely to be so for some time ◆*adj.* **1** not well; weak and sick [caring for an *invalid* parent] **2** of or for invalids [an *invalid* home]

in·val·id² (in val′id) *adj.* not valid; having no force or value [A check with no signature is *invalid*.]

in·vest (in vest′) *v.* **1** to use or lend money for some business, property, stock, etc. in order to get a profit **2** to spend in order to get something in return [to *invest* much time in a search for a cure] **3** to cause to have; furnish with [The law *invests* a governor with many powers.] —**in·ves′tor** *n.*

in·ves·ti·gate (in ves′tə gāt) *v.* to search into so as to learn the facts; examine in detail [to *investigate* an accident] —**in·ves′ti·gat·ed, in·ves′ti·gat·ing** —**in·ves′ti·ga′tion, in·ves′ti·ga′tor** *n.*

The Latin word from which we took our word **investigate** means "to search out by following the footprints of." Detectives, including a famous one in stories, Sherlock Holmes, have often followed tracks when investigating a crime.

i·o·dine (ī′ə dīn *or* ī′ə din) *n.* a mineral that is a chemical element: it is in the form of dark crystals which can be dissolved in alcohol and used as an antiseptic

I·on·ic (ī än′ik) *adj.* describing a style of Greek architecture in which the columns have decorations like scrolls at the top

☆**i·tem·ize** (īt′əm īz) *v.* to list the items of, one by one [Please *itemize* my purchases.] —**i′tem·ized, i′tem·iz·ing**

Jj

jar·gon (jär′gən) *n.* **1** the special words and phrases used by people in the same kind of work [Sportswriters have a *jargon* of their own, and so do scientists.] **2** talk that makes no sense; gibberish

Jargon comes from an old French word that meant "the sound of chattering by birds." From this it came to mean the kind of talk that one cannot understand any better than one can understand the sounds that birds make.

jeop·ard·y (jep′ər dē) *n.* great danger or risk [A firefighter's life is often in *jeopardy*.]

jour·nal·ism (jʉr′nəl iz′m) *n.* the work of gathering, writing, or editing the news for publication in newspapers or magazines or for broadcasting on radio or television

ju·bi·lant (joo′b'l ənt) *adj.* joyful and proud; rejoicing [*Jubilant* crowds celebrated the victory.] —**ju′bi·lant·ly** *adv.*

a	ask, fat
ā	ape, date
ä	car, lot
e	elf, ten
er	berry, care
ē	even, meet
i	is, hit
ir	mirror, here
ī	ice, fire
ō	open, go
ô	law, horn
oi	oil, point
oo	look, pull
o͞o	ooze, tool
yoo	unite, cure
yo͞o	cute, few
ou	out, crowd
u	up, cut
ʉ	fur, fern
ə	a in ago
	e in agent
	e in father
	i in unity
	o in collect
	u in focus
ch	chin, arch
ŋ	ring, singer
sh	she, dash
th	thin, truth
th	then, father
zh	s in pleasure
	as in (ā b'l)

judg·ment (juj′mənt) *n.* **1** a judging or deciding **2** a decision given by a judge or a law court [The *judgment* was for the defendant.] **3** an opinion; the way one thinks or feels about something [In my *judgment*, she will win the election.] **4** criticism or blame [to pass *judgement* on another] **5** a being able to decide what is right, good, practical, etc.: good sense [a person of clear *judgment*]: *sometimes spelled* **judgement**

ju·di·cial (jōō dish′əl) *adj.* **1** of judges, law courts, or their duties [*judicial* robes; *judicial* duties] **2** ordered or allowed by a court [a *judicial* decree] **3** careful in forming opinions or making decisions; fair [a *judicial* mind] —**ju·di′cial·ly** *adv.*

jun·ior (jōōn′yər) *adj.* **1** the younger: a word written after the name of a son who has exactly the same name as his father: abbreviated **Jr. 2** lower in position or rank [a *junior* executive] ☆**3** of juniors in a high school or college [the *junior* class] ◆*n.* **1** a person who is younger or has a lower rank than another [Her sister is her *junior* by three years.] ☆**2** a student in the next to last year of a high school or college

ju·ven·ile (jōō′və n′l *or* jōō′və nīl) *adj.* **1** young or youthful **2** of, like, or for children or young people [*juvenile* ideas; *juvenile* books] ◆*n.* **1** a child or young person ☆**2** a book for children

kil·o·li·ter (kil′ə lēt′ər) *n.* a unit of volume, equal to 1,000 liters or one cubic meter

kil·o·watt (kil′ə wät) *n.* a unit of electrical power, equal to 1,000 watts

lab·o·ra·to·ry (lab′rə tôr′ē *or* lab′ər ə tôr′e) *n.* a room or building where scientific work or tests are carried on, or where chemicals, drugs, etc. are prepared —*pl.* **lab′o·ra·to′ries**

☆**la·crosse** (lə krôs′) *n.* a ball game played by two teams on a field with a goal at each end: the players use webbed rackets with long handles

lar·ynx (lar′iŋks) *n.* the upper end of the windpipe, that contains the vocal cords

lat·er·al (lat′ər əl) *adj.* of, at, from, or toward the side; sideways [*lateral* movement] —**lat′er·al·ly** *adv.*

lathe (lāth) *n.* a machine for shaping a piece of wood, metal, etc. by holding and turning it rapidly against the edge of a cutting tool

laud·a·ble (lôd′ə b'l) *adj.* deserving praise [a *laudable* performance] —**laud′a·bly** *adv.*

le·gal·i·ty (li gal′ə tē) *n.* the condition of being legal or lawful

leg·end·ar·y (lej′ən der′e) *adj.* of, in, or like a legend [a *legendary* heroine]

length·wise (leŋkth′wīz) *adj., adv.* in the direction of the length [Carry the box in *lengthwise*.]

li·a·bil·i·ty (lī′ə bil′ə tē) *n.* **1** the condition of being liable [*liability* to error; *liability* for damages] **2 liabilities,** *pl.* money owed; debts **3** a condition that acts against one; disadvantage [Small hands can be a *liability* to a pianist.] —*pl.* **li′a·bil′i·ties**

li·a·ble (lī′ə b'l) *adj.* obliged by law to pay; responsible [We caused the accident and are *liable* for the damage done.]

li·bel (lī′b'l) *n.* **1** anything written or printed that harms a person's reputation in an unfair way **2** the act or crime of publishing such a thing ◆*v.* to publish a libel against —**li′beled** or **li′belled, li′bel·ing** or **li′bel·ling** —**li′bel·er** or **li′bel·ler** *n.*

li·bel·ous or **li·bel·lous** (lī′b'l əs) *adj.* containing or making a libel against someone

lib·er·al (lib′ər əl) *adj.* **1** giving freely; generous [a *liberal* contributor to charity] **2** open to new ideas; broad-minded; tolerant **3** broad in range; not limited to one subject or field of study [a *liberal* education] **4** in favor of reform or progress in politics, religion, etc. ◆*n.* a person who is in favor of reform and progress —**lib′er·al·ly** *adv.*

lib·er·ate (lib′ə rāt) *v.* to free as from slavery [to *liberate* prisoners of war] —**lib′er·at·ed, lib′er·at·ing** —**lib′er·a·tor** *n.*

li·brar·i·an (lī brer′ē ən) *n.* **1** a person who is in charge of a library **2** a person who has had special training in order to work in a library

lin·e·ar (lin′ē ər) *adj.* **1** of, made of, or using a line or lines [*linear* boundaries] **2** of length [*linear* measure]

liq·ui·date (lik′wə dāt) *v.* **1** to settle the affairs of a business that is closing, usually because it is bankrupt **2** to pay a debt in full **3** to get rid of, as by killing [The dictator *liquidated* enemies.] —**liq′ui·dat·ed, liq′ui·dat·ing** —**liq′ui·da′tion** *n.*

li·ra (lir′ə) *n.* the basic unit of money in Italy and Turkey —*pl.* **li·re** (lir′ā) or **li′ras**

lit·er·al (lit′ər əl) *adj.* **1** following the original, word for word [a *literal* translation of a French poem] **2** based on the actual words in their usual meaning; not allowing for idiom or exaggeration [The *literal* meaning of "lend an ear" is to let another borrow one's ear.] —**lit′er·al·ly** *adv.*

lit·er·a·ture (lit′ər ə chər) *n.* **1** all the writings of a certain time, country, etc.; especially, those that have lasting value because of their beauty, imagination, etc., as fine novels, plays, and poems **2** the work or profession of writing such things; also, the study of such writings

li·thog·ra·phy (li thäg′rə fē) *n.* the process of printing from a flat stone or metal plate whose surface is treated so that only the parts having the design will hold ink —**li·thog′ra·pher**

log·a·rithm (lôg′ə ri*th*′m) *n.* the figure that tells to what power a certain fixed number, as ten, must be raised to equal a given number [The *logarithm* of 100 is 2, when 10 is taken as the fixed number ($10^2 = 100$).]: such numbers are listed in tables to shorten the working of problems in mathematics

log·i·cal (läj′i k′l) *adj.* **1** based on logic or using logic [a *logical* explanation] **2** that is to be expected because of what has gone before [the *logical* result of one's actions] —**log′i·cal·ly** *adv.*

lu·mi·nous (lo͞o′mə nəs) *adj.* **1** giving off light; bright [the *luminous* rays of the sun] **2** filled with light [a *luminous* room] **3** glowing in the dark [*luminous* paint] —**lu·mi·nos·i·ty** (lo͞o′mə näs′ə tē) *n.*

mag·is·trate (maj′is trāt) *n.* **1** an official with the power to put laws into effect, as the president of a republic **2** a minor official, as a judge in a police court

mag·net·ic (mag net′ik) *adj.* **1** working like a magnet [a *magnetic* needle] **2** that can be magnetized **3** that attracts strongly [*magnetic* eyes]

ma·hog·a·ny (mə häg′ə nē *or* mə hôg′ə nē) *n.* **1** the hard, reddish-brown wood of a tropical American tree, used in making furniture **2** this tree **3** reddish brown —*pl.* **ma·hog′a·nies**

mal·ad·just·ed (mal′ə jus′tid) *adj.* badly adjusted; especially, not able to fit happily into the life around one —**mal′ad·just′ment** *n.*

ma·lev·o·lent (mə lev′ə lənt) *adj.* wishing harm or evil to others; malicious —**ma·lev′o·lence** *n.* —**ma·lev′o·lent·ly** *adv.*

mal·func·tion (mal funk′shən) *v.* to fail to work as it should ◆*n.* an instance of such failure [The launch was delayed by the *malfunction* of a rocket.]

mal·ice (mal′is) *n.* a feeling of wanting to hurt or harm someone; ill will; spite

man·date (man′dāt) *n.* **1** an order or command, especially one in writing **2** the will of the people as made known by their votes in elections **3** control over a territory as formerly given by the League of Nations to one of its member nations; also, the territory so controlled

man·da·to·ry (man′də tôr ē) *adj.* ordered or demanded by someone in power; required

man·i·cure (man′ə kyo͝or) *n.* the care of the hands; especially, the trimming and cleaning of the fingernails ◆*v.* to give a manicure to —**man′i·cured, man′i·cur·ing** —**man′i·cur′ist** *n.*

mar·i·o·nette (mar′ē ə net′) *n.* a puppet or small jointed doll moved by strings or wires and used in putting on shows on a small stage

mark (märk) *n.* the basic unit of money in Germany: *the full name is* **deut·sche mark** (doi′che märk)

mar·riage (mar′ij) *n.* **1** the state of being married; married life **2** the act or ceremony of marrying; wedding

ma·ter·nal (mə tur′n′l) *adj.* **1** of or like a mother; motherly **2** related to one on one's mother's side [my *maternal* aunt] —**ma·ter′nal·ly** *adv.*

ma·ter·ni·ty (mə tur′nə tē) *n.* the condition or character of being a mother; motherhood or motherliness ◆*adj.* for women who are about to become mothers or women who have just had babies [a *maternity* dress; a *maternity* ward in a hospital]

math·e·ma·ti·cian (math′ə mə tish′ən) *n.* an expert in mathematics

mat·ri·mo·ny (mat′rə mō′nē) *n.* the condition of being married; marriage —**mat′ri·mo′ni·al** *adj.*

ma·tron (mā′trən) *n.* **1** a wife or a widow, especially one who is not young **2** a woman who has charge of others, as in a prison

max·i·mum (mak′sə məm) *n.* **1** the greatest amount or number that is possible or allowed [Forty pounds of luggage is the *maximum* you can take.] **2** the highest degree or point reached [Today's *maximum* was 35°C.] —*pl.* **max′i·mums** or **max·i·ma** (mak′sə mə) ◆*adj.* greatest possible or allowed [*maximum* speed]

me·chan·i·cal (mə kan′i k′l) *adj.* **1** having to do with machinery, or having skill in its use **2** made or run by machinery [a *mechanical* toy] **3** acting or done as if by a machine and without thought; automatic [to greet someone in a *mechanical* way] —**me·chan′i·cal·ly** *adv.*

a	ask, fat
ā	ape, date
ä	car, lot
e	elf, ten
er	berry, care
ē	even, meet
i	is, hit
ir	mirror, here
ī	ice, fire
ō	open, go
ô	law, horn
σi	oil, point
o͝o	look, pull
o͞o	ooze, tool
yo͞o	unite, cure
yo͞o	cute, few
σu	out, crowd
u	up, cut
ʉ	fur, fern
ə	a in ago
	e in agent
	e in father
	i in unity
	o in collect
	u in focus
ch	chin, arch
ŋ	ring, singer
sh	she, dash
th	thin, truth
th	then, father
zh	s in pleasure
′	as in (ā b′l)

mel·o·dra·ma (mel′ə drä′mə *or* mel′ə dram′ə) *n.* **1** a play in which there is much suspense and strong feeling, and a great exaggeration of good and evil in the characters **2** any exciting action or talk like that in such a play

Melodrama comes from a Greek word meaning "song" and the French word for "drama." In the original melodramas there were songs sung at various points in the action of the play.

mem·oir (mem′wär) *n.* **1 memoirs**, *pl.* the story of one's life written by oneself; autobiography; also, a written record based on the writer's own experience and knowledge **2** a written story of someone's life; biography

men·u (men′yōō) *n.* a list of the foods served at a meal [a restaurant's dinner *menu*]

mer·can·tile (mur′kən til *or* mur′kən tīl) *adj.* having to do with merchants, trade, or commerce

☆**me·sa** (mā′sə) *n.* a large, high rock having steep walls and a flat top

Mesa is a Spanish word that came from a Latin word meaning "table." Some mesas looked like tables to the Spanish explorers in what is now the southwestern United States.

me·tab·o·lism (mə tab′ə liz′m) *n.* the process in all plants and animals by which food is changed into energy, new cells, waste products, etc. —**met·a·bol·ic** (mət′ə bäl′ik) *adj.*

met·al·lur·gy (met′′l ur′jē) *n.* the science of getting metals from their ores and making them ready for use, by smelting, refining, etc. —**met′al·lur′gi·cal** *adj.* —**met′al·lur′gist** *n.*

met·a·mor·pho·sis (met′ə môr′fə sis) *n.* **1** a change in form; especially, the change that some animals go through in developing, as of tadpole to frog or larva to moth **2** a complete change in the way someone or something looks or acts —*pl.* **met·a·mor·pho·ses** (met′ə môr′fə sēz)

met·a·phor (met′ə fôr) *n.* the use of a word or phrase in a way that is different from its usual use, to show a likeness to something else ["The curtain of night" is a *metaphor* that likens night to a curtain that hides something.]

me·te·or·ol·o·gy (mēt′e ə räl′ə jē) *n.* the science that studies weather, climate, and the earth's atmosphere —**me′te·or·ol′o·gist**

me·trop·o·lis (mə träp′′l is) *n.* **1** the main city of a state, country, or region **2** any large or important city —*pl.* **me·trop′o·lis·es**

Metropolis comes from the ancient Greek words for "mother" and "city." For the ancient Greeks a metropolis was the mother city of a colony.

met·ro·pol·i·tan (met′rə päl′ə t'n) *adj.* **1** of a metropolis [a *metropolitan* park] ☆**2** making up a metropolis [*Metropolitan* Chicago includes the central city and its suburbs.] ◆*n.* a person who lives in, or is at home in, a big city

mi·cro·or·gan·ism (mī′krō ôr′gə niz′m) *n.* any living thing too tiny to be seen without a microscope; especially, any of the bacteria, viruses, protozoans, etc.

mil·li·gram (mil′ə gram) *n.* a unit of weight, equal to one thousandth of a gram

mil·li·li·ter (mil′ə lēt′ər) *n.* a unit of volume, equal to one thousandth of a liter

mim·ic·ry (mim′ik rē) *n.* **1** the art of imitating, or an example of this **2** the way in which some living things look like another or like some natural object —*pl.* **mim′ic·ries**

min·i·a·ture (min′ē ə chər *or* min′i chər) *n.* **1** a very small copy or model [a *miniature* of the Liberty Bell] **2** a very small painting, especially a portrait ◆*adj.* that is a miniature [a *miniature* car]

mis·de·mean·or (mis′di mēn′ər) *n.* a breaking of the law that is less serious than a felony and brings a lesser penalty [It is a *misdemeanor* to throw litter in the streets.]

mo·bile (mō′b'l *or* mō′bīl *or* mō′bēl) *adj.* **1** that can be moved quickly and easily [a *mobile* army] **2** that can change rapidly or easily in response to different moods, conditions, needs, etc. [*mobile* features; *mobile* policies] ◆*n.* (mō′bēl) a kind of sculpture made of flat pieces, rods, etc. that hang balanced from wires so as to move easily in air currents —**mo·bil·i·ty** (mō bil′ə tē)

mod·er·a·tor (mäd′ə rāt′ər) *n.* a person who is in charge of conducting a discussion or debate

mod·i·fy (mäd′ə fī) *v.* **1** to make a small or partial change in [Exploration has *modified* our maps of Antarctica.] **2** to make less harsh, strong, etc. [to *modify* a jail term] **3** to limit the meaning of; describe or qualify [In the phrase "old man" the adjective "old" *modifies* the noun "man."] —**mod′i·fied, mod′i·fy·ing** —**mod′i·fi·ca′tion, mod′i·fi′er** *n.*

☆**mod·ule** (mäj′ōōl) *n.* **1** any of a set of units, as wall cabinets, that can be arranged together in various ways **2** a section of a machine or device that can be detached for some special use [the landing *module* of a spacecraft] —**mod·u·lar** (mäj′ə lər) *adj.*

mol·e·cule (mäl′ə kyōōl) *n.* **1** the smallest particle of a substance that can exist alone without losing its chemical form: a molecule consists of one or more atoms —**mo·lec·u·lar** (mə lek′yə lər) *adj.*

mo·men·tum (mō men′təm) *n.* **1** the force with which a body moves, equal to its mass multiplied by its speed [His sled gained *momentum* as it coasted downhill.] **2** strength or force that keeps growing [The peace movement gained *momentum*.]

mon·arch (män′ərk) *n.* **1** a ruler, as a king, queen, or emperor **2** a large North American butterfly, with reddish-brown wings with black edges

mon·e·tar·y (män′ə ter′e) *adj.* **1** in money; pecuniary [That old car has little *monetary* value.] **2** of the money used in a country [The *monetary* unit of France is the franc.]

mon·o·lith (män′ə lith) *n.* a large block of stone, or a statue, monument, etc. carved from a single, large stone —**mon′o·lith′ic** *adj.*

mon·o·logue or **mon·o·log** (män′ə lôg) *n.* **1** a long speech by one person during a conversation **2** a poem, part of a play, etc. in which one person speaks alone **3** a play, skit, etc. performed by one actor

mo·nop·o·ly (mə näp′ə lē) *n.* **1** complete control of a product or service in some place by a single person or group: a company with a monopoly has no competition and can set prices as it wishes **2** such control given and regulated by a government [The city gave the bus company a *monopoly* for ten years.] **3** the condition of having something all to oneself [No one has a *monopoly* on brains.] —*pl.* **mo·nop′o·lies**

mon·o·tone (män′ə tōn) *n.* **1** a keeping of the same tone or pitch without change, as in talking or singing **2** a person who sings with few if any changes of tone **3** sameness of color, style, etc. [The room was decorated in gray *monotones*.]

Mo·roc·co (mə rä′kō) a country in northwestern Africa —**Mo·roc′can** *adj., n.*

mor·tal (môr′t′l) *adj.* **1** that must die at some time [All men are *mortal*.] **2** of people as beings who must die; human [a *mortal* weakness] **3** causing death of the body or soul [a *mortal* wound; *mortal* sin] **4** lasting until death [*mortal* combat; *mortal* enemies] ◆*n.* a human being

mort·gage (môr′gij) *n.* **1** an agreement in which a person borrowing money gives the lender a claim to property as a pledge that the debt will be paid [The bank holds a *mortgage* of $15,000 on our house.] **2** the legal paper by which such a claim is given ◆*v.* **1** to pledge by a mortgage in order to borrow money [to *mortgage* a home] **2** to put a claim on; make risky [He *mortgaged* his future by piling up debts.] —**mort′gaged, mort′gag·ing**

Mortgage comes from two words in Old French, *mort* and *gage*, that meant "dead" and "pledge." The pledge would be "dead" to the lender if the borrower paid the debt and kept the property that had been pledged. And the pledge would be "dead" to the borrower if he or she failed to pay the debt and lost the property.

☆**mor·ti·cian** (môr tish′ən) *n.* another name for **funeral director**

mor·tu·ar·y (môr′choo wer′ē) *n.* a place where dead bodies are kept before the funeral —*pl.* **mor′tu·ar′ies** ◆*adj.* of death or funerals

☆**muck·rake** (muk′rāk) *v.* to search out dishonest acts of public officials, business people, etc. and make them known, as in newspapers —**muck′raked, muck′rak·ing** —**muck′rak·er** *n.*

mu·nic·i·pal·i·ty (myoo nis′ə pal′ə tē) *n.* a city or town that has self-government in local matters —*pl.* **mu·nic′i·pal′i·ties**

mur·mur (mur′mər) *n.* **1** a low, steady sound, as of voices far away **2** a complaint made in a very low voice ◆*v.* **1** to make a low, steady sound [The wind *murmured* through the trees.] **2** to speak or complain in a very low voice

mu·si·cian (myoo zish′ən) *n.* a person skilled in music, as a composer or one who plays a musical instrument or sings, especially for a living

myr·i·ad (mir′ē əd) *n.* **1** ten thousand: *used mostly in old stories* **2** any very large number [a *myriad* of locusts] ◆*adj.* of a very large number; countless

nar·ra·tive (nar′ə tiv) *n.* **1** a story; a report of happenings; tale **2** the telling of stories or events; narration ◆*adj.* in the form of a story [a *narrative* history of the United States]

neb·u·la (neb′yə lə) *n.* a cloudlike patch seen in the sky at night: it is either a large mass of thin gas or a group of stars too far away to be seen clearly —*pl.* **neb·u·lae** (neb′yə lē) or **neb′u·las** —**neb′u·lar** *adj.*

nec·es·sar·y (nes′ə ser′ē) *adj.* **1** that is needed or must be done; required; essential [Do only the *necessary* repairs.] **2** that cannot be avoided; inevitable [The accident was a *necessary* result of the driver's carelessness.] ◆*n.* something necessary —*pl.* **nec′es·sar′ies**

a	ask, fat
ā	ape, date
ä	car, lot
e	elf, ten
er	berry, care
ē	even, meet
i	is, hit
ir	mirror, here
ī	ice, fire
ō	open, go
ô	law, horn
σi	oil, point
σσ	look, pull
σ̄σ̄	ooze, tool
yσσ	unite, cure
yσ̄σ̄	cute, few
σu	out, crowd
u	up, cut
ʉ	fur, fern
ə	a in ago
	e in agent
	e in father
	i in unity
	o in collect
	u in focus
ch	chin, arch
ŋ	ring, singer
sh	she, dash
th	thin, truth
th	then, father
zh	s in pleasure
′	as in (ā b′l)

ne·ces·si·ty (nə ses′ə tē) *n.* **1** that which is necessary or needed or cannot be done without [Food and shelter are *necessities*.] **2** great need [Call only in case of *necessity*.] **3** poverty; want [to live in great *necessity*] —*pl.* **ne·ces′si·ties**

neg·a·tive (neg′ə tiv) *adj.* **1** saying that something is not so or refusing; answering "no" [a *negative* reply] **2** that does not help, improve, etc. [*negative* criticism] **3** opposite to or lacking something that is positive [He always takes a *negative* attitude and expects the worst.] **4** showing that a certain disease, condition, etc. is not present [The reaction to her allergy test was *negative*.] **5** describing a quantity less than zero or one that is to be subtracted ◆*n.* **1** a word, phrase, or action showing that one does not approve or agree ["No" and "not" are *negatives*.] **2** the film or plate from which a finished photograph is printed: the negative shows the light areas of the original subject as dark and the dark areas as light —**neg′a·tive·ly** *adv.*

neg·lect (ni glekt′) *v.* **1** to fail to do what one should do, as because of carelessness [In her hurry, Sharon *neglected* to lock the door.] **2** to fail to take care of as one should; give too little attention to [He became so busy with work that he began to *neglect* his family.] ◆*n.* the act of neglecting or the condition of being neglected [The old house suffered from *neglect*.]

neg·li·gent (neg′li jənt) *adj.* in the habit of neglecting things; not being careful; careless —**neg′li·gence** *n.* —**neg′li·gent·ly** *adv.*

ne·go·ti·ate (ni gō′shē āt) *v.* **1** to talk over a problem, business deal, dispute, etc. in the hope of reaching an agreement [to *negotiate* a contract] **2** to succeed in crossing, climbing, etc. [to *negotiate* a deep river] —**ne·go′ti·at·ed, ne·go′ti·at·ing** —**ne·go′ti·a′tion, ne·go′ti·a′tor** *n.*

ne·on (nē′än) *n.* a chemical element that is a gas without color or smell: it is found in the air in very small amounts

neu·tron (noo′trän *or* nyoo′trän) *n.* one of the particles that make up the nucleus of an atom: a neutron has no electrical charge

nic·o·tine (nik′ə tēn) *n.* a poisonous, oily liquid found in tobacco leaves: it is used to kill insects

nom·i·na·tive (näm′ə nə tiv) *adj.* showing the subject of a verb or the words that agree with the subject ◆*n.* the case in grammar that shows this

In Latin and some other languages, nouns, pronouns, and adjectives have special endings to show that they are in the **nominative** case. In English, only a few pronouns, such as *I*, *she*, *he*, and *who* are in the nominative case.

non·cha·lant (nän shə länt′ *or* nän′shə lənt) *adj.* not caring; not showing concern; casual [He is *nonchalant* about his debts.] —**non·cha·lance′** *n.* —**non·cha·lant′ly** *adv.*

Nonchalant is a word borrowed from French and comes from two Latin words meaning "to be not warm." A person who is nonchalant does not get warm or passionate about things, but seems always to be cool or lukewarm.

non·ex·ist·ent (nän′ig zis′tənt) *adj.* not existing; not real [to worry over *nonexistent* dangers] —**non′ex·ist′ence** *n.*

☆**no·ta·rize** (nōt′ə rīz) *v.* to sign a legal paper and stamp it with one's seal as a notary public —**no′ta·rized, no′ta·riz·ing**

nu·mer·i·cal (noo mer′i k'l *or* nyoo mer′i k'l) *adj.* **1** of or having to do with a number or numbers; by numbers [to arrange in *numerical* order] **2** shown as a number, not as a letter [In the equation $x + y = 10$, 10 is the only *numerical* quantity.] —**nu·mer′i·cal·ly** *adv.*

o·bit·u·ar·y (ō bich′oo wer′e) *n.* an announcement, as in a newspaper, that someone has died, usually with a brief story of the person's life —*pl.* **o·bit′u·ar′ies**

In talking about unpleasant things, people often try to use softer, or less harsh, words or phrases. Just as we sometimes say of someone who has died that the person "has passed on," the ancient Romans would use the verb *obit*, meaning "has gone forward." From this verb we get **obituary**.

ob·jec·tive (əb jek′tiv) *adj.* **1** not having or showing a strong opinion for or against something; without bias [A judge must remain *objective*.] **2** that shows the object of a verb or of a preposition [In "I gave them to her," "them" and "her" are in the *objective* case.] ◆*n.* **1** something that one tries to reach; goal; purpose [What are your *objectives* in this job?] **2** the objective case —**ob·jec′tive·ly** *adv.* —**ob·jec·tiv·i·ty** (äb′jek tiv′ə tē) *n.*

ob·serv·ant (əb zur′vənt) *adj.* **1** strict in observing, or keeping, a law, custom, etc. [*observant* of the rules of etiquette] **2** paying careful attention; alert [An *observant* student noticed the wrong spelling.] —**ob·serv′ant·ly** *adv.*

ob·serv·a·to·ry (əb zur′və tôr′ē) *n.* a building with telescopes and other equipment in it for studying the stars, weather conditions, etc. —*pl.* **ob·serv′a·to′ries**

ob·sid·i·an (əb sid′ē ən) *n.* a dark, glassy rock formed from the lava of volcanoes

ob·so·lete (äb sə lēt′ *or* äb′sə lēt) *adj.* no longer in use or fashion; out-of-date [an *obsolete* word; an *obsolete* airplane]

ob·sta·cle (äb′sti k'l) *n.* anything that gets in the way or keeps one from going ahead; obstruction [Lack of an education was the main *obstacle* to his success.]

oc·ca·sion·al·ly (ə kā′zhən'l ē) *adv.* now and then; once in a while

oc·cur (ə kur′) *v.* **1** to come into one's mind [The idea never *occurred* to me.] **2** to happen; take place [That event *occurred* years ago.] —**oc·curred′, oc·cur′ring**

oc·ta·gon (äk′tə gän) *n.* a flat figure having eight angles and eight sides

o·mit (ō mit′) *v.* to leave out [You may *omit* the raisins.] —**o·mit′ted, o·mit′ting**

o·paque (ō pāk′) *adj.* **1** that cannot be seen through; not letting light through; not transparent [an *opaque* screen] **2** not shiny; dull [The desk had an *opaque* surface.] **3** hard to understand [an *opaque* remark]

op·por·tu·ni·ty (äp′ər tōō′nə tē *or* äp′ər tyōō′nə tē) *n.* a time or occasion that is right for doing something; good chance [You will have an *opportunity* to ask questions after the talk.] —*pl.* **op′por·tu′ni·ties**

op·pose (ə pōz′) *v.* **1** to act or be against; fight or resist [The mayor *opposes* raising taxes.] **2** to put opposite or in contrast; set against [To each of his arguments the lawyer *opposed* one of her own.] —**op·posed′, op·pos′ing**

op·press (ə pres′) *v.* **1** to trouble the mind of; worry; weigh down [*oppressed* by a feeling of fear] **2** to keep down by the cruel use of power; rule in a very harsh way [Pharaoh *oppressed* the Israelite slaves.] —**op·pres′sor** *n.*

op·ti·cian (äp tish′ən) *n.* a person who makes or sells eyeglasses and other optical supplies

op·ti·mism (äp′tə miz'm) *n.* **1** a bright and hopeful feeling about life, in which one expects things to turn out all right **2** the belief that there is more good than evil in life —**op′ti·mis′tic** *adj.* —**op′ti·mis′ti·cal·ly** *adv.*

op·tion (äp′shən) *n.* **1** the act of choosing; choice [I had no *option* but to go.] **2** the right of choosing [They have the *option* of taking a vacation now or in the winter.]

op·u·lent (äp′yə lənt) *adj.* **1** wealthy; rich [an *opulent* nation] **2** in great amounts; abundant [an *opulent* growth of hair] —**op·u·lence** (äp′yə ləns) *n.*

or·di·nance (ôr′d'n əns) *n.* **1** an order, command, or rule ☆**2** a law, especially one made by a city government [an *ordinance* forbidding jaywalking]

or·na·ment (ôr′nə mənt) *n.* **1** anything added or put on to make something look better; decoration [Christmas-tree *ornaments*] **2** a person whose character or talent makes the whole group seem better [That teacher is an *ornament* to the profession.] ◆*v.* (ôr′nə ment′) to add ornaments to; decorate

Ot·to·man (ät′ə mən) *n.* **1** *another name for* **Turk** —*pl.* **Ot′to·mans 2 ottoman**, a low seat without back or arms; also, a padded footstool ◆*adj.* another word for **Turkish**

o·ver·lap (ō vər lap′) *v.* to lap over part of something or part of each other [The scales on a fish *overlap* one another. The two events *overlapped* in time.] —**o·ver·lapped′, o·ver·lap′ping** ◆*n.* (ō′vər lap) **1** the act of overlapping **2** a part that overlaps

pag·eant (paj′ənt) *n.* **1** a large, elaborate public show, parade, etc. **2** an elaborate play based on events in history, often performed outdoors

Pa·ki·stan (pä′ki stän′ *or* pak′i stan′) a country in southern Asia, on the Arabian Sea

par·a·ble (par′ə b'l) *n.* a short, simple story that teaches a moral lesson, as in the Bible

par·a·dox (par′ə däks) *n.* **1** a statement that seems to contradict itself or seems false, but that may be true in fact; *example*: "Water, water, everywhere, and not a drop to drink." **2** a statement that contradicts itself and is false; *example*: The sun was so hot we nearly froze. **3** a person or thing that seems full of contradictions —**par′a·dox′i·cal** *adj.*

par·al·lel (par′ə lel) *adj.* **1** moving out in the same direction and always the same distance apart so as to never meet, as the tracks of a sled in the snow **2** similar or alike [Their lives followed *parallel* courses.] ◆*n.* **1** a parallel line, plane, etc. **2** something similar to or like something else [Your experience is a *parallel* to mine.] **3** a comparison showing how things are alike [The teacher drew a *parallel* between the two books.] **4** any of the imaginary circles around the earth parallel to the equator that mark degrees of latitude [New Orleans is on the 30th *parallel* north of the equator.] ◆*v.* to be in a parallel line or plane with [The road *parallels* the river.] —**par′al·leled** or **par′al·lelled, par′al·el·ing** or **par′al·lel·ling**

a	ask, fat
ā	ape, date
ä	car, lot
e	elf, ten
er	berry, care
ē	even, meet
i	is, hit
ir	mirror, here
ī	ice, fire
ō	open, go
ô	law, horn
oi	oil, point
ōō	look, pull
ōō	ooze, tool
yōō	unite, cure
yōō	cute, few
ou	out, crowd
u	up, cut
ʉ	fur, fern
ə	a in ago
	e in agent
	e in father
	i in unity
	o in collect
	u in focus
ch	chin, arch
ŋ	ring, singer
sh	she, dash
th	thin, truth
th	then, father
zh	s in pleasure
′	as in (ā b'l)

pa·ral·y·sis (pə ral′ə sis) *n.* **1** a loss of the power to move or feel in any part of the body, as because of injury to the brain or spinal cord **2** a condition of being powerless or helpless to act [a *paralysis* of industry]

☆**par·a·med·ic** (par′ə med′ik) *n.* a person doing paramedical work

☆**par·a·med·i·cal** (par′ə med′i k'l) *adj.* being or having to do with persons whose work is helping doctors and nurses: paramedical workers, such as midwives or nurses' aides, get special training

par·a·phrase (par′ə frāz) *n.* a putting of something spoken or written into different words having the same meaning ◆*v.* to write or say in a paraphrase —**par′a·phrased, par′a·phras·ing**

par·a·site (per′ə sīt) *n.* **1** a plant or animal that lives on or in another plant or animal and gets food from it [Mistletoe and fleas are *parasites*.] **2** a person who lives at another's expense without paying that person back in any way

pa·ren·the·sis (pə ren′thə sis) *n.* **1** a word, phrase, etc. put into a complete sentence as an added note or explanation and set off, as between curved lines, from the rest of the sentence **2** either or both of the curved lines () used to set off such a word, phrase, etc. —*pl.* **pa·ren·the·ses** (pə ren′thə sēz)

Parenthesis comes from a Greek word meaning "to put beside." Words in parentheses are put beside other words to explain them.

par·o·dy (par′ə dē) *n.* a piece of writing or music that imitates another in such a way as to make fun of it —*pl.* **par′o·dies** ◆*v.* to make fun of by imitating —**par′o·died, par′o·dy·ing**

par·quet (pär kā′) *n.* **1** a flooring made of pieces of wood fitted together to form a pattern **2** the main floor of a theater; orchestra

par·tic·i·pate (pär tis′ə pāt) *v.* to take part with others; have a share [Sue *participated* in the school play.] —**par·tic′i·pat·ed, par·tic′i·pat·ing** —**par·tic′i·pa′tion, par·tic′i·pa′tor** *n.*

par·ti·ci·ple (pär′tə sip′'l) *n.* a form of a verb used as both a verb and an adjective: participles have tense and voice, and can take an object [In "He is humming a tune," "humming" is a present *participle* used as a verb. In "a man dressed in gray," "dressed" is a past *participle* used as an adjective.]

par·tic·u·lar (pər tik′yə lər) *adj.* **1** of only one person, group, part, or thing; not general; individual [What is your *particular* opinion?] **2** apart from any other; specific [Do you have a *particular* color in mind?] **3** more than ordinary; unusual; special [Pay *particular* attention.] **4** hard to please; very careful [They are *particular* about what movies they see.] ◆*n.* a detail; fact; item [Give full *particulars* about the robbery to the police.]

pa·trol (pə trōl′) *v.* to make regular trips around a place in order to guard it —**pa·trolled′, pa·trol′ling** ◆*n.* **1** a patrolling **2** a person or group that patrols **3** a group of soldiers, ships, or airplanes used to guard an area or to get information about the enemy

pe·cul·iar (pi kyōōl′yər) *adj.* **1** odd; strange; queer [Things look *peculiar* through these dark glasses.] **2** of a particular person, thing, or group; special; distinctive [These markings are *peculiar* to this bird.] —**pe·cul′iar·ly** *adv.*

ped·es·tal (ped′is t'l) *n.* **1** the piece at the bottom that holds up a statue, column, lamp, etc. **2** any base, especially a high one

pe·di·at·rics (pē′dē at′riks) *pl. n.* the branch of medicine that has to do with the care and treatment of babies and children; *used with a singular verb* —**pe′di·at′ric** *adj.*

pend·ant (pen′dənt) *n.* an ornament that hangs down, as a locket or earring

pen·du·lum (pen′doo ləm *or* pen′d'l əm) *n.* a weight hung so that it swings freely back and forth, often used to control a clock's movement

per·en·ni·al (pə ren′ē əl) *adj.* **1** that lives for more than two years: said of certain plants **2** returning or becoming active again and again [Raising money for new sports equipment is a *perennial* problem.] **3** lasting or going on for a long time [to seek *perennial* youth] ◆*n.* a plant that lives for more than two years —**per·en′ni·al·ly** *adv.*

per·ma·nent (pʉr′mə nənt) *adj.* lasting or meant to last for a very long time [One's *permanent* teeth should last as long as one lives.] ◆*n.* a hair wave put in by means of chemicals and lasting for months: *the full name is* **permanent wave** —**per′ma·nence** or **per′ma·nen·cy** *n.* —**per′ma·nent·ly** *adv.*

per·mit (pər mit′) *v.* **1** to give consent to; let; allow [Will you *permit* me to help you?] **2** to give a chance [We'll fly if the weather *permits*.] —**per·mit′ted, per·mit′ting** ◆*n.* (pʉr′mit) a paper, card, etc. showing permission; license [a *permit* to carry a gun]

per·pen·dic·u·lar (pʉr′pən dik′yə lər) *adj.*
1 at right angles [The wall should be *perpendicular* to the floor.] **2** straight up and down; exactly upright [a *perpendicular* flagpole] ◆*n.* a line that is at right angles to the horizon, or to another line or plane [The Leaning Tower of Pisa leans away from the *perpendicular*.]

per·pet·u·al (pər pech′ᴏᴏ wəl) *adj.* **1** lasting forever or for a long time **2** continuing; constant [a *perpetual* bore]
—**per·pet′u·al·ly** *adv.*

per·plex (pər pleks′) *v.* to make unsure of what to do; fill with doubt; confuse or puzzle [Your silence *perplexes* me.]

per·son·al·i·ty (pʉr′sə nal′ə tē) *n.* **1** all the special qualities which make a person different from other people **2** personal qualities that attract others to one; charm, energy, cleverness, etc. [Your friend is smart, but has no *personality*.] **3** a person; especially, a very unusual or famous person
—*pl.* **per′son·al′i·ties**

per·son·i·fy (pər sän′ə fī) *v.* **1** to think of or show some idea or thing as a person [A ship is *personified* when it is referred to as "she."] **2** to be a good example of some quality, idea, etc. [Tom Sawyer *personifies* the spirit of boyhood.] —**per·son′i·fied, per·son′i·fy·ing** —**per·son·i·fi·ca′tion** *n.*

per·spec·tive (pər spek′tiv) *n.* **1** the way things look from a given point according to their size, shape, distance, etc. [*Perspective* makes things far away look small.] **2** the art of picturing things so that they seem close or far away, big or small, etc., just as they look to the eye when viewed from a given point **3** a certain point of view in understanding or judging things or happenings, especially one that shows them in their true relations to one another [Working in a factory will give you a new *perspective* on labor problems.]

pe·so (pā′sō) *n.* the basic unit of money in Argentina, Colombia, Cuba, Mexico, etc.
—*pl.* **pe′sos**

pe·ti·tion (pə tish′ən) *n.* **1** a strong, serious request, as a prayer **2** a formal, written request to someone in authority, signed by a number of people ◆*v.* to make a petition to or a request for [The mayor of our town has *petitioned* the governor for flood relief.]
—**pe·ti′tion·er** *n.*

phar·ma·cist (fär′mə sist) *n.* a person who is trained to prepare and sell drugs and medicine according to the orders of a doctor; druggist

phar·ma·cy (fär′mə sē) *n.* **1** the work of preparing drugs and medicines according to a doctor's orders **2** a place where this is done; drugstore —*pl.* **phar′ma·cies**

phil·har·mon·ic (fil′här män′ik) *adj.* loving music [a *philharmonic* society] ◆*n.* a society that supports a symphony orchestra; also, such an orchestra

physical therapy (fiz′i k'l ther′ə pē) *n.* the treatment of disease or injury by physical means rather than with drugs, as by exercise, massage, heat, baths, etc.
—**physical therapist**

phys·ics (fiz′iks) *pl. n.* the science that deals with energy and matter, and studies the ways that things are moved and work is done: *used with a singular verb* [*Physics* includes the study of light, heat, sound, electricity, and mechanics.]

plan·e·tar·i·um (plan′ə ter′ē əm) *n.* a room with a large dome ceiling on which images of the heavens are cast by a special projector: the natural movements of the sun, moon, planets, and stars can be shown in these images

plaque (plak) *n.* **1** a thin, flat piece of metal, wood, etc. with decoration or lettering on it: plaques are hung on walls, set in monuments, etc. **2** a thin film that forms on the teeth: it hardens into tartar if it is not removed

pleas·ant (plez′'nt) *adj.* **1** that gives pleasure; bringing happiness; enjoyable [a *pleasant* day in the park] **2** having a look or manner that gives pleasure; likable [a *pleasant* person] —**pleas′ant·ly** *adv.*
—**pleas′ant·ness** *n.*

po·et·ic (pō et′ik) *adj.* **1** of, like, or fit for a poet or poetry [*poetic* talent; *poetic* language] **2** written in verse [*poetic* drama] *Also sometimes* **po·et′i·cal**
—**po·et·i·cal·ly** *adv.*

pol·i·tics (päl′ə tiks) *pl. n.* **1** the science of government; political science **2** the act of taking part in political affairs, often as a profession **3** the use of schemes to get what one wants, especially power [office *politics*]: *this word is used with a singular verb in meanings* 1, 2, *and* 3

pol·len (päl′ən) *n.* the yellow powder found on the stamens of flowers: it is made up of male cells which fertilize another flower when carried to its pistil, as by bees or the wind

por·ce·lain (pôr′s'l in) *n.* a fine, white, hard earthenware used in making bathtubs, sinks, tiles, etc.: porcelain used for dishes is called **china**

Por·tu·gal (pôr′chə gəl) a country in southwestern Europe, west of Spain: it includes the Azores and the Madeira Islands

pos·ses·sion (pə zesh′ən) *n.* **1** the fact of possessing, holding, or owning; ownership [to have *possession* of secret information] **2** something that one owns [This vase is my most prized *possession*.] **3** territory ruled by an outside country [Guam is a *possession* of the United States.]

a	ask, fat
ā	ape, date
ä	car, lot
e	elf, ten
er	berry, care
ē	even, meet
i	is, hit
ir	mirror, here
ī	ice, fire
ō	open, go
ô	law, horn
oi	oil, point
ᴏᴏ	look, pull
o͞o	ooze, tool
yᴏᴏ	unite, cure
y͞oo	cute, few
ou	out, crowd
u	up, cut
ʉ	fur, fern
ə	a in ago
	e in agent
	e in father
	i in unity
	o in collect
	u in focus
ch	chin, arch
ŋ	ring, singer
sh	she, dash
th	thin, truth
th	then, father
zh	s in pleasure
′	as in (ā b'l)

pos·ses·sive (pə zes′iv) *adj.* **1** having or showing a strong feeling for owning or keeping things [a *possessive* person] **2** in grammar, describing the case of words that shows ownership, origin, etc. [The *possessive* case of English nouns is formed by adding 's or ' (the *neighbor's* dog; *Jesus'* teachings). "My," "mine," "your," "yours," "its," etc. are *possessive* pronouns.] ◆*n.* **1** the possessive case **2** a word in this case
—**pos·ses′sive·ly** *adv.*
—**pos·ses′sive·ness** *n.*

pound (pound) *n.* **1** a unit of weight, usually equal to 16 ounces: one pound equals 453.59 grams **2** the basic unit of money in the United Kingdom, equal to 100 pennies; also, the basic unit of money in certain other countries, as Ireland, Israel, Sudan, etc. £ is the symbol for this unit of money

prac·ti·cal (prak′ti k'l) *adj.* **1** that can be put to use; useful and sensible [a *practical* idea; *practical* shoes] **2** dealing with things in a sensible and realistic way [Wouldn't it be more *practical* to paint it yourself than pay to have it painted?] **3** learned through practice or experience [*practical* nursing]
—**prac′ti·cal′i·ty** (-kal′ə tē) *n.*

pre·am·ble (prē′am′b'l) *n.* the part of the beginning of a document such as a constitution or law that tells its reason and purpose

pre·cinct (prē′siŋkt) *n.* ☆**1** any of the districts into which a ward or city is divided [a voting *precinct*; a police *precinct*] **2** usually **precincts**, *pl.* the grounds inside the limits of a church, school, etc. **3** a boundary or limit

pre·clude (pri klood′) *v.* to make impossible; shut out; prevent [His care *precluded* any chance of failure.]
—**pre·clud′ed, pre·clud′ing**

pred·i·cate (pred′ə kit) *n.* the word or words that say something about the subject of a sentence or clause: a predicate may be a verb, a verb and adverb, a verb and its object, etc. [The wind *blows.* The wind *blows hard.* The wind *blows the leaves down.*] ◆*adj.* of or in a predicate [In the sentence "Julie is ill," "ill" is a *predicate* adjective.] ◆*v.* (pred′ə kāt) to base upon certain facts, conditions, etc. [The decisions of the courts are *predicated* upon the Constitution.] —**pred′i·cat·ed, pred′i·cat·ing**

pre·fer (pri fur′) *v.* **1** to like better; choose first [He *prefers* baseball to football.] **2** to bring before a law court [She *preferred* charges against the thief who stole her car.]
—**pre·ferred′, pre·fer′ring**

preg·nan·cy (preg′nən sē) *n.* the condition of being pregnant —*pl.* **preg′nan·cies**

preg·nant (preg′nənt) *adj.* having an unborn child or offspring growing in the uterus; with young

prej·u·dice (prej′ə dis) *n.* **1** an opinion formed without knowing the facts or by ignoring the facts; unfair or unreasonable opinion [Some people have a *prejudice* against modern art.] **2** dislike or distrust of people just because they are of another race, religion, country, etc. ◆*v.* to fill with prejudice [Joan *prejudiced* her sister against their uncle.] —**prej′u·diced, prej′u·dic·ing**

pre·lim·i·nar·y (pri lim′ə ner′e) *adj.* leading up to the main action; introductory [the *preliminary* matches before the main bout] ◆*n.* something that is done first; preliminary step [When the *preliminaries* were over, the meeting began.]
—*pl.* **pre·lim′i·nar′ies**

prel·ude (prel′yood *or* prē′lood) *n.* **1** a part that comes before or leads up to what follows [The calm was a *prelude* to the storm.] **2** a part at the beginning of a piece of music, as of a fugue; also, a short, romantic piece of music

pre·ma·ture (prē mə toor′ *or* prē mə choor′) *adj.* before the usual or proper time; too early or too hasty
—**pre·ma·ture′ly** *adv.*

pre·mier (pri mir′) *n.* a chief official; especially, a prime minister ◆*adj.* first in importance or position; chief

pre·mo·ni·tion (prē′mə nish′ən) *n.* a feeling that something bad will happen; forewarning

prep·o·si·tion (prep′ə zish′ən) *n.* a word that connects a noun or pronoun to something else in the sentence, as to a verb [we went *to* the store], to a noun [the sound *of* music], or to an adjective [good *for* you]

pre·sup·pose (prē sə pōz′) *v.* **1** to suppose beforehand; take for granted [Her questions *presuppose* that we have read the book.] **2** to need or show as a reason [A healthy body *presupposes* a proper diet.]
—**pre·sup·posed′, pre·sup·pos′ing**
—**pre·sup·po·si·tion** (prē′sup ə zish′ən) *n.*

prev·a·lent (prev′ə lənt) *adj.* that exists, happens, etc. over a wide area; common; general [a *prevalent* belief]
—**prev′a·lence** *n.*

pri·ma·ry (prī′mer′e *or* prī′mər ē) *adj.* **1** first in time or order [the *primary* grades in school] **2** from which others are taken or made; basic [Red, yellow, and blue are the *primary* colors in painting.] **3** first in importance; chief [a matter of *primary* interest] ◆*n.* **1** something first in order, importance, etc. ☆**2** an election in which candidates are chosen for a later election
—*pl.* **pri′ma′ries**

prim·i·tive (prim′ə tiv) *adj.* **1** of or living in earliest times; ancient [Some *primitive* peoples worshiped the sun.] **2** like that of earliest times; crude; simple [*primitive* art] ◆*n.* a primitive person or thing
—**prim′i·tive·ly** *adv.*

pro·ce·dure (prə sē′jər) *n.* a way or method of doing something [the correct *procedure* to follow during a fire drill]

pro·ces·sion (prə sesh′ən) *n.* **1** a number of persons or things moving forward in an orderly way **2** the act of moving in this way

pro·duc·tion (prə duk′shən) *n.* **1** the act of producing [The new steel plant began *production* last week.] **2** the amount produced [The new machinery increased *production*.] **3** something that is produced, as a play that is staged for the public

pro·fes·sor (prə fes′ər) *n.* a teacher; especially, a college teacher of the highest rank —**pro·fes·so·ri·al** (prō′fə sôr′ē əl) *adj.* —**pro·fes′sor·ship** *n.*

pro·logue (prō′lôg) *n.* **1** an introduction to a poem, play, etc; especially, lines spoken by an actor before a play begins **2** any action or happening that serves as an introduction to another, more important happening

pro·pel·ler (prə pel′ər) *n.* a device made up of blades mounted on a shaft, which is turned by an engine for driving an airplane, ship, etc.

prop·er·ty (präp′ər tē) *n.* **1** something owned, especially land or real estate [There is much loss of *property* because of fire. We have a fence around our property.] **2** any of the special qualities by which a thing is known; characteristic [Oxygen has the *properties* of being colorless, odorless, and tasteless.] —*pl.* **prop′er·ties**

proph·et (präf′it) *n.* **1** a religious leader who is believed to speak for God or a god, as in giving messages or warnings [Isaiah was a *prophet*. The Greek oracles were *prophets*.] **2** a person who claims to tell what will happen in the future

pro·pos·al (prə pō′z'l) *n.* **1** the act of suggesting or offering **2** something proposed, as a plan or scheme [The council approved the mayor's *proposal*.] **3** an offer of marriage

pro·pri·e·tar·y (prə prī′ə ter′ē) *adj.* **1** owned by a person or company, as under a patent, trademark, or copyright [A *proprietary* medicine is patented.] **2** owning property [the *proprietary* classes] **3** of ownership [*proprietary* rights]

pro·pri·e·tor (prə prī′ə tər) *n.* a person who owns and sometimes also operates a store or business —**pro·pri′e·tor·ship′**

pro·pul·sion (prə pul′shən) *n.* **1** a propelling, or driving forward **2** a force that propels

prose (prōz) *n.* speech or writing that is not poetry; ordinary language.

Prose comes from a Latin phrase meaning "direct speech." Prose is the form of language we ordinarily speak and write to each other. It does not have a formal pattern of rhyme or meter, as poetry usually does.

pro·té·gé (prōt′ə zhā) *n.* a person who is helped and guided in his or her career by another

pro·to·col (prōt′ə kôl) *n.* the manners and forms that are accepted as proper and polite in official dealings, as between the ministers of different countries

Protocol comes from the Greek words for "first" and "glue," and originally meant the first leaf glued to a document, describing what was in it. From this it came to mean the document telling of points of agreement reached by countries making a treaty. Later it also came to mean the code of behavior in ceremonies and dealings between high officials.

pro·trude (prō trood′) *v.* to stick out; project; extend [*protruding* front teeth] —**pro·trud′ed, pro·trud′ing** —**pro·tru·sion** (prō troo′zhən) *n.*

prov·erb (präv′ərb) *n.* an old and familiar saying that tells something wise ["A stitch in time saves nine" is a *proverb*.]

prov·ince (präv′ins) *n.* **1** a region in or belonging to a country, having its own local government; especially, any of the ten divisions of Canada that are like the States **2** provinces, *pl.* the parts of a country away from the large cities **3** range of duties or work [Enforcing laws falls within the *province* of a police department.]

pro·voke (prə vōk′) *v.* **1** to annoy or make angry [It *provoked* me to see litter on the lawn.] **2** to arouse or call forth [The clown's antics *provoked* laughter from the crowd.] —**pro·voked′, pro·vok′ing**

Provoke comes from Latin words that mean "to call forth." One might say that to provoke someone is to call forth some kind of reaction, so that the person becomes curious, angry, amused, etc.

prox·y (präk′sē) *n.* **1** a person who is given the power to act for another, as in voting; agent **2** a statement in writing giving such power **3** the action of a proxy [to vote by *proxy*] —*pl.* **prox′ies**

pru·dent (prood′ənt) *adj.* careful or cautious in a sensible way; not taking chances; wise —**pru′dence** *n.* —**pru′dent·ly** *adv.*

pseu·do·nym (soo′də nim *or* syoo′də nim) *n.* a name used by a writer or other person in place of the real name [O. Henry is the *pseudonym* of William Sydney Porter.]

psy·chi·a·trist (sə kī′ə trist *or* sī kī′ə trist) *n.* a doctor who takes care of people who are mentally ill

psy·chol·o·gy (sī käl′ə jē) *n.* **1** the science that studies the mind and the reasons for the ways that people think and act **2** the ways of thinking and acting of a person or group [the *psychology* of the child; mob *psychology*] —*pl.* **psy·chol′o·gies** —**psy·chol′o·gist**

a	ask, fat
ā	ape, date
ä	car, lot
e	elf, ten
er	berry, care
ē	even, meet
i	is, hit
ir	mirror, here
ī	ice, fire
ō	open, go
ô	law, horn
oi	oil, point
oo	look, pull
o͞o	ooze, tool
yoo	unite, cure
yo͞o	cute, few
ou	out, crowd
u	up, cut
ʉ	fur, fern
ə	a in ago
	e in agent
	e in father
	i in unity
	o in collect
	u in focus
ch	chin, arch
ŋ	ring, singer
sh	she, dash
th	thin, truth
th	then, father
zh	s in pleasure
′	as in (ā b'l)

pub·lic·i·ty (pə blis′ə tē) *n.* ☆**1** information that brings a person, place, or thing to the attention of the public [The newspapers gave much *publicity* to our play.] **2** the attention of the public [A politician seeks *publicity*.] **3** things done or the business of doing things to get public attention [An agent handles the rock star's *publicity*.]

punc·tu·al (puŋk′choo wəl) *adj.* coming, or doing something, at the right time; prompt —**punc′tu·al′i·ty** *n.* —**punc′tu·al·ly** *adv.*

quad·ri·lat·er·al (kwäd′rə lat′ər əl) *adj.* having four sides ➤*n.* a flat figure with four sides and four angles

quar·an·tine (kwôr′ən tēn) *n.* **1** the act of keeping a diseased person, animal, or plant away from others so that the disease will not spread **2** a place where such persons, animals, or plants are kept **3** the time during which a ship is kept in port while the passengers, cargo, etc. are inspected for some disease ➤*v.* **1** to put in a place of quarantine **2** to cut off, as a country, from dealings with another or others —**quar′an·tined, quar′an·tin·ing**

Quarantine comes from an Italian word meaning "forty days." Originally a ship was kept in port for forty days when it was suspected of carrying a disease.

rack·et (rak′it) *n.* a light bat for tennis, badminton, etc., having a network as of catgut or nylon strung in a frame attached to a handle

This word **racket** comes from an Arabic word meaning "palm of the hand." The first "racket" used in games was certainly the palm of the hand, and it is still the one used in the game of handball.

rac·quet (rak′it) *n. another spelling of* **racket**

☆**rac·quet·ball** (rak′it bôl′) *n.* a game like handball, but played with a short-handled racket

ra·di·ol·o·gy (rā′dē äl′ə jē) *n.* the use of X-rays, radioactive drugs, etc. to discover and treat diseases —**ra′di·ol′o·gist** *n.*

ra·tion·al·ize (rash′ən ə līz′) *v.* to give a reasonable explanation without seeming to know that it is not the real one [We *rationalized* the small audience by blaming it on the weather.] —**ra′tion·al·ized′, ra′tion·al·iz′ing** —**ra′tion·al·i·za′tion** *n.*

re·cit·al (ri sīt′'l) *n.* **1** the act of reciting or telling with many details [a long *recital* of his troubles] **2** the story or report told in this way **3** a program of music or dances given by a soloist or soloists

re·dun·dant (ri dun′dənt) *adj.* **1** more than enough; not needed **2** using more words than are necessary to the meaning [It is *redundant* to say "Take daily doses every day."] —**re·dun′dant·ly** *adv.*

Redundant comes from a Latin word that means "to overflow." A redundant expression can be said to overflow with too many words.

re·flec·tor (ri flek′tər) *n.* a surface or part that reflects light, heat, sound, etc. [a *reflector* on a lamp]

re·frac·tion (ri frak′shən) *n.* the bending of a ray of light, etc. as it passes on a slant into a medium of a different density, as from air into water

re·gime *or* **ré·gime** (rə zhēm′ *or* rā zhēm′) *n.* a system of rule or government [a democratic *regime*]

re·ha·bil·i·tate (rē′hə bil′ə tāt) *v.* **1** to bring back to a normal or good condition [to *rehabilitate* a slum area] **2** to bring back to a former rank or reputation —**re′ha·bil′i·tat·ed, re′ha·bil′i·tat·ing** —**re′ha·bil′i·ta′tion** *n.*

rel·a·tiv·i·ty (rel′ə tiv′ə tē) *n.* **1** the condition of being relative **2** a theory of the universe developed by Albert Einstein, dealing with the relationship of matter, energy, space, and time

rel·e·vant (rel′ə vənt) *adj.* having to do with the matter at hand; to the point [a *relevant* remark] —**rel′e·vance** *or* **rel′e·van·cy** *n.*

rep·re·sent·a·tive (rep′rə zen′tə tiv) *adj.* **1** representing; standing for [a sculptured figure *representative* of Justice] **2** based on representation of the people by delegates [*representative* government] **3** being an example; typical [This building is *representative* of modern architecture.] *n.* **1** a typical example **2** a person chosen to act or speak for others [Judy is our *representative* on the student council.] ☆**3 Representative**, a member of the lower house of Congress or of a State legislature

re·pro·duc·tion (rē′prə duk′shən) *n.* **1** a reproducing or being reproduced **2** a copy or imitation [a *reproduction* of an ancient statue] **3** the process by which animals and plants produce others of their kind —**re′pro·duc′tive** *adj.*

re·pub·li·can (ri pub′li kən) *adj.* **1** of or having to do with a republic [a *republican* form of government] ☆**2 Republican**, of or belonging to the Republican Party ◆*n.* **1** a person who believes in and supports a republic ☆**2 Republican**, a member of the Republican Party

re·search (ri surch′ *or* rē′surch) *n.* careful, patient study in order to find out facts and principles about some subject [to carry on *research* into the causes of cancer] ◆*v.* to do research —**re·search·er** *n.*

res·i·den·tial (rez′ə den′shəl) *adj.* **1** used for residences, or homes, not businesses [a *residential* area] **2** of or having to do with residence [a *residential* requirement for voting]

res·pi·ra·tion (res′pə rā′shən) *n.* **1** the act or process of breathing **2** the process by which a living thing takes in oxygen from the air or water and gives off carbon dioxide, etc.

ré·su·mé (rez′oo mā′ *or* rā′zoo mā′) *n.* **1** a brief report that tells the main points ☆**2** a record of the work experience and education of a person applying for a job: *also written* **resumé**

res·ur·rect (rez′ə rekt′) *v.* **1** to bring back to life **2** to bring back into use [to *resurrect* an old custom]

ret·i·cent (ret′ə s'nt) *adj.* not saying much, especially about one's thoughts —**ret′i·cence** *n.*

re·ver·ber·ate (ri vur′bə rāt) *v.* to bounce back, as sound; echo [The guide's call *reverberated* in the cave.] —**re·ver′ber·at·ed, re·ver′ber·at·ing** —**re·ver′ber·a′tion** *n.*

re·viv·al (ri vī′v'l) *n.* **1** the act of bringing or coming back into use, being, etc. [the *revival* of an old custom] **2** a meeting at which there is excited preaching for the purpose of stirring up religious feeling

re·voke (ri vōk′) *v.* to put an end to, as a law, permit, license, etc.; cancel; repeal —**re·voked′, re·vok′ing**

rev·o·lu·tion·ar·y (rev′ə loo′shən er′ē) *adj.* **1** of, in favor of, or causing a revolution, especially in a government **2** bringing about very great change [a *revolutionary* new way to make glass] **3** revolving or rotating ◆*n.* another name for **revolutionist** —*pl.* **rev′o·lu′tion·ar·ies**

rhet·o·ric (ret′ər ik) *n.* the art of using words skillfully in speaking or writing **2** a book about this **3** a showy way of writing or speaking, especially when used to say something that is not important —**rhe·tor·i·cal** (ri tôr′i k'l) *adj.* —**rhe·tor′i·cal·ly** *adv.*

ru·ble (roo′b'l) *n.* the basic unit of money in Russia

Rug·by (rug′bē) a private school for boys in England ◆*n.* a kind of football first played at this school

ru·pee (roo pē′) *n.* the basic unit of money in India, and also in Pakistan

ru·ral (roor′əl) *adj.* having to do with the country or with people who live there, as on farms

sanc·tu·ar·y (saŋk′choo wer′ē) *n.* **1** a place set aside for religious worship, as a church or temple **2** the main room for services in a house of worship **3** a place where one can find safety and shelter; also, the safety found there [The criminals found *sanctuary* in a church.] **4** a place where birds and animals are protected from hunters [a wildlife *sanctuary*] —*pl.* **sanc′tu·ar′ies**

sap·phire (saf′īr) *n.* **1** a clear, deep-blue, costly jewel **2** deep blue

sar·casm (sär′kaz'm) *n.* **1** a mocking or sneering remark meant to hurt or to make someone seem foolish **2** the making of such remarks ["I only explained it five times," she replied in *sarcasm*.]

Sarcasm comes from the Greek word that means "to tear flesh the way dogs do." Sarcastic words are sometimes spoken of as biting words, for they are intended to bite into feelings and hurt, as a dog's teeth would hurt flesh.

sat·el·lite (sat′'l īt) *n.* **1** a heavenly body that revolves around another, larger one [The moon is a *satellite* of the earth.] **2** an artificial object put into orbit around the earth, the moon, or some other heavenly body **3** a country that depends on and is controlled by a larger, more powerful one **4** a follower of an important person

sat·is·fac·to·ry (sat′is fak′tə rē) *adj.* good enough to satisfy, or meet the need or wish —**sat′is·fac′to·ri·ly** *adv.*

sat·u·rate (sach′ə rāt) *v.* **1** to soak through and through [The baby's bib was *saturated* with milk.] **2** to fill so completely or dissolve so much of something that no more can be taken up [to *saturate* water with salt] —**sat′u·rat·ed, sat′u·rat·ing** —**sat′u·ra′tion** *n.*

sau·té (sō tā′) *v.* to fry quickly in a pan with a little fat —**sau·téed** (sō tād′), **sau·té·ing** (sō tā′iŋ) ◆*adj.* fried in this way [chicken livers *sauté*]

sa·vor·y¹ (sā′vər ē) *adj.* pleasing to the taste or smell [a *savory* stew]

sa·vor·y² (sā′vər ē) *n.* a kind of herb with a mint flavor, used in cooking

a	ask, fat
ā	ape, date
ä	car, lot
e	elf, ten
er	berry, care
ē	even, meet
i	is, hit
ir	mirror, here
ī	ice, fire
ō	open, go
ô	law, horn
oi	oil, point
oo	look, pull
oo	ooze, tool
yoo	unite, cure
yoo	cute, few
ou	out, crowd
u	up, cut
u	fur, fern
ə	a in ago
	e in agent
	e in father
	i in unity
	o in collect
	u in focus
ch	chin, arch
ŋ	ring, singer
sh	she, dash
th	thin, truth
th	then, father
zh	s in pleasure
′	as in (ā b'l)

181

scal·lop (skäl′əp *or* skal′əp) *n.* **1** a water animal with a soft body enclosed in two hard, ribbed shells hinged together: it has a large muscle, used as food **2** any of a series of curves that form a fancy edge on cloth, lace, etc. ◆*v.* **1** to bake with milk sauce and bread crumbs [*scalloped* potatoes] **2** to cut in scallops [a *scalloped* neckline]

scar·ci·ty (sker′sə tē) *n.* the condition of being scarce; lack; rareness, etc. —*pl.* **scar′ci·ties**

scav·eng·er (skav′in jər) *n.* **1** an animal that feeds on rotting meat and garbage [Vultures and hyenas are *scavengers.*] **2** a person who gathers things that others have thrown away

sce·nar·i·o (si ner′ē ō) *n.* ☆**1** the written script from which a movie is made **2** an outline for the way something might happen or is planned to happen —*pl.* **sce·nar′i·os**

sched·ule (skej′ool) *n.* ☆**1** a list of the times at which certain things are to happen; timetable [a *schedule* of the sailings of an ocean liner] ☆**2** a timed plan for a project [The work is ahead of *schedule.*] **3** a list of details [a *schedule* of postal rates] ◆*v.* **1** to make a schedule of [to *schedule* one's hours of work] ☆**2** to plan for a certain time [to *schedule* a game for 3:00 p.m.] —**sched′uled, sched′ul·ing**

scheme (skēm) *n.* **1** a plan or system in which things are carefully put together [the color *scheme* of a painting] **2** a plan or program, often a secret or dishonest one [a *scheme* for getting rich quick] ◆*v.* to make secret or dishonest plans; plot [Lee is always *scheming* to get out of work.] —**schemed, schem′ing** —**schem′er** *n.*

☆**schoon·er** (skoo′nər) *n.* a ship with two or more masts and sails that are set lengthwise

se·clu·sion (si kloo′zhən) *n.* a secluding or being secluded; isolation; privacy [to live in *seclusion*]

sec·re·tar·y (sek′rə ter′ē) *n.* **1** a person whose work is keeping records, writing letters, etc. for a person, organization, etc. **2** the head of a department of government [the *Secretary* of State] **3** a writing desk, especially one with a bookcase built at the top —*pl.* **sec′re·tar′ies** —**sec·re·tar·i·al** (sek′rə ter′ē əl) *adj.*

se·cu·ri·ty (si kyoor′ə tē) *n.* **1** the condition or feeling of being safe or sure; freedom from danger, fear, doubt, etc. **2** something that protects [Insurance is a *security* against loss.] **3** something given or pledged as a guarantee [A car may be used as *security* for a loan.] **4 securities**, *pl.* stocks and bonds —*pl.* **se·cu′ri·ties**

sed·i·men·ta·ry (sed′ə men′tər ē) *adj.* of, containing, or formed from sediment [*sedimentary* rock]

sem·i·an·nu·al (sem′i an′yoo wəl) *adj.* happening, coming, etc. twice a year [*semiannual* payment of taxes] —**sem′i·an′nu·al·ly** *adv.*

sem·i·pre·cious (sem′i presh əs) *adj.* describing gems, as the garnet or turquoise, that are of less value than the precious gems

sen·sa·tion·al (sen sā′shən'l) *adj.* stirring up strong feeling or great excitement [a *sensational* new theory] **2** meant to shock, thrill, excite, etc. [a *sensational* novel] **3** very good; *used only in everyday talk* —**sen·sa′tion·al·ism** *n.* —**sen·sa′tion·al·ly** *adv.*

sev·er·al (sev′ər əl *or* sev′rəl) *adj.* more than two but not many; a few [*Several* people called while you were out.] ◆*pron., n.* not many; a small number [Most of them left, but *several* stayed. *Several* of the windows were broken.]

shek·el (shek′'l) *n.* a gold or silver coin of the ancient Hebrews

Si·er·ra Le·one (sē er′ə lē ōn) a country on the western coast of Africa

sig·nif·i·cant (sig nif′ə kənt) *adj.* **1** important; full of meaning [The President gave a *significant* speech.] **2** having a meaning, especially a hidden one [She gave him a *significant* wink.] —**sig·nif′i·cant·ly** *adv.*

sim·i·lar·i·ty (sim′ə lar′ə tē) *n.* **1** the state of being similar; likeness **2** a similar point or feature —*pl.* **sim′i·lar′i·ties**

sim·i·le (sim′ə lē) *n.* a figure of speech in which two things that are different in most ways are said to be alike, by using either the word *as* or *like* ["He's as thin as a rail" and "She sings like a bird" are *similes.*] —*pl.* **sim′i·les**

sim·u·late (sim′yoo lāt) *v.* **1** to pretend to have or feel [to *simulate* anger] **2** to look or act like; imitate [The insect *simulated* a twig.] —**sim′u·lat·ed, sim′u·lat·ing** —**sim′u·la′tion** *n.*

si·mul·ta·ne·ous (sī′m'l tā′nē əs) *adj.* done or happening together or at the same time —**si′mul·ta′ne·ous·ly** *adv.*

sin·gu·lar (siŋ′gyə lər) *adj.* **1** being the only one of its kind; unique [a *singular* specimen] **2** showing that only one is meant [The *singular* form of "geese" is "goose."] ◆*n.* the singular form of a word in grammar —**sin·gu·lar·i·ty** (siŋ′gyə lar′ə tē) *n.* —**sin′gu·lar·ly** *adv.*

sit·u·a·tion (sich′oo wā′shən) *n.* **1** a place or position; location; site **2** condition or state, as caused by things that have happened [Her election as mayor has created an interesting *situation.*]

ski (skē) *n.* one of a pair of long, wooden runners fastened to the shoes for gliding over snow ◆*v.* to glide on skis, as down snow-covered hills —**skied** (skēd), **ski′ing** —**ski′er** *n.*

slang (slaŋ) *n.* words and phrases that are used in everyday talk but are out of place in fine or serious speech or writing

Slang words are usually popular for only a short time. A few slang words and meanings that have been in use for a longer time are included in dictionaries. "Crummy" is slang, and so are "rocky" when used to mean "weak or dizzy" and "grub" when used to mean "food."

so·journ (sō′jʉrn) *n.* a short stay; visit ◆*v.* (*also* so′jʉrn′) to stay for a while, as on a visit [We *sojourned* in Italy.] —**so′journ·er** *n.*

Sojourn comes from a Latin word that means "under a day." Originally a sojourn was a short visit or trip that would take less than a day. **Sojourn**, **journal**, and **journey** all come to us from the same Latin word for "day."

so·lil·o·quy (sə lil′ə kwē) *n.* **1** the act of talking to oneself **2** a speech in a play in which a character tells his or her thoughts to the audience by talking aloud, as if to himself or herself —*pl.* **so·lil′o·quies**

so·lo (sō′lō) *n.* a piece of music that is sung or played by one person —*pl.* **so′los** ◆*adj.* **1** for or by one singer or one instrument **2** made or done by one person [a *solo* flight in an airplane] ◆*adv.* without another or others; alone ◆*v.* **1** to fly an airplane alone **2** to play or sing a musical solo —**so′loed, so′lo·ing** —**so′lo·ist** *n.*

so·lu·tion (sə lōō′shən) *n.* **1** the solving of a problem **2** an answer or explanation [to find the *solution* to a mystery] **3** the dissolving of something in a liquid **4** a mixture formed in this way [Make a *solution* of sugar and vinegar.]

son·net (sän′it) *n.* a poem of fourteen lines that rhyme in a certain pattern

soph·o·more (säf′ə môr) *n.* a student in the tenth grade or in the second year of college

so·ror·i·ty (sə rôr′ə tē) *n.* a club of women or girls, especially a social club, as in a college —*pl.* **so·ror′i·ties**

souf·flé (sōō flā′) *n.* a baked food made light and fluffy by adding beaten egg whites before baking [a cheese *soufflé*]

source (sôrs) *n.* **1** a spring or fountain that is the starting point of a stream **2** a thing or place from which something comes or is got [The sun is our *source* of energy. This book is the *source* of my information.]

sou·ve·nir (sōō və nir′) *n.* an object kept to remind one of something; memento [We save our programs as *souvenirs* of plays we've seen.]

spec·i·fi·ca·tion (spes′ə fi kā′shən) *n.* **1** the act of specifying; detailed mention **2** something specified; a specific item **3** *usually* **specifications**, *pl.* a statement or a description of all the necessary details, as of sizes, materials, etc. [the *specifications* for a new building]

spec·ta·cle (spek′tə k'l) *n.* **1** something to look at, especially an unusual sight or a grand public show [The fireworks display was a *spectacle*.] **2** spectacles, *pl.* a pair of eyeglasses; *an old-fashioned meaning*

Spectacle, spectacular, spectator, spectroscope, and **spectrum** all come from the Latin word *spectare*, meaning "to behold" or "to watch." All of these words have to do with someone seeing or with something seen or used in seeing.

spec·u·late (spek′yə lāt) *v.* **1** to think about or make guesses; ponder; meditate [Scientists *speculate* on the kinds of life there may be on distant planets.] **2** to make risky business deals with the hope of making large profits —**spec′u·lat·ed, spec′u·lat·ing** —**spec′u·la′tion, spec′u·la′tor** *n.*

spir·it·u·al (spir′i chōō wəl) *adj.* **1** of the spirit or soul as apart from the body or material things **2** having to do with religion or the church; sacred ◆☆*n.* a religious folk song of the kind created by African Americans —**spir·it·u·al·i·ty** (spir′i chōō wal′ə tē) *n.* —**spir′it·u·al·ly** *adv.*

stage·coach (stāj′kōch) *n.* a coach pulled by horses that traveled a regular route, carrying passengers, mail, etc.

stan·za (stan′zə) *n.* a group of lines forming one of the sections of a poem or song; verse

Stanza is an Italian word for "stopping place." A poem or song stops between the stanzas, each of which has a further thought about the poem's subject.

sta·tis·ti·cal (stə tis′ti k'l) *adj.* having to do with statistics —**sta·tis′ti·cal·ly** *adv.*

staunch (stônch *or* stänch) *v.* to stop or slow down the flow of blood from a wound ◆*adj.* **1** strong, firm, loyal, etc. [*staunch* friendship] **2** watertight [a *staunch* ship] —**staunch′ly** *adv.*

stim·u·lant (stim′yə lənt) *n.* something that stimulates or excites one, as coffee or any of certain drugs

stri·dent (strīd′'nt) *adj.* harsh in sound; shrill or grating [a *strident* voice] —**stri′dent·ly** *adv.*

struc·tur·al (struk′chər əl) *adj.* **1** used in building [*structural* steel] **2** of structure [*structural* design] —**struc′tur·al·ly** *adv.*

sub·poe·na (sə pē′nə) *n.* an official paper ordering a person to appear in a court of law ◆*v.* to order with such a paper —**sub·poe′naed, sub·poe′na·ing**: *also spelled* **sub·pe′na**

sub·sid·i·ar·y (səb sid′ē er′ē) *adj.* **1** helping or useful, especially in a lesser way **2** of less importance; secondary ◆*n.* **1** a person or thing that helps or gives aid **2** a company that is controlled by another company [The bus company's *subsidiary* operates the lunchrooms in the stations.] —*pl.* **sub·sid′i·ar′ies**

a	ask, fat
ā	ape, date
ä	car, lot
e	elf, ten
er	berry, care
ē	even, meet
i	is, hit
ir	mirror, here
ī	ice, fire
ō	open, go
ô	law, horn
σi	oil, point
σο	look, pull
ōō	ooze, tool
yōō	unite, cure
yōō	cute, few
ου	out, crowd
u	up, cut
ʉ	fur, fern
ə	a in ago
	e in agent
	e in father
	i in unity
	o in collect
	u in focus
ch	chin, arch
ŋ	ring, singer
sh	she, dash
th	thin, truth
th	then, father
zh	s in pleasure
′	as in (ā b'l)

183

sub·urb (sub′ərb) **n.** a district, town, etc. on the outskirts of a city

The word for city in ancient Rome was *urbs*. The *sub-* in **suburb** means "near," so the word itself means literally "near the city."

sub·ur·ban (sə bʉr′bən) **adj.** **1** of or living in a suburb **2** typical of suburbs or of those who live in them [a *suburban* style of living]

suc·ces·sive (sək ses′iv) **adj.** coming in regular order without a break; consecutive [I won six *successive* games.] —**suc·ces′sive·ly adv.**

suc·cu·lent (suk′yoo lənt) **adj.** full of juice; juicy [a *succulent* peach] —**suc′cu·lence n.**

sum·mon (sum′ən) **v.** **1** to call together; call or send for [The President *summoned* the Cabinet.] **2** to call forth; rouse; gather [*Summon* up your strength.] **3** to order to appear in a court of law

su·per·flu·ous (soo pʉr′floo wəs) **adj.** more than is needed; unnecessary [*superfluous* motions; a *superfluous* remark] —**su·per′flu·ous·ly adv.**

su·per·in·tend·ent (soo′pər in ten′dənt) **n.** **1** a person in charge of an institution, school system, etc. **2** the manager of a building; custodian

su·pe·ri·or (sə pir′ē ər) **adj.** **1** higher in rank, position, etc. [Soldiers salute their *superior* officers.] **2** above average in quality, value, skill, etc.; excellent [a *superior* grade of cotton] **3** showing a feeling of being better than others; haughty ◆**n.** **1** a person of higher rank, greater skill, etc. **2** the head of a monastery or convent —**su·pe·ri·or·i·ty** (sə pir′ē ôr′ə tē) **n.**

su·per·vi·sor (soo′pər vi′zər) **n.** a person who supervises; director —**su′per·vi·so·ry adj.**

sup·ple·ment (sup′lə mənt) **n.** **1** something added, as to make up for something missing [Vitamin pills are a *supplement* to a poor diet.] **2** a section added to a book or newspaper, to give extra or more up-to-date information, special articles, etc. ◆**v.** (sup′lə ment) to be or give a supplement to; add to —**sup′ple·men′tal adj.**

sup·press (sə pres′) **v.** **1** to put down by force or power; crush [The ship's captain acted quickly to *suppress* the mutiny.] **2** to keep back; hide; conceal [to *suppress* a laugh; to *suppress* a news story] —**sup·pres·sion** (sə presh′ə n) **n.**

sur·geon (sʉr′jən) **n.** a doctor who specializes in surgery

sur·ger·y (sʉr′jər ē) **n.** **1** the treating of disease or injury by operations with the hands or tools, as in setting broken bones, cutting out tonsils, etc. **2** an operation of this kind **3** the room in a hospital where doctors do such operations —*pl.* **sur′ger·ies**

Surgery comes from a Greek word meaning "a working with the hands." The doctor who does surgery must be skillful in using the hands to treat patients.

sur·viv·al (sər vi′v'l) **n.** **1** the act or fact of surviving, or continuing to exist [Nuclear war threatens the *survival* of all nations.] **2** something surviving from an earlier time, as a custom

sus·pend (sə spend′) **v.** **1** to hang by a support from above [The keys were *suspended* by a chain from his belt.] **2** to keep out for a while as a punishment [She was *suspended* from school for misbehaving.] **3** to stop from operating for a time [to *suspend* bus service; to *suspend* a rule] **4** to hold back or put off [The judge *suspended* her sentence.]

sus·pense (sə spens′) **n.** **1** the condition of being anxious and uncertain [We waited in *suspense* for the jury's verdict.] **2** the growing excitement felt as a story, play, etc. builds to a high point or climax [a movie full of *suspense*]

syl·la·ble (sil′ə b'l) **n.** **1** a word or part of a word spoken with a single sounding of the voice ["Moon" is a word of one *syllable*. "Moonlight" is a word of two *syllables*.] **2** any of the parts into which a written word is divided to show where it may be broken at the end of a line [The *syllables* of the entry words in this dictionary are divided by tiny dots.]

Syllable comes from a Greek word that means "to put or hold together." Syllables are put together to form words.

syl·la·bus (sil′ə bəs) **n.** an outline or summary, especially of a course of study —*pl.* **syl′la·bus·es** or **syl·la·bi** (sil′ə bī)

sym·bol·ize (sim′b'l īz) **v.** **1** to be a symbol of; stand for [A heart *symbolizes* love.] **2** to represent by a symbol [This artist *symbolizes* the human spirit by means of figures with wings.] —**sym′bol·ized, sym′bol·iz·ing**

sym·me·try (sim′ə trē) **n.** **1** an arrangement in which the parts on opposite sides of a center line are alike in size, shape, and position [The human body has *symmetry*.] **2** balance or harmony that comes from such an arrangement

sym·pho·ny (sim′fə nē) **n.** **1** a long piece of music for a full orchestra, usually divided into four movements with different rhythms and themes **2** a large orchestra for playing such works: *its full name is* **symphony orchestra 3** harmony, as of sounds, color, etc. [The dance was a *symphony* in motion.] —*pl.* **sym′pho·nies** —**sym·phon·ic** (sim fän′ik) **adj.** —**sym·phon′i·cal·ly adv.**

sym·po·si·um (sim pō′zē əm) **n.** **1** a meeting for discussing some subject **2** a group of writings or opinions on a particular subject —*pl.* **sym·po′si·ums** or **sym·po·si·a** (sim pō′zē ə)

symp·tom (simp′təm) *n.* something showing that something else exists; sign [Spots on the skin may be a *symptom* of chicken pox.] —**symp·to·mat·ic** (simp′tə mat′ik) *adj.*

syn·a·gogue (sin′ə gäg *or* sin′ə gôg) *n.* a building where Jews gather for worship and religious study

syn·chro·nize (siŋ′krə nīz) *v.* **1** to move or happen at the same time or speed [The gears must *synchronize* when you shift.] **2** to make agree in time or rate of speed [Let's *synchronize* our watches. The movie film should be *synchronized* with the sound track.] —**syn′chro·nized, syn′chro·niz·ing**

Synchronize comes from two Greek words that mean "to be together in time." The shutter and flashbulb of a camera are synchronized so that they will both operate at the same time.

syn·co·pate (siŋ′kə pāt) *v.* in music, to shift the accent by putting the beat at a place that would normally not be accented and holding it into the next accented beat [Much jazz is *syncopated*.] —**syn′co·pat·ed, syn′co·pat·ing** —**syn′co·pa′tion** *n.*

syn·di·cate (sin′də kit) *n.* **1** a group of bankers, large companies, etc. formed to carry out some project that needs much money ☆**2** an organization that sells articles, stories, comic strips, etc. to a number of newspapers ◆*v.* (sin′di kāt) **1** to form into a syndicate **2** to publish through a syndicate in a number of newspapers —**syn′di·cat·ed, syn′di·cat·ing** —**syn′di·ca′tion** *n.*

syn·on·y·mous (si nän′ə məs) *adj.* of the same or almost the same meaning

syn·tax (sin′taks) *n.* the way words are put together and related to one another in sentences; sentence structure —**syn·tac′ti·cal** or **syn·tac′tic** *adj.*

syn·the·sis (sin′thə sis) *n.* the putting together of parts or elements so as to make a whole [Plastics are made by chemical *synthesis*.] —*pl.* **syn·the·ses** (sin′thə sēz)

sy·ringe (sə rinj′ *or* sir′inj) *n.* a device made up of a narrow tube with a rubber bulb or a plunger at one end, for drawing in a liquid and then pushing it out in a stream: syringes are used to inject fluids into the body, to wash out wounds, etc. ◆*v.* to wash out with a syringe —**sy·ringed′, sy·ring′ing**

Tt

tac·i·turn (tas′ə tʉrn) *adj.* not liking to talk; usually silent —**tac′i·tur′ni·ty** *n.*

tech·ni·cal·i·ty (tek′nə kal′ə tē) *n.* **1** a technical point, detail, etc. [the *technicalities* of radio repair] **2** a small point or detail related to a main issue [She was found guilty on a legal *technicality*.] —*pl.* **tech′ni·cal′i·ties**

tech·ni·cian (tek nish′ən) *n.* a person who has skill in the technique of some art or science

tech·nol·o·gy (tek näl′ə jē) *n.* **1** the study of the industrial arts or applied sciences, as engineering, mechanics, etc. **2** science as it is put to use in practical work [medical *technology*] **3** a method or process for dealing with a technical problem —**tech·no·log·i·cal** (tek′nə läj′i k'l) *adj.* —**tech′no·log′i·cal·ly** *adv.* —**tech·nol′o·gist** *n.*

tel·e·cast (tel′ə kast) *v.* to broadcast by television ◆*n.* a television broadcast —**tel′e·cast** or **tel′e·cast·ed, tel′e·cast·ing** —**tel′e·cast·er** *n.*

tel·e·vise (tel′ə vīz) *v.* to send pictures of by television [to *televise* a baseball game] —**tel′e·vised, tel′e·vis·ing**

tend·en·cy (ten′dən sē) *n.* the fact of being likely or apt to move or act in a certain way [There is a *tendency* for prices to go up. Pat has a *tendency* to complain.] —*pl.* **tend′en·cies**

ter·mi·nal (tʉr′mə n'l) *adj.* of, at, or forming the end [a *terminal* bud on a branch; the *terminal* payment of a loan] ◆*n.* **1** an end or end part **2** a main station of a railroad, bus line, or airline, where many trips begin or end **3** a machine like a typewriter, but with a kind of TV screen, for feeding information to, or getting it from, a computer

ter·race (ter′əs) *n.* **1** a flat platform of earth with sloping banks; also, any of a series of such platforms, rising one above the other, as on a hillside **2** a paved area near a house, that overlooks a lawn or garden; patio **3** a small, roofed balcony outside an apartment ◆*v.* to form into a terrace or terraces — **ter′raced, ter′rac·ing**

ter·rain (tə rān′) *n.* ground or an area of land [a farm with hilly *terrain*]

ter·ri·to·ry (ter′ə tôr′e) *n.* **1** the land ruled by a nation or state **2 Territory,** a large division of a country or empire, that does not have the full rights of a province or state, as in Canada or Australia [the Northwest *Territories*] **3** any large stretch of land; region **4** the particular area chosen as its own by an animal or group of animals —*pl.* **ter′ri·to′ries**

the·ol·o·gy (thē äl′ə jē) *n.* **1** the study of God and religious beliefs **2** a system of religious beliefs —*pl.* **the·ol′o·gies** —**the·o·lo·gian** (thē′ə lō′jən)

ther·a·peu·tic (ther′ə pyoot′ik) *adj.* having to do with or used in treating or curing diseases —**ther′a·peu′ti·cal·ly** *adv.*

a	ask, fat
ā	ape, date
ä	car, lot
e	elf, ten
er	berry, care
ē	even, meet
i	is, hit
ir	mirror, here
ī	ice, fire
ō	open, go
ô	law, horn
oi	oil, point
oo	look, pull
o͞o	ooze, tool
yoo	unite, cure
yo͞o	cute, few
ou	out, crowd
u	up, cut
ʉ	fur, fern
ə	a in ago
	e in agent
	e in father
	i in unity
	o in collect
	u in focus
ch	chin, arch
ŋ	ring, singer
sh	she, dash
th	thin, truth
th	then, father
zh	s in pleasure
′	as in (ā b'l)

ther·a·py (ther′ə pē) *n.* any method of treating disease [drug *therapy*; heat *therapy*] —*pl.* **ther′a·pies** —☆**ther′a·pist** *n.*

ther·mos (thur′məs) *n.* a container for keeping liquids at almost the same temperature for several hours: *the full name is* **thermos bottle**

ther·mo·stat (thur′mə stat) *n.* a device for keeping temperature even, especially one that automatically controls a furnace, etc. —**ther′mo·stat′ic** *adj.*

tim·bre (tim′bər *or* tam′bər) *n.* the quality of sound, apart from pitch or loudness, that makes one's voice or musical instrument different from others

tol·er·ance (täl′ər əns) *n.* **1** a willingness to let others have their own beliefs, ways, etc., even though these are not like one's own **2** the power of the body to keep a drug or poison from working [My body has built up a *tolerance* for penicillin, so that it can no longer help me.]

to·pog·ra·phy (tə päg′rə fē) *n.* **1** the surface features of a region, as hills, rivers, roads, etc. **2** the science of showing these on maps and charts —**to·pog′ra·pher** *n.* —**top·o·graph·i·cal** (täp′ə graf′i k'l) *adj.*

tour·na·ment (toor′nə mənt) *n.* **1** a contest in which knights on horseback tried to knock each other off the horses with lances **2** a series of contests in some sport or game in which a number of people or teams take part, trying to win the championship

tran·quil (traŋ′kwəl) *adj.* calm, quiet, peaceful, etc. [*tranquil* waters; a *tranquil* mood] —**tran·quil′li·ty** *or* **tran·quil′i·ty** *n.* —**tran′quil·ly** *adv.*

☆**trans·con·ti·nen·tal** (trans′kän tə nen′t'l) *adj.* that goes from one side of a continent to the other [a *transcontinental* airplane flight]

trans·fuse (trans fyo͞oz′) *v.* **1** to pass blood, blood plasma, etc. that has been taken from one person into a vein of another **2** to pour in or spread through; instill [Victory *transfused* courage into the team.] —**trans·fused′, trans·fus′ing** —**trans·fu′sion** *n.*

tran·si·tive (tran′sə tiv) *adj.* describing a verb that takes a direct object [In the sentence "He saved money for a car," "saved" is a *transitive* verb.]

trans·mit (trans mit′) *v.* **1** to send from one person or place to another; pass on; transfer [to *transmit* a disease; to *transmit* a letter; to *transmit* power from an engine by means of gears] **2** to pass or let pass, as light, heat, etc. [Water *transmits* sound.] **3** to send out radio or TV signals —**trans·mit′ted, trans·mit′ting**

trans·mit·ter (trans mit′ər) *n.* **1** a person or thing that transmits **2** the part of a telegraph or telephone that sends out sounds or signals **3** the apparatus for sending out electric waves in radio and TV

tran·spire (tran spīr′) *v.* **1** to give off vapor, moisture, etc., as through pores **2** to become known ☆**3** to take place; happen: *thought of by some people as a loose or incorrect meaning* [What *transpired* while I was gone?] —**tran·spired′, tran·spir′ing**

treach·er·ous (trech′ər əs) *adj.* **1** not loyal or faithful; betraying or likely to betray **2** seeming safe, reliable, etc. but not really so [*treacherous* rocks] —**treach′er·ous·ly** *adv.*

treas·ur·er (trezh′ər ər) *n.* a person in charge of a treasury, as of a government, company, club, etc.

tres·pass (tres′pəs *or* tres′pas) *v.* **1** to go on another's property without permission or right ["No *trespassing*" means "keep out."] **2** to break in on; intrude [Don't *trespass* on my privacy.] **3** to do wrong; sin ◆*n.* **1** the act of trespassing **2** a sin or wrong —**tres′pass·er** *n.*

trib·u·tar·y (trib′yo͞o ter′ē) *n.* **1** a stream or river that flows into a larger one **2** a nation that pays tribute or is under the power of another nation —*pl.* **trib′u·tar′ies** ◆*adj.* **1** flowing into a larger one [a *tributary* stream] **2** paying tribute to another, or under another's power [a *tributary* nation]

trig·o·nom·e·try (trig′ə näm′ə trē) *n.* the branch of mathematics dealing with the relations between the sides and angles of triangles

trite (trīt) *adj.* used so much that it is no longer fresh or new; stale ["Happy as a lark" is a *trite* expression.] —**trit′er, trit′est** —**trite′ly** *adv.*

Trite comes from a Latin word that means "to wear out." A trite phrase or saying has been used so much that it is worn out.

trop·i·cal (träp′i k'l) *adj.* of, in, or like the tropics [heavy *tropical* rains; *tropical* heat]

☆**troupe** (tro͞op) *n.* a band or company, especially of actors, singers, etc. —**troup′er** *n.*

tur·bine (tur′bin *or* tur′bīn) *n.* an engine in which the driving shaft is made to turn by the pressure of steam, water, or air against the vanes of a wheel fixed to it

tur·quoise (tur′koiz *or* tur′kwoiz) *n.* **1** a greenish-blue stone used as a jewel **2** a greenish blue

Turquoise comes from an Old French word meaning "Turkish." The first turquoise stones were brought to western Europe through Turkey and were thus thought to be Turkish although they really had come from Persia.

tweez·ers (twē′zərz) *pl. n.* small pincers for plucking out hairs, handling small things, etc.

Tweezers comes from an Old French word, now no longer used, that means a set of surgical instruments. That word came in turn from *etuis*, plural of a word for a small case used to hold needles or other small implements.

tyr·an·ny (tir′ə nē) *n.* **1** the government or power of a tyrant; harsh and unjust government **2** very cruel and unjust use of power **3** a tyrannical act —*pl.* **tyr′an·nies**

um·bil·i·cal cord (um bil′i k′l) the cord that connects a pregnant woman with her unborn baby: through it the baby gets nourishment, and at the point where it is cut at birth the baby's navel is formed

um·brel·la (um brel′ə) *n.* cloth, plastic, etc. stretched over a folding frame at the top of a stick, used to protect one from the rain or sun

un·doubt·ed·ly (un dout′id lē) *adv.* without doubt; certainly [It is *undoubtedly* a ruby.]

un·for·get·ta·ble (un′fər get′ə b'l) *adj.* so important, beautiful, shocking, etc. that it cannot be forgotten

u·ni·lat·er·al (yōō′nə lat′ər əl) *adj.* having to do with or done by only one of several persons, nations, etc. [a *unilateral* decision]

un·scathed (un skā*th*d′) *adj.* not hurt; unharmed [We got out of the accident *unscathed*.]

up·heav·al (up hē′v'l) *n.* **1** a forceful lifting up from beneath [the *upheaval* of ground in an earthquake] **2** a sudden, violent change [the *upheaval* begun by the French Revolution]

up·hol·ster·y (up hōl′stər ē *or* ə pōl′stər ē) *n.* the work of upholstering or materials used for this

ur·ban (ur′bən) *adj.* of, living in, or having to do with cities or towns [*urban* dwellers]

vac·ci·nate (vak′sə nāt) *v.* to inject a vaccine into, in order to keep from getting a certain disease, as smallpox —**vac′ci·nat·ed, vac′ci·nat·ing**

vag·a·bond (vag′ə bänd) *n.* **1** a person who moves from place to place **2** *another name for* **tramp** ◆*adj.* **1** wandering from place to place [a *vagabond* tribe] **2** of or having to do with a drifting, carefree life [*vagabond* habits]

va·grant (vā′grənt) *n.* a person who wanders from place to place, doing odd jobs or begging; tramp ◆*adj.* wandering from place to place, or living the life of a vagrant

vague (vāg) *adj.* not clear, definite, or distinct, as in form, meaning, or purpose [*vague* figures in the fog; a *vague* answer] —**va′guer, va′guest** —**vague′ly** *adv.* —**vague′ness** *n.*

var·i·a·tion (ver′e ā′shən) *n.* **1** the act of varying, changing, or differing [a *variation* in style] **2** the amount of a change [a *variation* of ten feet] **3** the repeating of a tune or musical theme, with changes as in rhythm or key

va·ri·e·ty (və rī′ə tē) *n.* **1** change; lack of sameness [I like *variety* in my meals.] **2** any of the various forms of something; sort; kind [many *varieties* of cloth; a cat of the striped *variety*] **3** a number of different kinds [a *variety* of fruits at the market] —*pl.* **va·ri′e·ties**

var·i·ous (ver′ē əs) *adj.* **1** of several different kinds [We planted *various* seeds.] **2** several or many [*Various* people have said so.] —**var′i·ous·ly** *adv.*

☆**vaude·ville** (vōd′vil *or* vôd′vil) *n.* a stage show made up of different kinds of acts, as comic skits, songs, dances, etc.

The word **vaudeville** was French to begin with. It comes to us from *Vau-de-Vire*, the name of a valley in Normandy, France. The people of the valley have been famous for their light, merry songs.

ven·dor *or* **vend·er** (ven′dər) *n.* a person who sells; seller [She is a *vendor* of drinks at baseball games.]

ve·neer (və nir′) *v.* to cover a common material with a thin layer of fine wood or costly material [piano keys *veneered* with ivory] ◆*n.* **1** a thin layer of fine wood or costly material put over a common material [a walnut *veneer* on a pine chest] **2** an outward look or show that hides what is below [a coarse person with a thin *veneer* of culture]

ven·ti·la·tor (ven′t'l āt ər) *n.* an opening or device for bringing in fresh air and driving out stale air

ver·bose (vər bōs′) *adj.* using too many words; wordy —**ver·bos·i·ty** (vər bäs′ə tē) *n.*

ver·dict (vur′dikt) *n.* **1** the decision reached by a jury in a law case [a *verdict* of "not guilty"] **2** any decision or opinion

ver·min (vur′min) *n.* **1** small animals or insects, such as rats and flies, that cause harm or are troublesome to people **2** a disgusting person —*pl.* **ver′min**

ver·nac·u·lar (vər nak′yə lər) *n.* **1** the native language of a country or place **2** the everyday language of ordinary people **3** the special words and phrases used in a particular work, by a particular group, etc. [In the *vernacular* of sailors, "deck" is the word for "floor."] ◆*adj.* of, using, or based on the everyday speech of ordinary people in a certain country or place [James Whitcomb Riley was a *vernacular* poet.]

a	ask, fat
ā	ape, date
ä	car, lot
e	elf, ten
er	berry, care
ē	even, meet
i	is, hit
ir	mirror, here
ī	ice, fire
ō	open, go
ô	law, horn
oi	oil, point
o͝o	look, pull
o͞o	ooze, tool
yo͞o	unite, cure
yo͞o	cute, few
ou	out, crowd
u	up, cut
ʉ	fur, fern
ə	a in ago
	e in agent
	e in father
	i in unity
	o in collect
	u in focus
ch	chin, arch
ŋ	ring, singer
sh	she, dash
th	thin, truth
th	then, father
zh	s in pleasure
′	as in (ā b'l)

ves·sel (ves′l) *n.* **1** anything hollow for holding something; container [Bowls, kettles, tubs, etc. are *vessels*.] **2** a ship or large boat **3** any of the tubes in the body through which a fluid flows [a blood *vessel*]

vet·er·i·nar·i·an (vet′ər ə ner′ē ən) *n.* a doctor who treats the diseases and injuries of animals

vi·bra·to (vi brät′ō) *n.* a slight throbbing in the sound of a singer's voice or of a musical instrument: it is produced by rapid, slight changes of the pitch back and forth

vice-pres·i·dent (vīs′prez′i dənt) *n.* **1** an officer next in rank to a president, who takes the place of the president if the president should die, be absent, etc. ☆**2 Vice-President**, such an officer in the United States government, who is also president of the Senate: *usually written* **Vice President**

vid·e·o·tape (vid′ē ō tāp′) *n.* a thin magnetic tape on which both the sound and picture signals of a TV program can be recorded by electronics

vin·dic·tive (vin dik′tiv) *adj.* **1** wanting to get revenge; ready to do harm in return for harm [A *vindictive* person holds a grudge.] **2** said or done in revenge [*vindictive* punishment] —**vin·dic′tive·ly** *adv.*

vin·e·gar (vin′i gər) *n.* a sour liquid made by fermenting cider, wine, etc., used to flavor or pickle foods

vir·tu·o·so (vur′chσo wō′sō) *n.* a person having great skill in the practice of some art, especially in playing music —*pl.* **vir′tu·o′sos** or **vir·tu·o·si** (vur′chσo wō′sē) —**vir·tu·os·i·ty** (vur′chσo wäs′ə tē) *n.*

vis·i·bil·i·ty (viz′ə bil′ə tē) *n.* **1** the condition of being visible **2** the distance within which things can be seen [Fog reduced the *visibility* to 500 feet.]

vo·cab·u·lar·y (vō kab′yə ler′ē) *n.* **1** all the words of a language, or all those used by a certain person or group [Jan's *vocabulary* is large. The word "fracture" is part of the medical *vocabulary*.] **2** a list of words, usually in alphabetical order with their meanings, as in a dictionary —*pl.* **vo·cab′u·lar′ies**

vo·cal·ize (vō′k'l īz) *v.* to make sounds with the voice; speak or sing —**vo′cal·ized, vo′cal·iz·ing**

vo·ca·tion (vō kā′shən) *n.* one's profession, occupation, trade, or career [He found his *vocation* in social work.] —**vo·ca′tion·al** *adj.*

A **vocation** is sometimes referred to as a "calling," and there is a connection between these words. The word **vocation** comes from a Latin word meaning "to call." People often feel as though they have been called upon to follow a certain kind of work.

vo·cif·er·ous (vō sif′ər əs) *adj.* loud and noisy in making one's feelings known; clamorous [a *vociferous* crowd; *vociferous* complaints]

☆**vol·ley·ball** (väl′ē bôl′) *n.* **1** a game played by two teams who hit a large, light ball back and forth over a high net with their hands **2** the ball used in this game

volt·age (vōl′tij) *n.* the force that produces electric current: it is measured in volts

vol·un·tar·y (väl′ən ter′ē) *adj.* **1** acting, done, or given of one's own free will; by choice [*voluntary* workers; *voluntary* gifts] **2** controlled by one's mind or will [*voluntary* muscles] —**vol′un·tar′i·ly** *adv.*

vul·ner·a·ble (vul′nər ə b'l) *adj.* **1** that can be hurt, destroyed, attacked, etc. [The wolf looked for a *vulnerable* spot into which to sink its fangs.] **2** likely to be hurt; sensitive [A vain person is *vulnerable* to criticism.] —**vul′ner·a·bil′i·ty** *n.*

war·rant (wôr′ənt) *n.* **1** a good reason for something; justification [She has no *warrant* for such a belief.] **2** something that makes sure; guarantee [His wealth is no *warrant* of happiness.] **3** an official paper that gives the right to do something [The police must have a *warrant* to search a house.] ⬥*v.* **1** to be a good reason for; justify [Her good work *warrants* our praise.] **2** to give the right to do something [His arrest was not *warranted*.] **3** to give a warranty for [This appliance is *warranted*.] **4** to say in a positive way: *used only in everyday talk* [I *warrant* they'll be late.]

wharf (hwôrf) *n.* a long platform built out over water so that ships can dock beside it to load and unload —*pl.* **wharves** (hwôrvz) or **wharfs**

whol·ly (hō′lē) *adv.* to the whole amount or degree; altogether; completely [You are *wholly* right. The building was *wholly* destroyed.]

win·some (win′səm) *adj.* attractive in a sweet, pleasant way; charming [a *winsome* girl]

with·hold (with hōld′) *v.* **1** to keep from giving or granting; refuse [She *withheld* her approval of the plan.] **2** to hold back; keep back; check [He *withheld* his anger.] **3** to take out or subtract from wages or salary, as taxes —**with·held′, with·hold′ing**

yeast (yēst) *n.* **1** a yellow, frothy substance made up of tiny fungi, used in baking to make dough rise **2** this substance dried in flakes or tiny grains, or made up in small cakes

yen (yen) *n.* the basic unit of money in Japan

Yu·go·sla·vi·a (yōō′gō slä′vē ə) a country in southeastern Europe, on the Balkan Peninsula

Zim·ba·bwe (zim bä′bwe) a country in southern Africa

zinc (ziŋk) *n.* a bluish-white metal that is a chemical element: it is used to coat iron, and in making certain alloys, medicines, etc.

zin·ni·a (zin′ē ə) *n.* a garden plant with brightly colored flowers having many petals

zo·ol·o·gy (zō äl′ə jē) *n.* the science that studies animals and animal life
—**zo·ol′o·gist** *n.*

a	ask, fat
ā	ape, date
ä	car, lot
e	elf, ten
er	berry, care
ē	even, meet
i	is, hit
ir	mirror, here
ī	ice, fire
ō	open, go
ô	law, horn
oi	oil, point
o͝o	look, pull
o͞o	ooze, tool
yo͝o	unite, cure
yo͞o	cute, few
ou	out, crowd
u	up, cut
ʉ	fur, fern
ə	a in ago
	e in agent
	e in father
	i in unity
	o in collect
	u in focus
ch	chin, arch
ŋ	ring, singer
sh	she, dash
th	thin, truth
th	then, father
zh	s in pleasure
′	as in (ā b'l)

Spelling Notebook

Spelling Notebook

Spelling Notebook

A a A a A a

Alphabet

alphabet

B b B b

banana

banana

C c C c C c

cocoa

cocoa

D d D d

dog dog

E e E e

Elephant

elephant

F f F f

fillet filly

g g g

goat

Goat

H h

Hot

hot

I i I i

igloo